*The Excellencie*
*of a Free-State*

Neptune, the Roman god of the sea,
inspiring the English republic to maritime greatness.

THE THOMAS HOLLIS LIBRARY

David Womersley, General Editor

# The Excellencie
# of a Free-State;
## Or, The Right Constitution
## of a Commonwealth

*Marchamont Nedham*

Edited and with an Introduction
by Blair Worden

LIBERTY FUND

*Indianapolis*

Introduction, editorial additions, and index
© 2011 by Liberty Fund, Inc.

Frontispiece: From *Of the Dominion, or, Ownership of the Sea,* by John Selden, 1652. Image is reproduced courtesy of The Bodleian Library, University of Oxford, shelfmark Vet.A3d.163.

Printed in the United States of America

C  10  9  8  7  6  5  4  3  2  1
P  10  9  8  7  6  5  4  3  2  1

Library of Congress Cataloging-in-Publication Data
Nedham, Marchamont, 1620–1678.
The excellencie of a free-state: or, the right constitution of a commonwealth/ Marchamont Nedham; edited and with an introduction by Blair Worden.
p. cm—(Thomas Hollis library)
Includes bibliographical references and index.
ISBN 978-0-86597-808-9 (hardcover: alk. paper)
ISBN 978-0-86597-809-6 (pbk.: alk. paper)
1. Political science—Early works to 1800.  2. Republicanism—Great Britain— History—17th century.  3. Great Britain—Politics and government—1642–1660. I. Womersley, David.  II. Title.  III. Title: The right constitution of a commonwealth.
JC153.N3 2010
321.8'6—dc22                                                        2010050874

LIBERTY FUND, INC.
8335 Allison Pointe Trail, Suite 300
Indianapolis, Indiana 46250-1684

# CONTENTS

# THE THOMAS HOLLIS LIBRARY

Thomas Hollis (1720–74) was an eighteenth-century Englishman who devoted his energies, his fortune, and his life to the cause of liberty. Hollis was trained for a business career, but a series of inheritances allowed him to pursue instead a career of public service. He believed that citizenship demanded activity and that it was incumbent on citizens to put themselves in a position, by reflection and reading, in which they could hold their governments to account. To that end for many years Hollis distributed books that he believed explained the nature of liberty and revealed how liberty might best be defended and promoted.

A particular beneficiary of Hollis's generosity was Harvard College. In the years preceding the Declaration of Independence, Hollis was assiduous in sending to America boxes of books, many of which he had had specially printed and bound, to encourage the colonists in their struggle against Great Britain. At the same time he took pains to explain the colonists' grievances and concerns to his fellow Englishmen.

The Thomas Hollis Library makes freshly available a selection of titles that, because of their intellectual power, or the influence they exerted on the public life of their own time, or the distinctiveness of their approach to the topic of liberty, comprise the cream of the books distributed by Hollis. Many of these works have been either out of print since the eighteenth century or available only in very expensive and scarce editions. The highest standards of scholarship and production ensure that these classic texts can be as salutary and influential today as they were two hundred and fifty years ago.

David Womersley

# PREFACE

The republican writings of Marchamont Nedham are a landmark in Western political thought. Writing in the years following the execution of King Charles I and the abolition of the monarchy in 1649, Nedham proposed an alternative to the improvised and short-lived constitutional expedients that followed the overthrow of the monarchy. Instead of clinging to remnants of the native constitution, urged Nedham, his countrymen should recover the principles and forms of republican rule that had prospered in classical antiquity. A disciple of Niccolò Machiavelli, whose methods of argument he imitated and whose reasoning he adapted to an English setting, Nedham opened the way for the more-searching or learned republican thinking of his contemporaries James Harrington, Henry Neville, and Algernon Sidney. *The Excellencie of a Free-State,* published in 1656, is the most coherent expression of Nedham's republican thought.

Nedham was no abstract political analyst. He was a hired journalist. Like his close friend and frequent literary ally John Milton, he published tracts in order to influence events. From 1650 to 1653 he wrote for the Commonwealth, which had replaced King Charles's rule. From 1653 onward he wrote for the protectorate of Oliver Cromwell. Yet behind his outward enthusiasm for the new governors of England lay sharp criticisms of their characters and measures. To recover his meanings we need to probe the political contexts of his writings and to explore his relations with the rulers who employed him.

My introduction will attempt those tasks. It will also explore the circumstances that led to the republication of *The Excellencie* in 1767, the version in which it has been primarily known. The reappearance of the work, under the sponsorship of the wealthy English bibliophile and "commonwealthman" Thomas Hollis, belonged to a literary enterprise that has had substantial consequences for political argument on both sides of the Atlantic. Liberty Fund, the publisher of the present volume, was founded by the widely read businessman Pierre Goodrich, with the aim of promoting understanding of ideas of liberty. Hollis had the same purpose. In pursuit of it he arranged the reproduction and dissemination of seventeenth-century writings that have become known as a canon of Whig literature. Although Hollis did not claim, or achieve, for Nedham a standing equal to that of Milton, Sidney, or Harrington, he maintained that Nedham's writing deserved attention alongside theirs. Modern perspectives on the history of political thought vindicate his assertion.

Blair Worden

# ACKNOWLEDGMENTS

Editors need the aid of experts and colleagues and are gladdened when, as in my case, it comes with kindness and generosity. I warmly thank Laura Goetz and David Womersley, my guides at Liberty Fund; Susan Halpert of the Houghton Library at Harvard and Colin Higgins of the Library of Christ's College, Cambridge; and scholars Rodney Allan, Harald Braun, Justin Champion, Mark Greengrass, Rachel Hammersley, Alan Houston, Paul Rahe, and David Wootton. Two debts, both of them to skillful and enterprising young historians, are exceptional: to Richard Foster, whose assistance in the preparation of the text and the textual apparatus has gone beyond his mechanical brief; and to Moses Tannenbaum, who has supplied me with invaluable information about the reception of the eighteenth-century edition of *The Excellencie* in America.

# ABBREVIATIONS

Blackburne   [Francis Blackburne,] *Memoirs of Thomas Hollis,* 2 vols., continuous pagination (London, 1780)

E   *The Excellencie of a Free-State* (London, 1656)

HD   Thomas Hollis, Diary, MS. Eng. 1191, Houghton Library, Harvard

Knachel   Marchamont Nedham, *The Case of the Commonwealth of England, Stated,* ed. Philip Knachel (Charlottesville, Va.: University Press of Virginia, 1969)

LP   Blair Worden, *Literature and Politics in Cromwellian England* (Oxford, U.K.: Oxford University Press, 2007, 2nd printing 2009)

MP   *Mercurius Politicus*

# INTRODUCTION

Marchamont Nedham (1620–1678) was the pioneer of English republicanism. His arguments for kingless rule were first published in brief essays written in 1650–52, during the rule of the Commonwealth that followed the execution of King Charles I in 1649. In 1656, when Oliver Cromwell had become lord protector, Nedham brought the essays together in his anonymously published tract *The Excellencie of a Free-State; Or, The Right Constitution of a Commonwealth*. His advocacy gave a new direction to English political thought. Posterity has paid less attention to him than to James Harrington, the other of the two most innovative republican writers of the 1650s. Harrington, whose treatise *Oceana* appeared five months after *The Excellencie*, was the more penetrating writer, but he followed where Nedham had led. The significance of *The Excellencie* was recognized in the reign of George III by the radical Whig bibliophile and antiquary Thomas Hollis, whose promotion of works favorable to his own conception of liberty made a large impact in Europe and, still more, in America. Hollis arranged the republication of Nedham's tract in 1767. The edition he sponsored was circulated in England, revolutionary America, and revolutionary France. Since then the tract has been largely neglected until recent times, when the expansion of interest in seventeenth-century political thought revived attention to it. Now *The Excellencie* is brought back into print.

In Nedham's time as in other historical periods, political thought was a response to political events. No writer's ideas have been more closely woven with events, or been framed with a keener eye to their course, than Nedham's. To understand the choice and purposes of his arguments we must re-create the circumstances that they addressed.[1]

## Marchamont Nedham and the English Republic

English republicanism was a creation, not a cause, of the English civil wars.[2] Before them, it is true, we can find much skepticism about princely rule, much complaint about the tendency of such rule to degenerate into tyranny, and much hostility to the evils of princely courts. We also find ample interest in the politics and virtues of ancient republics, as well as a thorough acquaintance with Machiavelli, their most adventurous modern interpreter. Yet those preoccupations were compatible with loyalty to, even veneration of, the English monarchy and the rights bestowed on kings by law and custom. The Parliament that resisted Charles I, known to posterity as the Long Parliament, sat from 1640 to 1653, though it was purged of its royalist members in 1642 and of the more cautious or conservative of its parliamentarian ones in 1648. During those thirteen years the revolution was transformed. It took directions, and found targets, that would have been unimaginable to its initiators. Men who went to war with Charles I in 1642 sought to preserve what they took to be the ancient constitution and

---

1. I have discussed aspects of Nedham's career more fully in "'Wit in a Roundhead': The Dilemma of Marchamont Nedham," in *Political Culture and Cultural Politics in Early Modern England,* ed. Susan Amussen and Mark Kishlansky (Manchester, U.K.: Manchester University Press, 1995), pp. 301–37; and in *LP.* The first publication is mostly concerned with the years before 1651; the second with 1651–60.

2. I offer accounts of seventeenth-century English republicanism in David Wootton, ed., *Republicanism, Liberty, and Commercial Society, 1649–1776* (Stanford, Calif.: Stanford University Press, 1994), chaps. 1–4; and "Republicanism, Regicide and Republic: The English Experience," in *Republicanism: A Shared European Heritage,* 2 vols., ed. Martin van Gelderen and Quentin Skinner (Cambridge, U.K.: Cambridge University Press, 2002), 1:307–27.

the shared authority of king and Parliament. In their eyes Charles had subverted that authority. He had brought novel and illegal challenges to the liberty of the subject, to parliamentary privilege, and to the rights of property. Charles himself believed the Parliamentarians to be the innovators. In the year or so before the outbreak of war, they certainly assumed startling powers, both legislative and executive. Yet their initiatives were emergency measures, justified in Parliament's view by the king's desertion of his regal obligations. Parliament's target was the misrule of a particular king, not the office of kingship.

No one in 1642 would have predicted the abolition of the monarchy seven years later. That development was the result of political events, not of political theory, which through the 1640s struggled to keep up with those events. The new model army, which by 1646 had won the first civil war for Parliament, was radicalized in its aftermath. It was further radicalized by the brief but bitter second civil war in 1648, which it likewise won. Now the army turned on its political masters, most of whom it suspected of entertaining too much respect for the defeated king and too little for the soldiery. In the fall of 1648, while a parliamentary delegation negotiated with Charles for his restoration, the army resolved to move against him. In December it occupied London and forcibly purged the Commons in the operation that would become known as Pride's Purge, after Colonel Thomas Pride, who carried it out. Next month the minority of Members of Parliament whom the army had allowed to remain, or the Rump as they came to be derisively called, erected a court to try the king. The court convicted Charles as a traitor to his people and as a tyrant who had declared war on them and bore the guilt of the blood they had shed. He was executed on 30 January 1649.

How would he be replaced? When, forty winters later, Charles's younger son James II lost his throne, his opponents had an alternative monarch in the Dutch Prince William of Orange, who was ready to rule with his wife, James's daughter Mary. In 1648–49 no member of the Stuart family, outraged as it was by what it viewed as the murder of its leader, would have accepted enthronement at the hands of the murderers. Charles's opponents were too divided to choose a monarch from among themselves, a move that anyway would have commanded no sense of legitimacy. Yet republican rule would be illegitimate too. The army's political leaders, Oliver Cromwell and his son-in-law Henry Ireton, did not seek it. In 1647 they had for a time been willing to restore the king himself, on terms in some respects more generous than Parliament's. It is true that by that time there were figures within the army's ranks, and among its civilian allies, who were sporadically expressing or implying an aversion to kingly government. But they did not devise, if indeed they even conceived of, an alternative system of rule.

Only when Charles was dead did the new rulers confront the question of constitutional settlement, and then in slow and gingerly fashion.[3] Republican rule was improvised. It emerged not by design but by default. On one reading, the cloudily worded preamble to the "act abolishing the office of king," which the Rump passed in March 1649, repudiated kingship only in the unlimited form to which Charles had allegedly aspired and left open the possibility of a return to the "mixed" monarchical constitution that Members of Parliament had believed themselves to be defending in 1642.[4] A further two months elapsed before the Rump passed an act declaring England "to be a Commonwealth and Free State." This time the government could not even agree on a preamble to vindicate the measure, which was consequently published without one.[5] The Rump would not have been able to reach any decision about the constitutional future at any point during the four years of its power, since from 1649 to 1651 it was preoccupied by the challenge of conquering Ireland and Scotland, where royalist armies kept the Stuart cause alive. Only with Cromwell's defeat of the invading Scots at Worcester in September 1651 was the regime secure. When Parliament's attention then turned to the settlement of England, divisions opened within it. The fatal split was between Parliament and its army. In April 1653 the army, which had forcibly

3. I have described the politics of the Commonwealth period in *The Rump Parliament 1648–1653* (Cambridge, U.K.: Cambridge University Press, 1977).

4. S. R. Gardiner, ed., *The Constitutional Documents of the Puritan Revolution, 1625–1660,* 3rd ed., rev. (Oxford, U.K.: Clarendon Press, 1962), pp. 385–86.

5. Ibid., p. 388.

destroyed the king, used its force to destroy the Parliament that had opposed him.

From 1649 to 1653 England was ruled not under a new constitution but by what was left of the old one. That rule was unicameral, for not only had kingship been abolished but at the same time so had the House of Lords, Parliament's upper chamber. The Lords would never have passed the legislation that sanctioned the trial of the king. To remove that obstacle the Rump had resolved on 4 January 1649 that the Commons, "being chosen by, and representing the people, have the supreme power in this nation," and were entitled to legislate unilaterally.[6] Yet the Rump's claim to represent the people was contradicted by the absence from the Commons of that majority of representatives whom the army had purged, and by the nation's plain hostility to a regime whose very existence, which only armed force could sustain, was at odds with the respect for the ancient constitution on which parliamentarianism had taken its stand in the civil wars.

How might the country be brought round to kingless rule? Not, the government knew, by professions of the legality of the regicide or the republic. The Rump in effect acknowledged its own illegality. In the aftermath of the regicide it drew on an argument that was widely circulated in 1649–52 and that found its most famous and accomplished expression in the *Leviathan* of Thomas Hobbes (1651). Hobbes wrote, not to justify a particular form of government, but to explain the obligation of subjects to obey any government, whatever its origins, that has acquired the protective power of the sword. In treatises and pamphlets written on the Rump's behalf, the same principle was adopted by a number of lesser-known writers.[7]

None of them articulated it more effectively than Marchamont Nedham, whose short book *The Case of the Commonwealth of England, Stated* was published in May 1650 and republished later in the year. "The power of the sword," explained Nedham, "is, and ever hath been,

6. *Journal of the House of Commons*, 4 January 1649.

7. Quentin Skinner, "Conquest and Consent: Hobbes and the Engagement Controversy," in *Visions of Politics*, 3 vols. (Cambridge, U.K.: Cambridge University Press, 2002–3), 3:287–307.

the foundation of all titles to government," and those who do not submit to its jurisdiction have no claim to "the benefits of its protection."[8] *The Case* has two parts. The first sets out five principles that vindicate the claims to obedience demanded by the Rump's command of the sword. The arguments of the second part warn readers against the inducements of enemies who conspire or wish for the Rump's overthrow. Each of four hostile groups, "the royal party," "the Scots," "the English Presbyterians," and "the Levellers," is accorded a chapter of refutation. The final chapter of part 2, offered "by way of conclusion," takes a different course. Titled "A Discourse of the Excellency of a Free State Above a Kingly Government," it urges the English to set aside their inherited prejudice in favor of monarchy and to grasp the superiority of republican rule. Nedham, who was an innovator on many intellectual and literary fronts,[9] brought his powers of innovation to the "Discourse." He used the title page of *The Case* to draw particular attention to the "Discourse" and its theme.[10]

Later in 1650 the young writer John Hall, who like Nedham was an employee of the Commonwealth, took up the republican case in his work *The Grounds and Reasons of Monarchy*. His career was so intimately bound with Nedham's, and the arguments and language of the two men resembled each other so often, that their writings can be hard to tell apart.[11] In 1650 Nedham and Hall introduced republicanism to English politics.

Marchamont Nedham (or sometimes "Needham," a spelling that probably indicates the contemporary pronunciation of the name, which likely would have rhymed with "freedom") is a figure troubling to readers who expect political thinkers to pursue a disinterested search for

8. Knachel, p. 5.
9. See p. xci, n. 259.
10. Knachel, p. 1; compare ibid., pp. 116–17.
11. Hall's political writings and their affinity with Nedham's are discussed in David Norbrook, *Writing the English Republic: Poetry, Rhetoric and Politics 1627–1660* (Cambridge, U.K.: Cambridge University Press, 1999), and in *LP*. For Hall's career and writings see also Nicholas McDowell, *Poetry and Allegiance in the English Civil Wars* (Oxford, U.K.: Oxford University Press, 2008).

truth. He is the serial turncoat of the civil wars. In the first war he wrote for Parliament. In the second he wrote for the king. In 1649 he was caught printing royalist material and was threatened with a charge of treason. He averted it by switching his allegiance to the new rulers, who rescued him from penury with a handsome stipend. In the 1650s he supported every regime in its turn: the Rump; Barebone's Parliament, the assembly with which Cromwell replaced the Rump in July 1653 but which endured only until December of that year, when it, too, succumbed to a military coup; the protectorate, which succeeded Barebone's and which held power, first under Oliver and then, after his death in September 1658, under his son Richard, until Richard's deposition in May 1659; then the Rump again, which was restored by the army that had expelled it six years earlier; then the army after it had expelled the Rump again in October 1659; and once more the Rump when it resumed power at the end of the same year. Thereafter he supported the restored monarchy.

Nedham airily acknowledged his transfers of allegiance. Most of his political writings—*The Excellencie of a Free-State* among them—were published anonymously, but in 1650 *The Case of the Commonwealth*, his first treatise for the republic, appeared under his own name and drew attention to his conversion. "Perhaps," its opening words declare to the reader, "thou art of an opinion contrary to what is here written. I confess that for a time I myself was so too, till some causes made me reflect with an impartial eye upon the affairs of this new government." The passage would reappear almost verbatim in a publication of 1661 that rejoiced in the king's return.[12]

Nedham's career, which repeatedly made him the friend or enemy of politicians and writers with whom he had at least once had the opposite relationship, challenges the categories of allegiance and conduct that govern our perceptions of both the political and the literary history of the civil wars. Nedham did have one point of consistency. It lay in his aversion, which he shared with Milton, to Presbyterianism, the parliamentarian grouping that had favored the return of the king

---

12. *The True Character of a Rigid Presbyter* (London, 1661), preface.

in 1648 and that was the common enemy of royalism and the republic. He detested it less for its political goals than for its commitment to religious intolerance and for the scope it gave to clerical dogmatism. Yet no other enemy of Presbyterianism swung so blatantly between the alternatives to it. To contemporaries he was "that speckled chameleon," "a mercenary soul,"[13] "a cat that (throw him which way you will) still light[s] on his feet."[14] Nevertheless, it would be a mistake to think of Nedham merely as a hack polemicist, tamely obedient to the demands of his successive employers. If he needed their payment and protection and the outlets his masters gave him for literary expression, the masters themselves needed his exceptional skills of persuasion. Even as he supplied the propaganda they required of him, he found a means of asserting, with resourceful obliqueness, an individuality and independence of voice. Where, if anywhere, his own convictions lay cannot be authoritatively decided. What we can say is that within each public position he adopted, and most of all in his republican writing, he contrived to open a gap between opinions he was called on to propagate and ones he simultaneously fostered. "In our late wars," he recalled in 1652, "the pen militant hath had as sharp encounters as the sword, and borne away as many trophies."[15] No writer, not even the dazzling royalist journalist Sir John Berkenhead, who was a rival of Nedham's in the first civil war and a collaborator in the second,[16] bore off as many trophies as he. Nedham won them largely through his management of news. But it was his polemic that politicians valued or feared most. His success enabled him to test to the limit the patience of his employers, or anyway the more conventional or mainstream of them, who found in his writings much to anger or trouble them.

13. *LP,* p. 27.

14. Quoted from the fourth page of (the confusingly paginated) *A Word for All: Or, The Rumps Funeral Sermon* (1660) in Paul A. Rahe, *Against Throne and Altar: Machiavelli and Political Theory Under the English Republic* (New York: Cambridge University Press, 2008), p. 177.

15. Epistle dedicatorie in *Of the Dominion of the Seas* by John Selden, trans. and ed. Nedham (London, 1652).

16. Peter W. Thomas, *Sir John Berkenhead 1617–1679: A Royalist Career in Politics and Polemics* (Oxford, U.K.: Clarendon Press, 1969).

Nedham was born in Burford in Oxfordshire. After a period at Oxford University and at Gray's Inn, London, he rose to prominence in his early twenties as editor of the weekly parliamentarian newsbook *Mercurius Britanicus,* which began in 1643. The collapse of censorship in 1640–42, and the impact on the population of the civil wars and their attendant controversies, created a wide literary market that thrived on the vivid reporting of news and on plain, direct, earthy reasoning. The genre suited Nedham's gifts, as did the war of pamphlets that paralleled that of the newsbooks. *Britanicus* championed the radical element within the parliamentarian cause. It attacked "lukewarm wretches," "moderate friends," and "neuters" who regretted the outbreak of the war or who wanted to end it on terms that would leave the king scope for renewed misrule. The war, Nedham urged, must be fought to the finish. He risked Parliament's displeasure by indicating that Charles might be deposed and replaced by his eldest son, the future Charles II. In 1645–46, as the war neared its end, Nedham went too far. Parliament, in its dealings with the king and in its depictions of him, had clung to the conventions of deference, referring reverently to "his majesty" and mainly blaming his misrule not on him but on evil advisers around him. Nedham, however, wrote of Charles's "guilty conscience" and "bloody hands."[17] Parliament's response was to close down *Britanicus* and have Nedham briefly jailed.

Now Parliament discovered the force of his motto, *Nemo me impune lacessit:* no one strikes me with impunity. First he lent his pen to the emergent Leveller movement, which was protesting the emergence of a parliamentary tyranny in place of the defeated regal one. Then in August 1647 he wrote, possibly with the connivance of the leaders of the new model army,[18] *The Case of the Kingdom, Stated,* a tract designed to facilitate negotiations between the army and the king through which both sides hoped to outmaneuver the Presbyterians. By the next month he was in the king's employment. Charles made him editor of a new weekly newsbook, *Mercurius Pragmaticus,* which would run until

17. Worden, "'Wit in a Roundhead,'" pp. 315–16.
18. *LP,* p. 183.

1649, and whose professed aim was "to write his majesty back into his throne." It was secretly written and published in London, a city that Parliament ostensibly controlled. It did not advance a royalist theory of government. Nedham's substantial essays in political theory were all written on the parliamentarian side. The weapon of *Pragmaticus* was satire, a talent that Nedham exuberantly aimed at his Puritan and parliamentarian former employers.

His transfer of allegiance to the Commonwealth in 1649 was contrived by John Bradshaw, who had presided over the trial of the king and was now president of the executive arm of the regime, the council of state. Nedham became—if he was not already—an intimate, devoted friend of Bradshaw's[19] and of Bradshaw's equally devoted associate, the poet John Milton, who was the council's Latin Secretary. Soon Nedham and Milton were literary partners on the Commonwealth's behalf. In June 1650, a month after the appearance of Nedham's *The Case of the Commonwealth*, the former editor of *Mercurius Britanicus* and *Mercurius Pragmaticus* launched a third newsbook, *Mercurius Politicus*. Milton, on the state's behalf, was soon supervising the production of *Politicus* and working closely with Nedham in the preparation of its content, which frequently echoed prose written by Milton himself on behalf of the regicide and the republic.[20] From September 1650 on, material from *The Case* began to appear as weekly editorials (an anachronistic but unavoidable term) in *Politicus*. Anthony Wood, whose every political instinct was repelled by the newsbook, conceded that it made Nedham "the Goliah of the Philistines . . . whose pen was in comparison with others a weaver's beam. 'Tis incredible what influence [it] had upon numbers of inconsiderable persons."[21] Most of the material in *The Excellencie of a Free-State* first appeared four years earlier in weekly editorials of *Politicus*, between September 1651 and August 1652. That period and the developments of 1649–51 which preceded it are the first of two contexts that shall be explored in order to grasp the purposes of

---

19. Ibid., pp. 45–47.
20. Ibid., chap. 9.
21. Wood's account of Nedham is found in Anthony Wood, *Atheniae Oxonienses*, 4 vols. (London, 1813–20), 3:1180–90.

Nedham's republican arguments. The second is the period of the protectorate preceding the publication of *The Excellencie*.

## Nedham and *Mercurius Politicus*

Like *Mercurius Britanicus* in the first civil war, *Mercurius Politicus* spoke for the bolder spirits among Nedham's employers. Within the new regime there were two opposing impulses. The first was a desire to entrench the revolution that had been achieved by Pride's Purge, the regicide, and the abolition of kingship and the House of Lords. Those deeds, it was urged, should be remembered and celebrated in print, while membership of central and local government should be confined to men ready to endorse them. The nation should be bound by oath to support the Commonwealth. Royal statues and other visual survivals of monarchy should be destroyed. The opposite impulse was toward the broadening, not the restriction, of the regime's base. Many Members of Parliament who had been expelled from the Commons at Pride's Purge or had then voluntarily withdrawn from it returned to it after the execution of the king. Even among those who had remained at Westminster during the king's trial, there were a number who had resented the purge and were troubled by the regicide. Returning members held those sentiments more keenly. They wanted to relegate the execution of Charles to the past and to heal the wounds that it had caused. The purge, they hoped, would be at least partly undone and an attempt would be made to return to the original, limited goals of Parliament in 1642, from which the regicide and the establishment of the republic had deviated.

In that contest John Bradshaw was a leading figure on the radical side. Milton's and Nedham's publications backed his stance.[22] Like *Britanicus* before it, *Politicus* disparaged "lukewarm," "neutral," "moderate" men. It urged that power and voting rights should be the prerogative of the Commonwealth's "party of its own," "men of valour and virtue," "sensible of liberty," who had dared to carry out or endorse the regicide and who now resisted the temporizing instincts of their colleagues.

22. *LP,* pp. 195–99.

Nedham hailed the memory of Pride's Purge, that "noble act," and of the regicide, so "noble" and "heroic an act of justice," "one of the most heroic and exemplary acts of justice that was ever done under the sun."[23] To royalists, the regicide had been a deed of sacrilege against the divinely appointed ruler. Nedham, determined to strip kingship of its mystery, laughed at Charles's heir, "young Tarquin."

In the editorials of 1651–52 that would reappear in *The Excellencie*, Nedham developed and expanded the republican thinking that he had announced in *The Case of the Commonwealth* in 1650. Now *The Excellencie*'s argument appeared in a sprightlier form, one designed to attract a wider readership than *The Case*. The learned apparatus of *The Case* was omitted. There were individuals in the Rump, chief among them Henry Marten, Thomas Chaloner, and James Harrington's literary partner Henry Neville, who likely encouraged Nedham's republican advocacy.[24] *Politicus* backed adventurous social and commercial policies that were pursued by those figures in Parliament. It also shared their irreverent wit and their detachment from the Puritan solemnity that characterized the run of parliamentary opinion. They were travelled men, of cosmopolitan outlook, ready to look beyond the traditions and perspectives of native political thought. Powerful as those Members of Parliament could sometimes be, they stood outside the parliamentarian mainstream. Nedham's friend Milton noticed how few of England's new leaders had been abroad.[25] The nation, he believed, would never gain political health until it imported "ripe understanding and many civil virtues . . . from foreign writings and examples of best ages."[26] *Politicus* concurred.

But would the majority in the Commons welcome Nedham's editorials? And could his newsbook convert the public rather than antagonize it? Margaret Judson has observed that, as a rule, "republican

23. Ibid., p. 182.

24. Ibid., pp. 73–75, 111.

25. Leo Miller, *John Milton and the Oldenburg Safeguard* (New York: Loewenthal Press, 1985), p. 172.

26. *Complete Prose Works of John Milton*, 8 vols., ed. D. M. Wolfe et al. (New Haven, Conn.: Yale University Press, 1953–82), 5:451.

ideology" had "only a minor role" in the literature written on behalf of the Rump.[27] The republican arguments that Nedham first voiced in *The Case of the Commonwealth* may have been formulated in his mind long before its publication. *Mercurius Britanicus* had slyly cast admiring glances at the Dutch republic and other "free states."[28] In November 1646 Nedham contributed to a tract, *Vox Plebis; or, The Peoples Out-Cry Against Oppression, Injustice, and Tyranny,* which was written on behalf of the Leveller leader John Lilburne. There Nedham used arguments derived from the *Discourses* of Machiavelli. On that occasion he did not employ Machiavelli's thinking to argue for kingless rule. However, he did deduce from it points that in *Politicus* would reappear, in similar language, to support that purpose.[29] Nevertheless, it was not until 1650 that he espoused republicanism in print. Much of the republican material that would resurface in *Politicus* may already have been drafted when *The Case* appeared, or it may have been first written in the year or so after the publication of that tract.[30] But it was not until September 1651, when Cromwell's victory at Worcester achieved the final defeat of the royalist cause, that the republican editorials began. It seems likely that the "Discourse" of 1650 had tested the water and that only after Worcester was the water deemed warm or safe enough for the adventurous campaign of *Politicus.*[31]

The campaign was conducted against a background of mounting international self-assertion by the Commonwealth. Alongside its exploits

---

27. Margaret Judson, *From Tradition to Political Reality: A Study of the Ideas Set Forth in Support of the Commonwealth Government in England, 1649–1653* (Hamden, Conn.: Archon, 1980), p. 11.

28. Worden, "'Wit in a Roundhead,'" p. 317.

29. Nedham's involvement in the pamphlet is evident not only from the distinctive style and vocabulary of the passage but from his re-use of material from it in later writings. *LP,* p. 42.

30. H. Sylvia Anthony, "*Mercurius Politicus* under Milton," *Journal of the History of Ideas* 27 (1966): 593–609, at pp. 602–3.

31. Material from the republican chapter of *The Case* would reappear in *Politicus,* but only after Worcester. Nedham reproduced a passage of it (p. 16; Knachel, pp. 116–17) in the editorial of 25 September 1651; and a further brief passage (claiming that virtues in hereditary rules are "very rare": p. 41; Knachel, pp. 117–18) reappears on 5 February 1652. The second extract, and much of the first, would be reproduced in *The Excellencie.* Nedham thus published that material three times.

on the battlefield, it had built a formidable navy and was ready to use it. In 1652 it embarked on an epic naval war with the Dutch, whose rapid rise to commercial and maritime prosperity had been the economic miracle of the age. Algernon Sidney (or Sydney), an energetic member of the Rump in its later stages, and a writer as eager as *Politicus* that the English should emulate the wisdom and virtue of republican Rome, would rejoice to recall in his *Discourses Concerning Government*, written under Charles II, the exploits of the Rump, which "in a few years' good discipline . . . produced more examples of pure, complete, incorruptible, and invincible virtue than Rome or Greece could ever boast."[32] The republicanism of *Politicus* drew on the Commonwealth's achievements too. Nedham had already proclaimed in *The Case* that England's new rulers were in "every way qualified like those Roman spirits of old." In 1652 *Politicus* avowed that England's "high achievements" since "the extirpation of tyranny" "may match any of the ancients" (p. 145); in another publication of the same year Nedham described England as "the most famous and potent republic in this day in the world," indeed, "the greatest and most glorious republic that the sun ever saw," though he here made an exception of Rome.[33]

Yet if the editorials congratulated England's new rulers, they also had less comfortable messages for them. The overt and primary purpose of *Politicus*, the one for which Nedham was paid, was to assist the entrenchment of the republic and the overthrow of its royalist enemies. He presented his proposals as means to "preserve" the Commonwealth from its enemies abroad, and as "banks" or "bars" or "bulwarks" against the return of monarchy. Behind his endorsement of the regime, however, there lay criticism of it, in which Nedham's individuality of voice asserts itself. The Rump sought to preserve its power by clinging to the improvised settlement of 1649. That settlement, Nedham indicated, could not last. He made it clear that it was not enough for the Rump to have declared England a Commonwealth and Free State, as it had done in May

32. Algernon Sidney, *Discourses Concerning Government*, ed. Thomas G. West (Indianapolis, Ind.: Liberty Fund, 1990), p. 216; compare ibid., pp. 143–44, 472.

33. *LP*, pp. 182, 219; Epistle dedicatorie and p. 483, *Of the Dominion of the Seas* by John Selden.

1649. The nation must become "free indeed" (pp. 46, 50, 139), "a state . . . really free" (pp. 45, 144, 149, 156). It must set aside its insular preoccupations and explore the histories of republics ancient and modern. It must emulate their virtues and shun their mistakes. It thus would not only secure liberty at home but would export it through its might and arms and ships, and thus free England from the threats posed by foreign kings. The Dutch war must be fought in the cause not only of national might and prosperity but of republicanism. *Politicus* yearned for the extinction of monarchs and of monarchical interests and instincts in the Netherlands, in Scotland, in France, and in Italy. Nedham's statements on that theme mirror lines of the "Horatian Ode" on Cromwell's return from Ireland in 1650 by Andrew Marvell, a poet whose writings bear many other resemblances to Nedham's.[34] Anticipating the emancipation of Scotland, France, Italy, and "all states not free," the poem summons old visions, to which the abolition of monarchy gave a fresh intensity, of the liberation by English force of foreigners eager to rise against their native oppressors. *Politicus* beats the same drum.[35]

Nedham's editorials roamed history for illustrations to support his thesis. In that practice he followed Machiavelli, to whose *Discourses* the editorials were indebted in form and content. In the popular mind Machiavelli's was a dirty name. Nedham, like many other writers who learned from him, remembered to disavow the ruthless affront to political morality which Machiavelli's *The Prince*, "that unworthy book" (p. 120), was commonly taken to constitute, though Nedham also contrived to turn Machiavelli's depictions of statecraft to his own polemical uses. However, the Machiavelli who mainly interests Nedham is not the analyst of princely rule but the celebrator of republican virtue. Nedham's historical examples were spread across a wider range of place and time than Machiavelli's, but at the center of his historical attention, as of Machiavelli's, was ancient Rome. There was nothing new in the drawing of parallels between English and Roman history. The political and imaginative literature of the Renaissance had often

34. *LP,* chaps. 3–6.
35. Ibid., pp. 67–69.

dwelled on them. But Renaissance writers had written under monarchy. Though they detected innumerable instructive resemblances of
character or circumstance between the Roman republic and modern
times, they discovered deeper and more pressing modern correspon-
dences in the imperial monarchy, the empire that had succeeded the republic. By contrast Nedham, like Machiavelli, centered his arguments
on that Roman republic, of which modern England could now be seen
as a counterpart. In the spirit of Machiavelli he commends the "active,"
"magnanimous," "gallant" character of free citizens, their love of "glory
and virtue," their "lofty" aspirations and the "edge" to their spirits. He
follows Machiavelli in linking republicanism to austerity, in observing
the classical distinction between "liberty" and "license," and in aligning
freedom with "discipline," "virtuous poverty," "honest poverty" and the
denial of "luxury."[36]

Nedham follows Machiavelli more daringly on another front. Machiavelli had dwelled on the conflicts in republican Rome between the
aristocracy, or the senatorial class or order, and the people. Nedham
portrayed a parallel conflict in civil-war England. Machiavelli not only
helped Nedham to free himself from insular and traditional ways of
political thinking but assisted his emancipation from familiar habits of
social thinking. The civil wars had not been fought in the cause of republicanism, but neither had they been wars between classes. They had
been fought between sides whose leaders accepted the hierarchies and
deferences of a society dominated by landlords and, in the towns, by
aldermanic oligarchies. The wars had, it is true, provoked a great deal of
social protest. The most conspicuous protesters were the Levellers, who
in the second half of the 1640s assailed abuses of the legal system that
favored the rich and powerful at the expense of the poor. They did not,
however, think of themselves as contending for one order of society at
the expense of another. It was Nedham who injected that perspective
into political debate.

Nedham's relations with the Levellers, being mostly hidden from
posterity's view, are a tantalizing subject. They went back at least as far

36. Ibid., pp. 25, 186–87.

as 1645, when he composed a preface to a tract written by John Lilburne, or written on his behalf.[37] Nedham's contribution to *Vox Plebis*, another pamphlet in Lilburne's cause, followed in 1646. In his writings both for the royalists and for the Commonwealth, Nedham attacked and derided the Levellers, as his employers would have expected or required him to do. Despite his outward hostility, his accounts of them sometimes hint at a personal sympathy. In *Politicus* his withering assaults are aimed not at the Leveller program but at the "odious signification" so misleadingly carried by "the common usage and application" of the term (p. 48), which implied the levelling of property and the community of estates. In this he echoed the sentiments of the Leveller leaders themselves. For "Leveller," though a convenient shorthand term for us, was a pejorative label, indignantly disowned by those to whom it was applied. No more than Nedham were the Levellers opposed to the tenure or protection of property. As a political party they were broken by the end of 1649, yet Nedham retained his sympathy for them. In *Politicus* he not only extended Leveller ideas but, innovating again, gave them a classical and Machiavellian framework.[38] He also widened the readership for them. Acquaintance with classical history was not confined to the minority of the population who attended universities, even if popular knowledge of the ancient past was uneven in depth. Largely perhaps through Nedham's influence, appeals to classical and especially Roman history became a familiar feature of popular literary production in the 1650s.[39]

In one sense Nedham's championship of the people went further than Machiavelli's. Although Machiavelli despised the parasitic gentry

37. Worden, "'Wit in a Roundhead,'" p. 320.

38. *Mercurius Politicus* was quoted in the cause of "honest Levelling" by Charles Hotham, *Corporations Vindicated in Their Fundamental Liberties* (1651), 22–33.

39. Nigel Smith, "Popular Republicanism in the 1650s: John Streater's 'Heroic Mechanicks,'" in *Milton and Republicanism*, ed. David Armitage, Armand Himy, and Quentin Skinner (Cambridge, U.K.: Cambridge University Press, 1995), pp. 137–55; Joad Raymond, "John Streater and *The Grand Politick Informer,*" *Historical Journal* 41 (1998): 567–74. In 1654–59 various newsbooks alerted a popular readership to classical parallels to current affairs, though on a less ambitious scale than *Politicus*.

and favored the people's cause, he maintained that Rome had thrived on the conflict between the two orders. The senators had thus been as necessary to Rome's greatness as the people. Nedham at one or two points implicitly endorses that view, but his populism (as for simplicity we shall call it) had a still stronger partisan thrust than Machiavelli's. He gives the term "the people" a double edge, which is achieved, like much else in his writings, by his talent for ambiguity. In his editorials the phrase can mean all the inhabitants of the nation, or it can exclude those who are socially privileged. The assertion in *Politicus* that "the original of all just power is in the people" was not in itself a populist claim. It echoes the resolutions of 4 January 1649 through which the Commons, whose members were mostly gentry, asserted its right, as the representatives of "the people," to try the king. In the Rump's thinking, the interests of "the people" are assumed to be those of their leaders. Likewise Nedham's claim that "all states are founded" for the sake of "the people" was compatible with much parliamentarian argument of the 1640s that had had no contentious social dimension. Even so, like the Levellers, he presents Parliament as the servant, not the master, of the people, for "all majesty and authority is really and fundamentally in the people, and but ministerially in their trustees, or representatives" (p. 96). The ideas of consent and representation that he brings to his accounts of ancient republics owe much more to his own society than to classical thought. He places those principles at the center of his argument and gives them a socially radical dimension.[40]

Nedham does not count all adult males as "the people," as one or two of the Levellers were ready to do. For him "the rabble" are beyond the political pale. Yet the tone of his statements frequently brings Leveller perceptions of the people's rights to mind. Fluctuating and sociologically imprecise as his vocabulary is, it recasts the political contests of the time. The Rump, asserts Nedham, has removed "the name of king" but not "the thing king." For "the interest of monarchy," whose "custom" it "hath been to lurk under every form" of government, "may reside in the

40. David Underdown, *Pride's Purge* (Oxford, U.K.: Clarendon Press, 1971), p. 263.

hands of many, as well as of a single person" (p. 79). It is discernible in oppression by nobles, or by "grandees," as much as by monarchs. Only when the "interest" is "plucked up root and branch" will the "rights and freedoms" that befit a republic be secured. Those truths have been hidden, under monarchical or aristocratic rule, by the addiction to "custom" and the ill "education" that are fostered by governors who have kept "the people in utter ignorance what liberty is" (pp. 13, 30, 164).

Writing against a fluid political background, and for a regime within which the balance of power recurrently shifted, Nedham found imprecision and malleability of language indispensable tools. On one subject his ambiguities create perplexity, perhaps by design. In ancient Rome, he maintains, the initial rule of kings gave way, not to popular rule, but to the dominance of the senate. Although "the Nation" had been "accounted free" under senatorial rule, the people became "free indeed" only when they challenged it and established their own officers and their own power. In turn they were "wormed out" of their liberty at times when senatorial or noble "encroachments" undermined that achievement (p. 15). Other seventeenth-century writers took as their models ancient Sparta or modern Venice, republics renowned for stability. Those commentators distanced themselves from the memory of Athens, or at least from the anarchical aspect of its democracy. But in Nedham's eyes the Spartan people were oppressed by "the pride of the senate." The "multiplied monarchy" or "grandee government" of contemporary Venice left the people "little better than slaves under the power of their senate," whereas Athens—on which Nedham hoped to write at length elsewhere—was "the only pattern of a free state, for all the world to follow," having been free not only from "kingly tyranny" but from "senatical encroachments" (p. 11). In Rome the people's liberties were won by the creation, in opposition to senatorial power, of "the tribunes," "that necessary office," and by the legislative role of "the people's assemblies" (pp. 10, 26). Only then could Rome, which had long been "declared" a free state, be properly called one.

What then of England's constitutional arrangements? Most of the time Nedham vindicates, at least implicitly, the principle of unicameral rule on which his masters had alighted. At times we might suppose his allusions to tribunes and popular assemblies to be intended to further that goal. After all, the House of Commons claimed to rule as the representative body of the people. *Vox Plebis,* the anonymous tract on Lilburne's behalf of 1646, to which Nedham had contributed and which had attacked the jurisdictional powers of the House of Lords, had appealed to the House of Commons as "the most honourable tribunes of the people."[41] During the proceedings against Charles I, John Bradshaw explained that England's parliament—which when Bradshaw spoke had been reduced to the Commons—was "what the tribunes of Rome were heretofore to the Roman Commonwealth."[42] Does Nedham mean, then, that the House of Lords has been England's senate, and that in 1649 the Commons, England's tribunes, rightly triumphed at the senate's expense? Some passages of the editorials may have been prudently intended to allow for that interpretation, but there are more that confound it. In them Nedham makes it plain that the English "senate" has remained in being since 1649 and that its power and failings are the basic problem of the republic. The inescapable message, though he is careful not to spell it out, is that the equivalent to Rome's senate is not the Lords but the Commons. Conventional parlance often referred to the Commons, flatteringly, as the senate.[43] Nedham's equation of the two is unflattering. He impels us to deduce that England will be truly free and have a true republic only when it has acquired some equivalent to Rome's "necessary" tribunes and its popular assemblies. It is a revolutionary proposal, and to most or all members of the Rump it would have been a horrifying one. There is no surprise in its having been advanced only briefly and imprecisely.

Running throughout Nedham's editorials is an implicit contrast between a truly free state and the oligarchical regime in power in England that claims to have created one. The contrast becomes explicit in a tract of 1651 by a collaborator of Nedham's, Charles Hotham, a scholar of

41. *Vox Plebis* (London, 1646), p. 58; see, too, Eric Nelson, *The Greek Tradition in Republican Thought* (Cambridge, U.K.: Cambridge University Press, 2004), p. 91n.

42. Milton, *Complete Prose Works,* 3:589n.; compare ibid., 3:46.

43. See, for example, *LP,* pp. 149, 224, 347.

Cambridge University who was aggrieved by his recent removal from a post there. Hotham sets his ideal of "a right republican government" against the "absolute oligarchy of a Hogen Mogen" that is now in power in England.[44] Nedham's own purpose is clarified when we return to his relations with the Levellers. In raising the subject of Rome's tribunes in *Vox Plebis*, the tract of 1646 written on Lilburne's behalf, Nedham advanced an argument that strikingly anticipated his claims of the 1650s. The pamphlet recalled that after the expulsion of Rome's "hereditary kings," the Tarquins, "the nobility began to take upon them the rule of the people: and by a greater tyranny than the Tarquins had done." So "the people," "enforced by a necessity of their preservations," "created Tribunes, as guardians of the publick liberty, whereby the insolence and arbitrary power of the nobility was restrained."[45]

By 1653 Lilburne was himself making the same case in his own name. During the publication of the editorials of *Politicus* of 1651–52 he was exiled by the Rump. He went to Holland, and thence to Flanders, before returning to England in June 1653. In 1652, writing abroad, Lilburne praised the "notable preambles"—the editorials—of *Politicus*.[46] They appear to explain the fascination he developed, during his exile, with classical history, about which he read "with so much delight and seriousness." His chief inspiration was Machiavelli, whose books, "for the excellency and usefulness in corrupt times and places," he discovered to be the best "for the good of all mankind" that he had read, worth their weight "in beaten gold" and "as useful, advantageous, necessary, and requisite to me, as a compass or perspective glass."[47] But Lilburne read Machiavelli through Nedham's eyes, and he repeated Nedham's arguments, often in Nedham's wording. From the outset of its rule, Lilburne had regarded the Rump as the replacement of a regal tyranny

44. Hotham, *Corporations Vindicated*, pp. 26–28, 33.

45. *Vox Plebis*, p. 3.

46. John Lilburne, *As You Were* ([Amsterdam?], 1652), p. 29; Rahe, *Against Throne and Altar*, p. 334. Samuel Dennis Glover, "The Putney Debates: Popular Versus Elitist Republicanism," *Past and Present* 164 (1999): 47–80, valuably draws attention to the interest of Lilburne and other Levellers in classical history. See, too, Smith, "Popular Republicanism."

47. Lilburne, *The Upright Mans Vindication* ([London], 1653), pp. 7, 23.

by a parliamentary one. Now classical history proved to him that the people of England had even better reason than "the old plebeians, or common people of Rome" to "contest even to the death, for the election from amongst themselves of tribunes, or keepers, or defenders of the people's liberties, indued with ample power, to preserve them against the annihilating encroachments, that their present tyrannical riders have already made upon them." Thus must they assert themselves, as the Roman people had done, against "the greatest . . . patricians, noblemen, senators."[48]

Nedham avowed that republics flourish when the interest of the people is "more predominant than the other" (p. 15). The people, "who best know where the shoe pinches" (p. 25), are equal, on their own, to the task of drafting and passing laws. Legislation, requiring as it does "no great skill," is "the proper work of the people in their supreme assemblies" (p. 55). Yet there will remain a need for some institution, parallel to Rome's senate, with which the machinery of popular involvement will "share" power. It will supply, as the Roman senate did, the "wisdom" that is requisite for the management of the executive and for the handling of "the secrets of government" (p. 15). In such statements Nedham qualifies his populism, perhaps with the aim of offering reassurance or concessions to his masters or to conventional opinion. In other passages, perhaps for the same reason, his republicanism is itself softened. Sometimes it seems that the modern deprivation of the people's liberties has been brought about not by kingship itself but by the erosion of restraints imposed on it in earlier times. Nedham's Machiavellian language is tempered, too, by a more comforting vocabulary, which promises the English not the animated political conflict that Machiavelli favored but the attainment of tranquillity and safety and the preservation of inherited "rights and liberties" (pp. 15, 98, 166). Machiavelli had insisted on the benefits brought to Rome by the "tumults" occasioned by its social and political divisions. To most readers in England, where fear of public disorder was an ancient and dominant feature of the political landscape, that was an alarming assertion. James

---

48. John Lilburne, *L. Colonel John Lilburne Revived* ([Amsterdam?], 1653), pp. 9–10.

Harrington, who followed Machiavelli on other fronts, renounced him on that one. Nedham by contrast does invoke Machiavelli's teaching on tumults, yet his espousal of it is hesitant and qualified.

Even so, his claims for "the people" must have caused unease in the Rump. The unease would have been intensified by his appeal to disaffected members of the army, a body whose hostility to the Parliament grew during the period of the republican editorials and culminated in the coup of April 1653. Officers and soldiers saw themselves as champions or defenders of the cause of the people, which in their eyes the Rump was betraying. They also had grievances of their own. We know from other evidence that there was "murmuring" among the officers "that they are not rewarded according to their deserts," that "they have neither profit, nor preferment," that Members of Parliament were "engrossing all places of honour and profit to themselves."[49] Nedham recalled that in republican Rome the people had overthrown the monopoly of office held by the senatorial families. They had ensured that "the road of preferment lay plain to every man" (p. 28), and that "all places of honour and trust were exposed to men of merit, without distinction" (p. 29).

To the extent that the army stood for the Commonwealth's "party of its own," *Politicus* can be seen as its mouthpiece. Of the army's political demands, none was keener or more prominent than its requirement that the Rump, the remnant of the Parliament that had sat since 1640, should dissolve itself. In its place there must be regular parliamentary elections that would root authority in the nation's consent. "Roman stories," urged *Politicus,* showed that the "people never had any real liberty" under "a standing power" (p. 10). For "the very life of liberty lies in a succession of powers and persons (p. 55)" and in the people's possession of "a constant succession of their supreme assemblies" (p. 10). Nedham repeatedly insinuates that the Rump, in resisting the pressure to dissolve, is proving itself to be a "standing senate," whose survival is incompatible with freedom. To the demand for fresh elections, however,

---

49. Bulstrode Whitelocke, *Memorials of the English Affairs,* 4 vols. (Oxford, U.K.: Oxford University Press, 1853), 3:470; and see *Writings and Speeches of Oliver Cromwell,* 4 vols., ed. W. C. Abbott (Cambridge, Mass.: Harvard University Press, 1937–47), 3:57.

there was an obvious objection. Would not an electorate so antago-
nistic to the Rump return a Parliament eager to destroy the cause for
which the army had fought? Almost everyone accepted that former
royalists would be disqualified from voting until the wounds of the
recent conflict had healed. But what of Presbyterians and neutrals,
who had themselves been outraged by Pride's Purge and the regicide?
Much depended on the outlook of Cromwell, lord general of the army,
who was also the most powerful figure, if far from an omnipotent one,
in the Commons. Recognizing the difficulties that elections would
bring, he half-connived at their postponement, and by doing so in-
curred mistrust among the Commonwealth's "party of its own," which
was generally less ready to acknowledge the problem. Nedham's argument that the vote should be confined to those who had actively supported the parliamentarian war effort—the "party"—at least offered a
straightforward solution. Though this proposal could not be expected
to broaden the base of the Commonwealth's support, it would remove
the obvious impediment to the rapid dissolution of the Parliament for
which *Politicus* pressed. The Rump was not convinced. In November
1651 the Parliament pledged not to sit for more than a further three
years. For Nedham, that was too long.[50]

If the Rump remained in power, he warned, power would contract, if
it had not already done so, into the hands of a clique of grandees. Naturally he did not say whom he meant, but a coalition of civilian and military grandees is perhaps the likeliest answer.[51] It was not only the Rump,
however, whose continuation in office Nedham challenged. Machiavelli
had warned of the dangers to republican liberty posed when the power

50. His newsbook reported the decision with outward deference but with evident restlessness: Worden, *Rump Parliament*, p. 289.

51. In 1653 Lilburne, drawing on a Roman example that Nedham also used,
directed a similar point solely against military grandees: against not only Cromwell but the officers John Lambert and Thomas Harrison, whom, with him, he
portrayed as England's equivalent to the triumvirate of Octavian, Anthony, and
Lepidus (*Upright Mans Vindication*, pp. 6–9). However, that was after the expulsion of the Rump, for which the three men had borne most responsibility.
Edmund Ludlow, *Memoirs of Edmund Ludlow*, 2 vols., ed. C. H. Firth (Oxford,
U.K.: Clarendon Press, 1894), 1:346.

of military leaders is "prolonged." His argument, which Nedham had taken up in *Vox Plebis*,[52] appears again in *Politicus*, which repeatedly counsels against the "prolonging" or "continuing" or "protracting" of power, and against "continuing power too long in the hands of particular persons." Nedham particularly warns, in his customary interlinear manner, against the extension of the authority of the lord general of the army. Cromwell would certainly have been one of the grandees he had in mind, for Cromwell had, on this front too, earned mistrust among the soldiery, where it was feared that his self-promotion would destroy the army's political virtue. Nedham presents Cromwell as another Julius Caesar, whose command, like that of generals at other moments of its history, Rome fatally "lengthened." In 1650 Marvell's "Horatian Ode" warned that Cromwell might cross a Rubicon, "grow stiffer with command," and acquire supreme rule.[53] Nedham cites Caesar's crossing of the Rubicon to the same end (pp. 91, 98). It was after that event, he contends, that the bearing of arms, which hitherto had been a mark of citizenship, was "kept . . . out of the hands of the people." On the same principle, intimates Nedham, Cromwell's army might become a mercenary force, a "Praetorian" rather than a "popular militia" (p. 92).

While the editorials were being published, Cromwell was assiduously courting popular support by promises of social and legal reform.[54] *Politicus* allows us to understand his behavior as a bid for the power base from which to acquire single rule. Cromwell had indeed done heroic service for his country, as Caesar and other Roman leaders named by Nedham did for theirs, but it is precisely in the "ambition" of such men, and in the "temptation" to pursue it that will beset them, that the largest danger to liberty may lie. Caesar, after all, "who first took arms upon the public score, and became the people's leader, le[t] in ambitious thoughts to his unbounded power" and "soon shook hands with his first friends and principles, and became another man: so that upon the first fair opportunity, he turned his arms on the public liberty"

52. *Vox Plebis*, p. 66.
53. *LP*, p. 96.
54. Ibid., pp. 94–95.

(p. 102). Likewise, "what more excellent patriot could there be than Manlius, till he became corrupted by time and power? Who more noble, and courteous, and well-affected to the common good, than was Appius Claudius?" (p. 27).

The danger to England is that the people's "negligence, in suffering themselves to be deluded" will allow them to be "won by specious pretences, and deluded by created necessities" (p. 80) and that a "supposed great patron of liberty" (p. 97) will prove to be its enemy. Although Cromwell's elevation would in the event be achieved through military coups, there seemed at least as much likelihood, during the period of the republican editorials, that it would emerge through the scenario against which Nedham repeatedly warns: the gradual contraction of power into a few hands and thence into a single person. The danger was the greater for being barely perceptible. Nedham recalls Tacitus's description of the Emperor Augustus, who "never declared himself, till, after many delays and shifts, for the continuation of power in his own hands, he got insensibly into the throne" (pp. 94–95). There is also a more sinister parallel. In the opening issue of *Politicus* Nedham had described Cromwell as "the only"—that is, the outstanding or archetypal—"*Novus Princeps* I ever met with in all the confines of history." The words unmistakably alluded to the model of the "new prince" whose rule is the subject of Machiavelli's *The Prince*. Now, in 1652, the newsbook reproduced the chapter of *The Prince* that recalls the wicked devices by which the "new prince" Dionysius of Syracuse, the Sicilian tyrant of the fourth century B.C., achieved and maintained his tyranny. When writing on the king's behalf Nedham had explicitly compared Cromwell to Dionysius.[55] He could not name him now, but discerning readers could hardly have missed the identification. It is heightened by Nedham's recollection that Dionysius had won his tyranny by "cloathing himself with a pretence of the people's liberties" and had been "by that means made their general" (p. 58).

Some of Nedham's boldest observations about the protraction of Cromwell's command were offered in May 1652 (pp. 81–82, 85–88). They

55. Ibid., pp. 91–92.

were sharply topical, for in that month the Commons resolved that the office of the lord lieutenant of Ireland, a survival from the monarchy that he had acquired in 1649, "be not continued."[56] It was in May, too, that Lilburne mentioned the "notable preambles" of *Politicus*. Their warnings about Cromwell were the passages invoked by Lilburne, who suspected, as perhaps Nedham did, that the lord general's foot-dragging over the holding of parliamentary elections derived from a fear that a newly elected parliament would feel more confident than the present one in resisting his own aggrandizement. Lilburne and the Levellers had long hated Cromwell, whom they believed to have turned ruthlessly against them; they had long been dismayed by the protraction of his military authority; they had long observed the "Machiavellian pretences" by which he advanced his own power.[57] The terms "junta" and "grandee," which *Politicus* aims at both him and the Rump, had been used to convey their own detestation of them. They had likewise directed the term "lordly interest," which recurrently appears in *Politicus*, at Cromwell.[58]

Lilburne returned to those subjects in a tract of 1653, in passages that again deploy the arguments and language of Nedham's republican editorials. "Great and glorious things . . . for the people's good," Lilburne writes, have been "pretended" by Cromwell, so that he might thwart the people's hopes of "constant successive parliaments" and, "Julius Caesar–like," usurp power for himself. Lilburne himself reproduced the chapter of *The Prince* about Dionysius of Syracuse—and made mischievous adjustments to it that heightened its pertinence to Cromwell.[59] Lilburne's literary campaign against Cromwell in 1653 included a public letter to "my very good friend" the Member of

---

56. *Journal of the House of Commons*, May 19, 1652. I am grateful to John Morrill for discussions of this point.

57. Walter Scott, ed., *Somers Tracts*, 13 vols. (London, 1806–13), 6:49.

58. Ibid., 6:45.

59. Lilburne, *Upright Mans Vindication*, pp. 6–8. See, too, Scott, *Somers Tracts*, 6:45, 168; *The Leveller* (London, 1659), pp. 80–89 (a tract published by Thomas Brewster, the publisher of Nedham's *The Excellencie* in 1656); *A Collection of the State Papers of John Thurloe*, 7 vols., ed. Thomas Birch (London, 1742), 7:754.

Parliament Henry Marten, who had long been a fellow sympathizer of Nedham's. Marten acted as a teller against the prolongation of Cromwell's lord lieutenancy in May 1652.[60] In Marten's papers there survives a manuscript that was composed, evidently with a view to publication or circulation, in the summer of 1653, shortly after Cromwell's forcible expulsion of the Rump. Written, or ostensibly written, by a member of the Parliament, perhaps by Marten himself and certainly by someone who held a number of his views, the paper recalled that the Rump had "lived in perpetual apprehension of what is now happened." The Parliament, the paper added, had brought destruction on itself by its elevation of Cromwell to supreme command of the army that occupied England and that conquered Ireland and Scotland. For "nothing did render the parliament more unfit to, and indeed more uncapable to settle the government than their putting all the power into the three nations into one hand," a decision by which it was "manifested to the world" that the parliament "understood nothing of a Commonwealth but the name."[61] Its ignorance on that subject was Nedham's complaint too.

Alongside Nedham's indications that Cromwell was a "kingly aspirer" (p. 21) there lay another foreboding. In the weeks before the regicide, and on occasions in the years of the Commonwealth and then of the protectorate, a proposal surfaced, sometimes within Cromwell's circle, sometimes outside it, that he or the republic should strike a deal with the exiled court. The outcome would be the return of the Stuart line, now or at some future date, on terms that would guarantee the survival of the parliamentarians, or Cromwell himself, in power.[62] It was an unlikely prospect but, Nedham evidently sensed, not an impossible one. In February 1651, when the antagonism of his patron John Bradshaw to Cromwell was sharpening, Nedham published an editorial recalling the unscrupulous achievement during the Wars of the Roses of that

60. *Journal of the House of Commons*, 21 May 1652.

61. C. M. Williams, "The Political Career of Henry Marten" (Ph.D. thesis, Oxford University, 1954), pp. 546–47.

62. Whitelocke, *Memorials*, 3:373–74; James Howell, *An Admonition to my Lord Protector* (London, 1654); Cromwell, *Writings and Speeches*, 3:524–25.

self-interested deposer and enthroner of kings, Richard Neville, Earl of Warwick (p. 17).

Although mostly concerned with advancing a political program, the editorials of *Politicus* advance a religious program too. It is a no less radical one. On no subject was Nedham closer to Milton, whose demand for the separation of church from state is echoed in two editorials of *Politicus*.[63] Though Nedham's writing has none of the spiritual dimension of Milton's, it shares his friend's aversion to what the two men saw as the power and bigotry of the clerical estate, especially in its Presbyterian form. As in politics, so in religion, the rulers of the Commonwealth were divided. Most Members of Parliament wanted reform of the church, but within existing structures and conceptions of state control. Only a minority took Milton's and Nedham's more far-reaching position. The first of the two editorials appeared on 29 April 1652, just when the Commonwealth's debates on religious reform had reached their decisive moment. In response to that crisis Milton wrote the sonnet to Cromwell that urges him to protect the passage of God's spirit from the contaminations of the world. The second of the editorials, on 12 August 1652, was the last one that the newsbook would publish. Perhaps its passionately worded anticlericalism, which in its audacity recalls the suicidal attacks on Charles I in the last stage of Nedham's earlier newsbook *Britanicus*, explains or helps to explain the demise of the editorials. Or perhaps Nedham already knew that his sequence of republican arguments, which he may anyway have felt to have run its course, was about to be terminated, and he decided to conclude with a defiantly explosive outburst. By August 1652 the intensification of divisions within the regime had paralyzed the government's capacity for polemical initiatives. Henceforth *Politicus* confined its indications of opinion to the slanting of the news it carried.[64]

63. *LP,* pp. 249–54.

64. Students of *Politicus* may wish to note a run of variant issues found at the Harvard College Library: see H. Weber, "On a File of *Mercurius Politicus* in the Harvard College Library," *Notes and Queries* 164 (1933): 364–66.

## Nedham and *The Excellencie* (1656)

Journalism, for which Nedham had such gifts, never satisfied him. He longed to write "treatises" that would give scope for more reflective writing and would command more public respect. "Serious truth," he complained, "is not regarded in a pamphlet," "the very name whereof is enough to raise a prejudice upon any other notions, how reasonable soever they be."[65] In August 1652 he concluded the last of his editorials in these words: "being confined to a few pages weekly, I have been able to give you but the bare hints of things done in haste, which may (perhaps) appear abroad in a more accomplished manner hereafter."[66] Four years later, on or around 29 June 1656, *The Excellencie of a Free-State* appeared.[67] Most of it consisted of material reproduced, mostly in the same order, from the editorials that had run from September 1651 to August 1652, though on three occasions he returned to editorials published earlier in 1651 (one of which contained the material about Warwick the kingmaker).

Unlike the editorials, the republication presents Nedham's material in a coherent and convenient form. It is, alas, not "more accomplished" than the earlier venture, and it is not the expanded version that is apparently anticipated by his statement that the editorials have contained only "bare hints" of his thinking. Although he made a number of adjustments to the editorials in 1656, he left their essential character and content intact. Journalists, who know that their material is soon forgotten, can afford to repeat it. If they write with a polemical purpose, as Nedham did, repetition may be necessary. To readers who encounter the editorials in their gathered form, the repetitions may be an irritant.[68] Another deficiency, which lies in the opportunism and

---

65. Worden, "'Wit in a Roundhead,'" p. 303.

66. A comparable passage had appeared in April 1652 (p. 157): perhaps the editorials had nearly been terminated at that time.

67. For the approximate date of publication see G. K. Fortescue, ed., *Catalogue of the Pamphlets . . . collected by George Thomason, 1640–1661*, 2 vols. (London, 1908), 2:153.

68. The repetitions irritated a reviewer upon the book's republication in 1767. *Monthly Review*, January 1767, p. 39.

the distortions that characterize his historical illustrations, is likewise heightened when the editorials are viewed alongside each other. Perhaps those weaknesses help to explain why, as far as we can judge, *The Excellencie* made far less contemporary impact than the editorials had done. It did, however, resonate in two significant works by other writers. The title of Milton's tract of 1660, *The Readie and Easie Way to Establish a Free Commonwealth, and the Excellence Thereof,* a book in whose composition and promotion Nedham was closely involved,[69] echoes Nedham's title: *The Excellencie of a Free-State; or, The Right Constitution of a Commonwealth.*[70] The second writer is the Puritan politician Bulstrode Whitelocke, another associate of Nedham, whose reflections on the English constitution would acquire an eighteenth-century following. Whitelocke reproduced passages that appear in *The Excellencie,* without naming the book or its author, in his manuscript "Historie of the Parlement of England," which he probably drew up after the Restoration, but in which he is likely to have drawn on notes made before it. Its main debt was to Nedham's condemnation of the oppression of the people by classical oligarchies and to his discussion of the emergence of Rome's tribunes and popular assemblies. On the subject of oligarchy Whitelocke "follow[ed] most the history of Rome," "as affording most examples, and perhaps too many resemblances," to English history.[71]

69. *LP,* pp. 349–53.
70. Ibid., pp. 77n, 133–36, 409.
71. Stowe MS 333, fols. 103–20, British Library. While Whitelocke's longer extracts from Nedham seem to have been taken from the text of *The Excellencie* rather than of *Politicus* (for on the two pertinent occasions when the texts of those two publications diverge, Whitelocke's wording is that of the tract rather than of the newsbook), there is one brief passage in which Whitelocke carries an echo of *Politicus* (fol. 113ᵛ, on Appius Claudius; see p. 177, below), and another that has material also to be found in Nedham's *The Case of the Commonwealth* (fol. 120ᵛ, on Sallust; Knachel, pp. 116–17). While Whitelocke, in composing his manuscript, may simply have moved among Nedham's publications, there is perhaps an alternative possibility: that he drew on a compendium of notes made available to him by Nedham. There is a hint elsewhere of literary collaboration between the two men. In 1652 Nedham, in dedicating his translation of John Selden's *Mare Clausum* to Parliament in 1652, said that his work for the book had been much "indebted," "(as I also am for many other favours), to a Right

The publication of *The Excellencie* in 1656 is not to be understood merely as a bid to give permanence or status to arguments previously offered in an ephemeral form. It had another purpose. *Politicus* had been a vehicle for criticism of a regime of which it was simultaneously the most influential weekly organ. *The Excellencie* carried sharper, and more startling, criticism of the present power.[72] Unlike *Politicus* it was not a government publication. Since Cromwell's elevation to single rule in December 1653, Nedham had been working for the protectorate, still with Milton at his side, in the office of Cromwell's secretary of state John Thurloe. From the beginning to the end of the Cromwellian regime, *Politicus* gave it unequivocal support. In February 1654 there was published, by the government printer Thomas Newcomb, who also printed *Politicus*, Nedham's pamphlet *A True State of the Case of the Commonwealth*. It was the ablest and most influential work to appear in vindication of the new government. The regime and its supporters did what they could to promote it.[73] Cromwell, in one of a number of indications that the protector turned to Nedham for help in the preparation of his speeches, would himself commend it and draw on its arguments in an address to Parliament in January 1655.[74] The pamphlet was the only contemporary work to which he ever referred in such a way. It may be—for the evidence is inconclusive—that a copy of the tract was handed to each Member of Parliament during the critical debates over the authority of the protectorate in the same Parliament four months

---

Honourable Member of your own great assembly" (Selden, *Of the Dominion*, sig. A2v). The obvious candidate is Selden's friend and devoted admirer Whitelocke, whose own writing drew extensively on Selden's. Though Whitelocke was no republican, he, like Nedham, defies the customary categorizations of Puritan politics. Like him he worked for, and was paid by, the protectorate while regarding it as a tyranny. Like him he had Leveller connections and sympathies that can surprise readers accustomed to his other faces. See Ruth Spalding, *Contemporaries of Bulstrode Whitelocke 1605–1675* (Oxford, U.K.: Oxford University Press, 1990), pp. 457–63; Whitelocke, *Memorials*, 4:187. For the connections between Whitelocke and Nedham see, too, Spalding, *Contemporaries of Bulstrode Whitelocke*, pp. 215–18; *LP*, pp. 134–36.

72. *LP*, pp. 305–13.

73. *State Papers of John Thurloe*, ed. Birch, 2:164; John Goodwin, *Peace Protected* (London, 1654), pp. 71–72.

74. *LP*, p. 141.

earlier.[75] By contrast, the publication of *The Excellencie* was furtive. It made no mention of the earlier appearance of the material in *Politicus*. Its authorship was disguised by the pretense—or semipretense, for Nedham's language has characteristically clever ambiguity—that the anonymous writer is a member of the army (p. 7).[76] The publisher, Thomas Brewster, had a line in unorthodox or radical publications, and had fallen from government favor upon Cromwell's elevation. Nedham took many risks in his career but none braver or rasher than the publication of *The Excellencie*. The treatise is an attack on the protectorate. That it did not cost him his freedom or even his job is intelligible only on the supposition that the government grasped what earlier powers had discovered: that politicians had more to gain from employing his gifts of propaganda, even at the cost of overlooking his departures from the official line, than from driving him into open opposition.[77] In his survival as much as in the "tergiversations" that imperilled it, his career unseats our perceptions of Puritan politics.

*The Excellencie* presents itself in its preface as a response to "high and ranting discourses of personal prerogative and unbounded monarchy" that have recently been published. Nedham singles out a work that appeared in September 1655, a month before *The Excellencie* was registered for publication.[78] This was *Som Sober Inspections . . . of the*

---

75. *A Perfect Diurnall; or, Occurrences of Certain Military Affairs* (London, 1654), 4–11 September 1654, p, 152; *A Perfect Account* (London, n.d.), 6–13 September 1654, p. 1535.

76. It is uncertain whether another republican attack on the protectorate, the Harringtonian tract carrying the title *A Copy of a Letter from an Officer of the Army in Ireland* (London, 1656), was really written by a soldier. *The Political Works of James Harrington,* ed. J. G. A. Pocock (Cambridge, U.K.: Cambridge University Press, 1977), pp. 10–12.

77. He served the protectorate adroitly not only as a writer but as an informer and as a ruthless orchestrator of favorable addresses to the regime from the localities. *LP,* pp. 25–26. For his manipulation of news in the government's interests see Patrick Little, "John Thurloe and the Offer of the Crown to Oliver Cromwell," in *Oliver Cromwell: New Perspectives,* ed. Patrick Little (Basingstoke, U.K.: Palgrave Macmillan, 2009), pp. 223, 226–27.

78. For the registration see *A Transcript of the Registers of the Worshipful Company of Stationers,* 3 vols. (London, 1913–14), 2:20. The fact that *The Excellencie* was registered can be taken to eliminate any possibility that the book was somehow published without Nedham's willing involvement.

*Late-long Parliament* (London, 1655) by the royalist James Howell. In his royalist phase in 1648, Nedham's newsbook *Mercurius Pragmaticus* had called Howell "that rare gentleman" and had commended a "seasonable" antiparliamentarian publication by him, "full of high reason and satisfaction." [79] A work by Howell of 1651 about the republic of Venice had been twice endorsed in editorials of *Politicus* (pp. 149, 161). Now, as so often, Nedham turned against a former literary ally. In 1654 Howell had urged Cromwell to follow the course against which Nedham, in *Politicus*, had warned in his allusions to Warwick the kingmaker. The protector, Howell proposed, should reach an agreement with the exiled court that would allow Charles II to assume the throne on Cromwell's death.[80] *Som Sober Inspections* has other advice for Cromwell, of a kind that would have been equally unsavory to republicans. He should rid himself, urged Howell, of the obstructive capacity of parliaments that had blighted Stuart rule.

Nedham quickly admits that *The Excellencie* is "not intended for a particular answer" to Howell's tract. His decision to begin with it, however, brings him two opportunities. First, he is able to give the initial impression that his book is directed, as the government would have liked it to be, against "the family and interest of the Stuarts," and that his own sympathies are with "his Highness," the protector. Disloyal to the protectorate as *The Excellencie* is, the disloyalty is never explicit. Its extent becomes evident when we recognize the second advantage that Nedham takes of the publication of Howell's tract. He cleverly lets Howell's plea for unfettered single rule, and his attack on parliamentary government and on the Parliament that Cromwell had dissolved in April 1653, set the terms of his own argument. Nedham agrees with Howell that the nation faces a choice between "unbounded monarchy" and rule by a parliament—and reaches the opposite answer. Two years earlier, in *A True State*, Nedham had portrayed the protectorate as a middle way between those choices. He had commended the Instrument of Government, the constitution on which the protectorate

---

79. *Mercurius Pragmaticus*, 26 September 1648, p. 16.
80. Howell, *Admonition*.

based its authority, for returning to the traditional balance of power between a single ruler and Parliament. In *The Excellencie* the middle way is forgotten. Readers of Nedham's preface are now invited to decide which of two courses will "best secure the liberties and freedoms of the people from the encroachments and usurpations of tyranny, and answer the true ends of the late wars": Howell's program, or "a due and orderly succession of the supreme authority in the hands of the people's representatives."

It soon becomes evident that the unbounded ruler that Nedham has in mind is not a Stuart. It is the usurper and tyrant Cromwell. It also soon becomes evident that the alternative Nedham offers is a return to the parliamentary sovereignty that Cromwell has broken. His purpose is achieved by a sleight of hand adroit even by his standards. *A True State* had reminded parliamentarian readers that "the original ground of our first engaging in the war" against Charles I had not been the attainment of parliamentary or republican government. The king's opponents had fought against tyranny, not kingship. They had sought to "regulate" the "disorders and excesses" of Charles I's rule.[81] The preface to *The Excellencie* likewise has passages that seem reassuring to mainstream parliamentary opinion. Claiming to speak for "all" the "friends and adherents" of the Long Parliament, Nedham remembers that it took up arms "not to destroy magistracy, but to regulate it; nor to confound propriety, but to enlarge it: that the prince as well as the people might be governed by law." Yet before we know where we are he has contrived to indicate that "the true ends of the late war" will be "answered" by the rule of sovereign parliaments, which will make England "a glorious commonwealth." For in *The Excellencie* the "due and orderly succession . . . in the hands of the people's representatives" is a defining feature, even the defining one, of a "free state," of which the book celebrates the "excellencie." It was the sovereign parliament of 1649–53, and it alone, that had declared England a "free state." The protectorate shunned the term.

No more than *Politicus* does *The Excellencie* provide an unambiguous vindication of the imperfect free state of 1649–53. Almost all the

---

81. *A True State of the Case of the Commonwealth* (London, 1654), pp. 5–6.

criticisms of the Rump that are visible in the newsbook reappear in *The Excellencie*. But the most damaging criticism, which had been directed at the Parliament's reluctance to hold elections, had lost much of its force as a result of the Rump's expulsion. Once removed from power, the victims of the coup committed themselves to the "constant succession" of parliaments that *Politicus* had demanded. Nedham now stands with its former members against Cromwell's destruction of parliamentary supremacy and against the tyranny with which the protector was alleged to have replaced it. Former prominent members of the Commonwealth regime, John Bradshaw among them, protested and conspired against Cromwell's rule. They liked to remind the protector that his expulsion of the Long Parliament had breached the treason act passed by the Commonwealth in 1649. *Politicus* had warned him that in accumulating power he risked "the guilt of treason against the interest and majesty of the people." *The Excellencie*, by repeating that passage (p. 102), confirms his crime. Another linguistic echo works to similar effect. Under the protectorate, men of Bradshaw's outlook, standing on the principle of parliamentary supremacy, were called "commonwealthmen" or "commonwealthsmen." *Politicus* had urged the English to "learn to be true commonwealth's-men." That plea, too, reappears in *The Excellencie* (p. 81).

We cannot say why Nedham, or his publisher, delayed nine months between registering *The Excellencie* and publishing it. It seems likely that the book, when it went to the printer in 1656, stood as it had done, or much as it had done, the previous year[82]—but with one exception. The concluding passage of the tract looks like a late addition. It reverts from the concluding editorials of *Politicus* to an earlier one, of November 1651, which now reappears as "a word of advice" to the electorate. The decision to call the parliament of 1656 was made at the end of May. The council's order for the issuing of electoral writs was agreed, as *Politicus* informed the nation, on or around 1 July.[83] *The Excellencie* (published on or around 29 June) appeared as an election manifesto. Its advice

82. The book carried an advertisement for three of the publisher's other productions, all of them carrying the date 1655. See Appendix A.

83. Cromwell, *Writings and Speeches*, ed. Abbott, 4:169, 198.

was to elect commonwealthmen. They were active in the election campaign, none more so than Henry Neville, who had been an ally of Nedham under the Commonwealth, and the quashing of whose election by the protectorate became a *cause célèbre*. Cromwell's executive council forbade all those commonwealthmen who won election in 1656 to sit in the Parliament, which in 1657 gave legislative sanction to the protectorate, brought it closer to the traditional forms of monarchy, and made Cromwell "king in all but name." [84]

Around six weeks before the publication of *The Excellencie*, another tract hostile to the protectorate had appeared: *A Healing Question Propounded* (London, 1656) by Sir Henry Vane. A hero of Milton, Vane was a former member of the Long Parliament who had been a crucial ally of Cromwell in it, but who had broken bitterly with him in 1653. *The Excellencie* carried an advertisement for another work by Vane that was unsympathetic to the protector, *The Retired Mans Meditations*, which Thomas Brewster had published in 1655. In November 1656 there appeared the *Oceana* of James Harrington, to which Harrington's intimate friend Henry Neville reportedly contributed, and which conformed to Neville's own views. *Oceana*, like Nedham's editorials in *Politicus* and like *The Excellencie*, has an anti-Cromwellian purpose that is intelligible only when its wording is set against its immediate political background. [85] It seems that Harrington had drafted it not long after the regicide, and that in 1656 the draft was adapted, as the editorials of *Politicus* were in *The Excellencie*, to the circumstances of the protectorate. Amid a number of differences between *Oceana* and *The Excellencie*, the most pronounced of them arising from Harrington's dislike of the spirit of political partisanship that Nedham's propaganda espoused, there is a striking series of parallels between the republican arguments of the two men. [86] If Harrington's treatise indeed originated,

---

84. Roy Sherwood, *Oliver Cromwell: King in All But Name* (Stroud, U.K.: Sutton, 1997).

85. Wootton, *Republicanism*, pp. 113–26; *LP*, pp. 105–15.

86. I have explained the point in Wootton, *Republicanism*, pp. 111–14, although I should have paid more attention to the resemblances between the proposals and arguments advanced by the two writers for dividing and balancing the functions

like Nedham's, under the Rump, we are left to remark on the fertility of that era in political thought and reflection, producing as it also did Hobbes's *Leviathan,* the debate over the sovereignty of the sword, Marvell's "Horatian Ode," and the rhetorical triumph of the *Defensio* published by Milton on behalf of the regicide.

If Nedham was not the profoundest of the thinkers of the Commonwealth, he could at least have claimed, under the protectorate, to have been the most prophetic of them. The reappearance in *The Excellencie* of the warnings that *Politicus* had given Cromwell imparts a quality of dramatic irony to the work. But Nedham was not content to repeat those warnings. By deft adjustments of wording he points to the difference of context and of purpose between the editorials, which were written to secure and extend republican rule, and the book, which was intended to restore it. Having reminded the reader, in the first sentence of the preface, that England has been "declared" to be a "free state," Nedham time and again alters the wording of *Politicus* so as to bring the term "free state" before the reader's eye (pp. 83, 95, 98, 105). Even on occasions when the term is reproduced from *Politicus,* Nedham redeploys it so as to underline Cromwell's destruction of the republic. *Politicus,* in urging the English not to re-admit the Stuarts, had advised them "to keep close to the rules of a free state, for the barring out of monarchy," and had commended the founders of commonwealths, such as England's rulers of 1649, who "have blocked up the way against monarchal tyranny, by declaring for the liberty of the people." In 1656, when England had, or was getting, a new monarchy (under whatever name), Nedham amended his wording and cited "the rules of a free state, for the turning out of monarchy" and commended founders of commonwealths "who shall block up the way against monarchic tyranny" by declaring—as Nedham would have wanted the parliament of 1656 to do—"for the liberty of the people" (p. 82). Other changes likewise draw

---

and powers of a senate and a popular assembly. Note, too, in Harrington's account in *Oceana* of the age when "the world was full of popular governments" (Harrington, *Political Works,* l. 3, p. 312), the echo of Nedham's allusion to the times when "the world abounded with free-states" (p. 35; compare p. 73).

hostile attention to Cromwell's usurpation. In *Politicus* "it is good commonwealth language" to maintain "that a due and orderly succession of power and persons" is the only means to preserve freedom and avoid tyranny. In *The Excellencie* "it was, and is, good commonwealth language" to do so (p. 23). In *Politicus,* the people are "now invested" in the possession of the "excellent" government of a free state: in the tract, they "but the other day were invested" in it (p. 81). The arguments of *Politicus* were replies to "all objecting monarchs and royalists": *The Excellencie,* to remind readers that a new kind of kingly power had arisen in the Stuarts' place, answered "all objecting monarchs and royalists, of what name and title soever" (p. 52). Another change enabled Nedham to glance at what he, and not he alone,[87] mockingly called the "holy war" which from the end of 1654 Cromwell had been fighting against Spain and which *The Excellencie* ascribes not to the zealous anti-Catholic motives professed by the regime but to the sinister principle of "reason of state" (p. 108). Further alterations enabled Nedham to use two terms that the commonwealthmen habitually applied to Cromwell's regime after his assumption of the protectorate. First, like them he alludes to the "apostacy" of those who support it (p. 42). Second, like the commonwealthmen, who refused to call Cromwell "protector," he instead alludes to him as the "general" (p. 58), the military title which his own ambition had prolonged, and by virtue of which he had seized power in April 1653.[88] He does, however, reproduce from *Politicus* his commendation of Rome's tribunes as the "protectors" of the people—but the noun is now italicized, a change that hints at the unhappy contrast between the Roman past and the English present (p. 13).[89]

When, in October 1655, Nedham registered *The Excellencie,* the protectorate's fortunes were low. Its attempt to secure parliamentary

87. Patrick Little and David L. Smith, *Parliaments and Politics During the Cromwellian Protectorate* (Cambridge, U.K.: Cambridge University Press, 2007), p. 257.

88. For the practice of making barbed interlinear allusions to Cromwell as the "general" see *LP,* pp. 317–18. It had begun before 1653 (p. xl), and was used in Lilburne's anti-Cromwellian tracts.

89. Compare Nedham's ingeniously hostile deployment of the same noun in 1659. *LP,* p. 44.

sanction for the Instrument of Government in the previous winter had been rebuffed, and it had resorted instead to the military rule of the major-generals. Over the summer of 1655 there seem to have been discussions within the regime, perhaps born of desperation, of a proposal to return to hereditary rule under the Cromwell family, a prospect that could have prompted or speeded the composition of *The Excellencie*. Late in the summer news came through of the humiliating defeat of an ambitious expedition sent by Cromwell to attack the Spanish empire in the new world. The political and fiscal paralysis that would induce the government to call the parliament of 1656 was already apparent. Perhaps Nedham, as at other times in his career, was preparing to jump ship. But there is an alternative, or additional, possibility. Under the Rump his arguments, offensive or troubling as they must have been in varying degrees to a high proportion of the nation's rulers, would have had support or protection from such radical figures as John Bradshaw and Henry Marten. Perhaps he had protectors, or even supporters, in Whitehall now. The protectorate, like the Rump before it, was a divided regime. Alongside those who wanted to steer it toward the resumption of monarchy, there were men, the military leaders Charles Fleetwood and John Desborough—Cromwell's son-in-law and brother-in-law—at their fore, who saw the protectorate as a means to preserve the nation and the Puritan cause from the anarchy into which it had descended in 1653, but who resisted the monarchical trend that had followed Cromwell's elevation. In opposition to it they were ready, in the manner of many politicians of the era, to endorse the publication of arguments bolder than their own positions. Fleetwood gave Sir Henry Vane encouragement to write *A Healing Question Propounded*. In 1654 Desborough had striven to protect a writer, John Streater, whose statements of republican principles were remarkably close to Nedham's.[90] He was, however, more vulnerable than Nedham. Being inflexibly committed to his principles, he had nothing to offer the government in return for toleration of his arguments. In 1654 he got into trouble for publishing a "discourse" in which "the excellence of a

90. *LP*, pp. 313–16; Wootton, *Republicanism*, p. 138 and n. 88.

free state was maintained, and the inconveniences of a tyranny or single person were fully demonstrated." Troops were sent to Streater's house, perhaps at Thurloe's behest, to silence him.[91] In 1656 Streater would be the printer of Harrington's *Oceana.*

Fleetwood and Desborough, however troubled they might have been by Nedham's main argument, could have been expected to welcome certain of the adjustments that were made in *The Excellencie* to material that had appeared in *Politicus.* In *The Excellencie* Nedham fleetingly and tentatively allows for a possibility that he had ruled out in 1651–52 and that the tract of 1656 otherwise excludes: the appointment of a king, who would be "chosen by the people's representatives, and made an officer of trust by them" (p. 41). In some men's eyes, at least, that proposal would have been compatible, as the principles laid down on behalf of the protectorate in Nedham's *A True State* in 1654 would not have been, with the sovereignty of Parliament, to which the king would be subordinate. The wording recalls that of the army when, before its march on London in December 1648, it contemplated the enthronement of an elected monarch.[92] *Politicus* had insisted that England's republic be kept free from "mixture" with any other form of government. That stipulation was omitted from *The Excellencie* (p. 141). Perhaps the reminder in the preface that parliament had fought the king so that "the prince as well as the people might be governed by law" was another hint that the unqualified republicanism demanded by the main body of the tract was not nonnegotiable. Support could have been found within *The Excellencie* for the continuation of Cromwell in office, with reduced powers defined and delegated by a sovereign parliament.

Not only was it a solution that might have satisfied Fleetwood and Desborough. It would have more or less accorded with the goals of Presbyterian members of the Parliament of 1654–55 who had been appalled by the pure republicanism of the commonwealthmen, and who had accordingly been ready to help keep the protectorate in being, but who had insisted that the definition of the protector's powers was a

91. John Streater, *Secret Reasons of State* (London, 1659), p. 18; *LP,* p. 312.
92. Worden, "Republicanism, Regicide and Republic," pp. 320–21.

matter for Parliament alone. The editorials of *Politicus* had recalled the misconduct of those Members of Parliament and their allies in 1647. *The Excellencie* dropped those accusations (pp. 139, 158, 170, 173), which in any case now belonged to the past. Nedham does nothing to indicate any diminution of his aversion to Presbyterian bigotry, but he does omit the last of the editorials of *Politicus,* the more inflammatory of the two that he had directed at the clerical estate, which the Presbyterians championed. In other places on the periphery of its argument his tract likewise offers concessions, or the hope of them, to political groups distant from the commonwealthmen.

In their despair and anger at Cromwell's usurpation, commonwealthmen had tried to form an anti-Cromwellian front, a tactic that would be repeated by Henry Neville and allies of his in the elections of 1656.[93] The commonwealthmen even appealed, as Levellers had sometimes done in the years since 1649, to those fellow victims of Cromwellian or military rule, the royalists, whom *The Excellencie* also aspired to win over. Even though it remained hostile to the memory of Charles I, and even though it offered royalists, at least for the time being, no prospect of participation in politics, the tract took a much softer line against the Stuart cause than *Politicus* had done. The phrase "the late tyrant," used of Charles I in *Politicus,* became, in 1656, "the late king" (pp. 37, 67, 92, 98). In the same year Harrington's republican treatise *Oceana* likewise shielded Charles from the charge of tyranny. To Harrington, as to Nedham in *The Excellencie,* the tyrant was Cromwell.[94] *Politicus* had vilified "the odious . . . name of Stuart," but *The Excellencie* replaced it with that of Richard III, the usurping king and former lord protector, whose name stood, in antiprotectoral thinking, for the usurper Cromwell.[95] The social radicalism of the newsbook, which had corresponded to a marked trend of the political writing and agitation of 1651–52, but which would have exercised less public appeal by 1656, was toned down in *The Excellencie.* Criticisms of the social oppression which *Politicus*

93. *Thurloe State Papers,* 5:296.
94. *LP,* pp. 105–14.
95. William Prynne, *King Richard the Third Revived* (London, 1657), PRO 31.3/92, fol. 197, The National Archives.

had discerned in the oligarchical republic of Venice were now reduced. The term "public popular militia" gives way to the tamer "public militia" (p. 92). Even as Nedham prepares, in the preface to *The Excellencie,* to argue for a contentious and animating political programme, he offers the prospect that the nation can become "a quiet habitation" where "none might make the people afraid." By such tactics does he seek to portray the republicanism of *Politicus* as the natural creed not only of the radicals in parliament and army but of the broad, essentially conservative parliamentarian cause. To that end the republicanism is presented in what, at least to outward appearances, is a diluted form. Neville and other republicans would adopt the same tactic in Parliament in 1659.[96]

## The Republication of *The Excellencie* (1767)

The republication of *The Excellencie* in 1767 has its context too. Behind it there lies a story that goes back about seventy years to 1698–1700, a decade or so after the Revolution that deposed James II and brought William III and Mary II to the throne. In those years a group of radical Whig writers and publicists, of whom the most active was the deist John Toland, revived the republican arguments of the Cromwellian and Restoration eras by publishing or, in most cases, republishing books that had advanced them. Writings by John Milton, Algernon Sidney, James Harrington, Henry Neville, and Edmund Ludlow were brought or brought back into print.

It was a brave venture.[97] Since the Restoration the memory of the regicide, and of the military and sectarian anarchy that followed it, had discredited republican arguments. In the 1690s two rival views of the midcentury convulsion emerged among the Whigs. Mainstream Whigs

---

96. Wootton, *Republicanism,* pp. 126–38.

97. I have described this venture, and the political setting and purposes of the republications, in Blair Worden, *Roundhead Reputations: The English Civil Wars and the Passions of Posterity* (London: Allen Lane, Penguin Press, 2001) and in "Whig History and Puritan Politics: The *Memoirs of Edmund Ludlow* Revisited," *Historical Research* 75 (2002): 209–37.

were eager, in the face of Tory accusations of seditious purpose, to demonstrate their affection for the established constitution. They dwelled on the memory not of 1649 but of the Revolution of 1688, which had brought them to power and which had preserved rather than destroyed the monarchy. To radical Whigs, by contrast, 1688 had been a missed opportunity to reassert the principles that had brought Charles I to account and to achieve the radical curtailment, possibly even the elimination, of the monarchy. So long as the post-Revolutionary regime of William III was fighting for survival against France, which had taken up the cause of the exiled Stuarts, the radical case was only intermittently advanced. After the Peace of Ryswick in 1697 it was boldly articulated. The Peace handed an inflammatory issue to republicans. They castigated the determination of the Whig ministry to retain an army in peacetime, a move, they alleged, that recalled the military rule of Cromwell. As in the 1650s, it was implied, so in the 1690s: a regime that had claimed to replace a tyranny had acquired its own tyrannical properties.

Of the republican writers who had had roles in the civil wars and whose works were published or revived at the end of the century, one name is conspicuously absent: Nedham's. The omission not only confined his tract to obscurity but also restricted the impact of the edition of 1767. By that time the republican writings that Toland and his allies did publish had become well known, so much so that it would be difficult for Nedham's writing to add much to them. But if Toland and his allies never mentioned Nedham's name, they did make silent use of him. In 1697 one of the principal tracts of the standing army controversy, apparently written by Toland in association with Walter Moyle and John Trenchard, appropriated, without acknowledgment, paragraphs in which Nedham had sung the praises of citizen militias, the republican alternative to standing armies.[98] In 1698 a separate

---

98. Compare *An Argument, Shewing, that a Standing Army is inconsistent with a Free Government* (London, 1697), pp. 7–9, with p. 90. Nedham's wording was altered, but the debt to him is clear and extensive. See too the passages that recall Nedham's wording in Moyle's treatise of 1698, *An Essay upon the Constitution of the Roman Government.* Caroline Robbins, ed., *Two English Republican Tracts* (London: Cambridge University Press, 1969), pp. 235, 239–40.

contribution to the standing army debate by Toland, his tract *The Militia Reform'd,* borrowed briefly from the same passage by Nedham.[99] The material on which Toland, Moyle, and Trenchard drew had appeared both in *Politicus* and in *The Excellencie,* and it is impossible to be certain from which of the two sources the passage was taken. The likely answer is *Politicus,* a work that had been drawn to public attention in 1692 in a biographical account of Nedham by the antiquary Anthony Wood—although Wood's text does not name *The Excellencie* among Nedham's other publications. Wood also mentions Nedham's authorship of *Politicus,* but again does not refer to *The Excellencie,* in his brief life of Milton, in which Nedham figures as a friend of the poet. Wood's descriptions of Nedham lodged themselves in the public mind. Thanks to them, *Politicus* would be much more widely known about than *The Excellencie* until the republication of the tract in 1767.[100] *The Excellencie* itself seems to have come close to disappearance between the Restoration and the republication of 1767.[101] Toland's circle may not have been aware of its existence. Toland did, however, republish a work that had been closely connected to Nedham's republican writings: *The Grounds and Reasons of Monarchy* (1650) by John Hall, who had been a contributor to *Mercurius Politicus.* It was included in the edition of the works of James Harrington published by Toland in 1700. In the

99. John Toland, *The Militia Reform'd* (London, 1698), p. 72. The interest of Toland's circle in Nedham is suggested, too, by bookseller Richard Baldwin's 1692 republication of a previously anonymous tract, *Christianissimus Christianandus* (1678), with Nedham attributed as author. Baldwin, a central figure in the publishing community that produced the canonical texts of the late 1690s, identifies Nedham as the author. There were other anonymous editions: 1691 (published as *The German Spie*), 1701, and 1707. For Baldwin see Edmund Ludlow, *A Voyce from the Watch Tower,* ed. Blair Worden (London: Royal Historical Society, 1978), pp. 18–19, 25, 34n, 54, and Worden, "Whig History and Puritan Politics," pp. 211–13.

100. A biweekly paper of political commentary by J[ames] Drake was published as *Mercurius Politicus* in 1705, and another periodical with the same title, launched by Daniel Defoe, ran from 1716 to 1720.

101. Copies of the 1656 edition very occasionally appear in eighteenth-century book catalogs. When Thomas Hollis presented a copy of the 1656 text to Christ's College Cambridge in 1768 (HD, 14 December 1768), his inscription described it as "rarissima," though he seems to have acquired at least one other copy. See *London Chronicle* 6 October 1772; Blackburne, *Memoirs,* pp. 659, 772–73.

original version the authorship had been indicated solely by the initials "J.H." Perhaps Toland, when he decided to reprint the tract, supposed that Harrington was the author, or else believed that the status of the work would be enhanced if it could be passed off as his. If so, he must have withdrawn the attribution before publication. The preface to the volume acknowledges that the work is not Harrington's but does not say what it is doing in an edition of Harrington's works.[102]

The spirit and energy of Hall's tract, and the vigor and candor of its republicanism, would have appealed to Toland. So would the liveliness of Nedham's prose. But even if Toland did know of *The Excellencie*, would he have considered publishing it? Nedham's social radicalism, though it might have had some appeal to Toland himself, would have gone against the grain of the political and social thought of the late seventeenth century, when radicals felt either inclined or obliged to acknowledge the dependence of liberty on the power of magnates with the wealth to sustain the independence of the crown.[103] Further and perhaps stronger reasons against the republication of *The Excellencie* would have been supplied by the immediate political context in which, and the political purpose for which, Toland worked. The proposal to maintain the army in peacetime provoked a reaction not only among radical Whigs but among Tories. Toland's patron Robert Harley, a statesman with a Whig past and a Tory future, saw in the issue an opportunity to create a "country" alliance, drawn from both parties. It would be united by opposition to the recent expansion of the executive and of its resources of patronage, developments that, it was alleged, had weakened both the virtue and the independence of Members of Parliament. The country party would attack not only the potential of a standing army to oppress the nation but the accompanying corruption and venality of

---

102. James Harrington, *The Oceana of James Harrington and his Other Works*, ed. John Toland (London, 1700), p. xxviii. Some eighteenth-century readers, coming across the tract in that edition or in the ones that followed it, and missing the prefatory disclaimer, would suppose it to be Harrington's. It was sometimes attributed to him in book catalogs, as it was in John Milner, *Virtue the Basis of Publick Happiness* (London, 1747), p. 32n.

103. Wootton, *Republicanism*, pp. 183–86.

the government and the court. Toland wanted to present his heroes of the civil wars not as incendiary figures but as men—preferably landed men—whose virtue and constancy had been impervious to corruption by either Charles I or Cromwell.

Like Nedham (and like Henry Neville) before him, Toland diluted a radical message to broaden its appeal. Yet, again like Nedham (and Neville), he did so with the purpose of luring moderate opinion toward radical solutions. The champions of liberty in the civil wars, Toland invites readers to infer, had not been firebrands. Solemn and responsible reflection had convinced them that only by bringing tyranny to account, or by fundamental constitutional change, could the freedom of the subject be achieved or maintained. He made the views of those heroes seem the natural companion to their uprightness of character. By taking huge editorial liberties he transformed Ludlow's personality to bring it into line with "country" values.[104] It would have been impossible to do the same with Nedham. The account of his life that Wood published in 1692 had brought the venal mutations of "this most seditious, notable and reviling author" to public attention. It is no surprise that the writers of the tract that five years later appropriated Nedham's arguments for citizen militias concealed their source. In the following year Toland's laudatory biography of Milton absorbed material from the earlier lives of the poet by Wood and by Milton's nephew Edward Phillips, but omitted the recollection of those writers that Nedham had been among Milton's friends.[105]

In the eighteenth century the editions of seventeenth-century writers that Toland and his friends did bring into print—Milton, Sidney, Harrington, Neville, Ludlow—were the dominant works in what Caroline Robbins, in her seminal book *The Eighteenth-Century Commonwealthman* half a century ago, called a "sacred canon" of "Real Whig" texts.[106] Their long-term influence, especially their place in

104. Worden, *Roundhead Reputations*, chaps. 1–4.

105. Helen Darbishire, ed., *Early Lives of Milton* (London: Constable, 1932), pp. xxxviii, 44–45, 74.

106. Caroline Robbins, *The Eighteenth-Century Commonwealthman* (1959; repr. New York: Atheneum, 1968), pp. 4–5.

"the ideological origins of the American Revolution," is now widely recognized.[107] But by the mid-eighteenth century the impact of Toland's publications, in England at least, had begun to fade. Toland had sought to merge republicanism with hostility to corruption. Under the first two Georges, hostility to corruption intensified, but republicanism was in retreat.[108] The revival and the renewed impact of the canon were the achievement of a second series of publications, this one spread over a longer period. Two men were responsible for it: Richard Baron and Thomas Hollis. It was they who achieved the republication of *The Excellencie* in 1767. Although they had their allies and sympathizers, they can hardly be said to have led a movement. Hollis's "dissemination of ideas," as Caroline Robbins remarked, "was a strictly private enterprise."[109] Although he had many connections in the antiquarian and bookselling worlds, his allies in the promotion of his program were very few.[110] There is something of the eccentric loner about both him and Baron. There is also a streak of oversensitivity, perhaps of paranoia. And there is an absence of guile, a feature that sharply distinguishes both men from their predecessor in the field, Toland. Hollis was called by Horace Walpole "as simple a soul as ever existed"[111] and by Dr. Johnson "a dull, poor creature as ever lived."[112] Yet by his own lights his labors on liberty's behalf had far-reaching results.

107. On the American side the seminal work was Bernard Bailyn, *The Ideological Origins of the American Revolution* (Cambridge, Mass.: Harvard University Press, 1967).

108. Worden, *Roundhead Reputations*, chaps. 5–6.

109. Caroline Robbins, "The Strenuous Whig, Thomas Hollis of Lincoln's Inn," in *Absolute Liberty: A Selection from the Articles and Papers of Caroline Robbins*, ed. Barbara Taft (Hamden, Conn.: Archon, 1982), p. 173. The material in Taft's selection, particularly this essay, remains the best introduction to Hollis and his work.

110. D. P. Sainsbury, *Disaffected Patriots: London Supporters of Revolutionary America, 1769–82* (Kingston and Montreal: McGill-Queen's University Press, 1987), p. 12; Bridget Hill, *The Republican Virago: The Life and Times of Catharine Macaulay, Historian* (Oxford, U.K.: Clarendon Press, 1992), p. 164.

111. Bernard Knollenberg, "Thomas Hollis and Jonathan Mayhew: Their Correspondence, 1759–1766," *Collections of the Massachusetts Historical Society* 69 (1956): 102–93, at p. 103.

112. W. H. Bond, *Thomas Hollis of Lincoln's Inn: A Whig and His Books* (Cambridge, U.K.: Cambridge University Press, 1990), p. 1.

We know much less about Baron[113] than about Hollis. Born at Leeds and educated at Glasgow, Baron was an impecunious writer, plagued by ill health and family misfortune, a man of artless and uncompromising idealism and of impetuous and splenetic temperament. In his youth he was a devotee of Thomas Gordon, the author, with John Trenchard, of *Cato's Letters*.[114] In 1751 Baron began the revival of the "sacred canon" by producing new editions of the *Memoirs of Edmund Ludlow* and the *Discourses* of Algernon Sidney.[115] His views on seventeenth-century history were notably outspoken. In the Ludlow edition, which enabled the reader, explained Baron, to admire the "principles" on which "those men acted, who passed sentence on King Charles I,"[116] he included the speech which John Cook, whom the Rump had appointed to conduct the prosecution of Charles I, had planned to deliver at the trial. In 1752 Baron edited a collection of tracts, *The Pillars of Priestcraft and Orthodoxy Shaken* (London, 1752), which included a sermon delivered in New England two years earlier by Jonathan Mayhew that had famously applauded Charles's execution. In 1753 Baron produced a new edition, in two volumes, of Milton's prose works.[117] In 1756 he published a hitherto unknown second edition, from 1650, of Milton's attack on the recently executed Charles I, *Eikonoklastes*. Baron announced his own principles and purposes in a preface, where he explained that the edition was designed to "strengthen and support" "the good old cause." "The good old cause" was the label that seventeenth-century regicides and commonwealthmen had claimed for themselves. It was also the

---

113. The best sources for Baron are Blackburne, pp. 61–63, 75–76, 145–46, 356, 361–65, 391, 492–93, 516, 721; HD; *The Protestant Dissenter's Magazine* 6 (1799): 166–68; Sylas Neville, *The Diary of Sylas Neville 1767–1788*, ed. Basil Cozens-Hardy (Oxford, U.K.: Oxford University Press, 1950); see, too, Hill, *Republican Virago*, s.v. "Baron." The brief article in the *Oxford Dictionary of National Biography* is not reliable.

114. John Trenchard and Thomas Gordon, *Cato's Letters: Essays on Liberty*, 2 vols., ed. Ronald Hamowy (Indianapolis: Liberty Fund, 1995).

115. He, and the promotion of the canon, were indebted to the editorial labors of the antiquary Thomas Birch, whose cautious politics were disliked by Baron and by Hollis's circle, but whose contribution they intermittently acknowledged.

116. *Memoirs of Edmund Ludlow* (London, 1751), p. xii.

117. *The Works of John Milton, Historical, Political, and Miscellaneous*, 2 vols., ed. Thomas Birch (London, 1753).

ideal, announced Baron's preface, "which in my youth I embraced, and
the principles whereof I will assert and maintain whilst I live."

He presented a copy of the publication to "my much honoured and
esteemed friend, Thomas Hollis."[118] Hollis was born in 1720 and died
in 1774, six years after Baron (whose year of birth is unknown). Like
Baron he had Yorkshire connections, but his background was otherwise
quite different. He was rich, Baron poor. Hollis, though he lived in
London, had estates in Dorset. Maintaining that the political corruption of the age ran so deep as to incapacitate virtue at Westminster, he
decided not to seek a seat in Parliament. Instead he sought to influence opinion through the publication and republication of works in
"the cause of liberty" or "the cause of truth and liberty." Thus would he
champion—in the phrase he highlighted when remembering the mar-
tyrdom of Algernon Sidney, who had been executed for treason after a
rigged trial in 1683—"the OLD CAUSE."[119] The canon, and the values
it represented, would be profoundly indebted to Hollis's munificence.
He subsidized expensive editions of canonical works. He had handsome
copies, individually bound and inscribed, sent to individuals and libraries in Britain; in North America (where the principal beneficiary was
the library of Harvard College);[120] and on the European Continent,
where they reached the Netherlands,[121] Sweden, France, Germany,

118. Blackburne, p. 62. Another presentation copy, given by Baron to a Mr.
Trueman, is in the Bodleian Library, Oxford: Vet A5 c. 100. It may be that only a
small number of copies were printed, for distribution to Baron's friends: see the
flyleaf of the copy of the second edition, of 1770, in the Bodleian, classmark 22856
e. 124. Hollis was probably responsible for the second edition and probably also
arranged for the second edition, in 1768, of Baron's *The Pillars of Priestcraft and
Orthodoxy Shaken*, 4 vols. (London, 1768) (HD, 11 June 1767).

119. HD, 2 May 1764; Robbins, "Strenuous Whig," pp. 171, 186; Sidney, *Discourses Concerning Government*, ed. Thomas Hollis (London 1763 ed.), p. 40. In
my references to this edition of the *Discourses*, page numbers will be those of the
Introduction, which is separately paginated.

120. Caroline Robbins, "Library of Liberty," in *Absolute Liberty*, pp. 206–29.
William H. Bond's study, *From the Great Desire of Promoting Learning: Thomas
Hollis's Gifts to Harvard College Library* (Cambridge, Mass.: Harvard University
Press, 2010), appeared after this introduction was written.

121. Kees van Strien, "Thomas Hollis and His Donation to Leiden University
Library, 1759–70," *Quaerendo* 30 (2000): 3–34.

Russia, Italy, and Corsica. "Books of government," he explained, were what he "delighted most to send," for "if government goes right all goes right."[122] He arranged and financed the publication of excerpts from the canonical works in the gazettes. He had fresh editions of Ludlow and Harrington printed; he planned new ones of Milton and Neville; and he tried to get the political works of Andrew Marvell republished. Although Hollis normally left the bulk of the editorial work to others, there were two significant exceptions. In 1761 he produced his own edition of Toland's life of Milton, together with *Amyntor,* the sequel Toland had published in 1699.[123] Then, in 1763, came the most laborious and perhaps the most influential of his publishing ventures, his loving edition of Sidney's *Discourses,* which he had undertaken, as he recorded in his diary, "without a single bye view, and ALONE for the love I bear to liberty and his memory" and for "the benefit of my countrymen and mankind."[124] The editions of Sidney and Toland carried extensive annotations that reinforced the texts with pleas for liberty extracted from other works, often from other times.

When Baron's edition of *Eikonoklastes* appeared in 1756, his friendship with Hollis, warm as it evidently was, was of recent origin.[125] At least by 1759, when Hollis's diary begins and we can follow its course, the relationship had become close.[126] The two men would meet frequently and at length, sometimes at Hollis's chambers in Lincoln's Inn, sometimes near Baron's home at Blackheath. They found much common ground in their dismay at the condition of "the times"—a favorite lament of Hollis.[127] They were appalled by the crown's treatment of

---

122. Charles W. Akers, *Called unto Liberty: A Life of Jonathan Mayhew, 1720–1766* (Cambridge, Mass.: Harvard University Press, 1964), p. 145.

123. John Toland, *The Life of John Milton . . . with Amyntor, or, A Defense of Milton's Life* (London, 1761).

124. HD, 31 March 1763.

125. Blackburne, p. 61.

126. I am most grateful to David Womersley for lending me microfilms of the diary.

127. HD, 26 June 1764, 6 December 1766, 15 September 1768; Hollis to Timothy Hollis, 23 February 1771, MS Eng. 1191/1/1, Houghton Library, Harvard University.

the American colonies, and went out on a limb in their ardent support for the colonists' cause.[128] Jonathan Mayhew, whose explosive sermon of 1750 had been reprinted by Baron and invoked by Hollis,[129] became Hollis's principal contact with the American movement of resistance.[130] In the colonists' cause he "found himself," as Robbins wrote, "slowly but inexorably cast in the new role of interpreter to England of American sentiments."[131] His American ally Andrew Eliot told him that, were it not for the information sent over by him, "we should be quite ignorant of what is said either for us or against us" in England.[132] There was much else to unite Hollis and Baron. Both men, preoccupied by the venality of contemporary English politics, looked to the abolition of borough constituencies as the sole means to end it.[133] The political radicalism of the two friends was partnered by a vigorous and vigilant antipathy, on which a rounded account of their lives would have much to say, to clericalism and to ecclesiastical and doctrinal intolerance, evils of which they likewise discerned a revival in their own time. Both men presented themselves as assertors of "civil and religious liberty,"[134] a phrase Hollis liked to inscribe in presentation copies of the books he promoted. They were dismayed not merely by the political and religious tendencies of the age but by its moral character and by the degeneration of public and private virtue. They were scandalized by the appeal of novels and romances to young men who preferred reading them to the strenuous study of the texts of liberty.[135]

128. HD, 6 December 1766; for the eccentricity of their position see Sainsbury, *Disaffected Patriots*, p. 13.

129. Toland, *Life of John Milton*, p. 248; Blackburne, pp. 73, 92–93, 763; HD, 2 April 1764; Robbins, "Strenuous Whig," p. 190.

130. Blackburne, p. 81; Akers, *Called unto Liberty*, s.v. "Hollis."

131. Robbins, "Strenuous Whig," p. 186.

132. 7 September 1769, MS Am. 882.5F, Houghton Library, Harvard University.

133. Blackburne, pp. 321–22; HD, 28 May 1770.

134. Blackburne, pp. vi, 27, 66, 76, 81, 362 (compare pp. 470, 577); Bond, *Thomas Hollis*, p. 121; HD, 28 March 1765; 21 June, 5 November 1766; 23 August 1767; 28 January, 24 December 1768. Compare *Political Register*, June 1768, p. 405, and another publication in which Hollis was involved: *Collection of Letters and Essays in Favour of Public Liberty*, 3 vols. (London, 1774), title page and 1:253.

135. Milton, *Eikonoklastes*, ed. Baron (London, 1756), preface, and Hollis's annotations on p. iv of the preface in the copy in the Houghton Library, EC75.

Their closest bond, however, was the hold of the seventeenth century on their minds. They sought out scarce tracts from the period. Hollis, who also tracked down civil-war manuscripts, compiled a large collection of pamphlets of that time. He made selections from them available to two historians whose writings on the seventeenth century he did what he could to assist: Catharine Macaulay, the author of a prodigiously successful *History of England,* and Hollis's own friend William Harris, the biographer of Cromwell and Charles II.[136] Hollis took Baron's edition of *Eikonoklastes* to his heart. He inserted his own extensive annotations between the leaves of copies of the work. In a copy he sent to Harvard he also inserted a copy of Charles I's death warrant, which had been printed by the Society of Antiquaries in 1750.[137] He delighted in the intended speech of John Cook that Baron had reprinted. He heavily annotated Cook's tract of 1652, *Monarchy No Creature of God's Making,* which vindicated, as Hollis exultantly remarked, "that famous piece of justice of January 30 164[9]," the regicide, "in which we have great cause to rejoice." He drew attention to other vindications of the king's execution and publicized the desire of the regicide Thomas Scot, as recorded in Ludlow's *Memoirs,* to have inscribed on his tomb the words "Here lieth one who had a hand and a heart in the execution of Charles Stuart late King of England."[138]

Hollis sighed to remember the courage, and the vigilance for liberty, that in the seventeenth century had emboldened men to bring a tyrant to account. It dismayed him to compare those elevated figures with their "progeny," the men of his own time, who had "arrived" "to such a comfortable pitch of inattention and insensibility, to such a total extinction

H7267. Zz756m3 (hereafter "Houghton *Eikonoklastes*"); Sidney, *Discourses* (1763 ed.), p. 45; Blackburne, p. 377.

136. Hill, *Republican Virago,* explores the relationship of Hollis and Macaulay. Mutually admiring letters between them are in the Houghton Library, MS Eng. 1191/2. Hollis's diary provides information about his communications with, and admiration for, both Macaulay and Harris.

137. Houghton, *Eikonoklastes;* Blackburne, pp. 759–60.

138. Cook, *Monarchy No Creature of Gods Making* (1652; EC75. H7267. Zz652c, Houghton Library), esp. p. 131; Blackburne, pp. 749–78; Sidney, *Discourses* (1763 ed.), pp. 8–13, 45.

of the public spirit."[139] Not only were freedom and virtue now insufficiently valued, but the principles that had sustained the Stuart tyranny were reasserting themselves. The overthrow of the Whig ascendancy after the accession of George III in 1760 provoked many comparisons between the king's favorite minister, the Earl of Bute, and the Duke of Buckingham under Charles I;[140] many anxieties about the return of "the Laudean-times";[141] many fears that divine-right or patriarchal theories of government were returning. "The rod of oppression," it was remarked, "may as well be held over [the people's] head by a Charles as a George."[142] Since the Restoration, church and law had commanded the annual remembrance of the blasphemous execution of Charles I on 30 January 1649 and the happy enthronement of Charles II on 29 May 1660. The commemorations, which often brought public controversy, seemed to Hollis to be arousing worrying new sentiments. In the mid-1760s, noticing the "great singularity and boldness" with which "Jacobites and Papists" had come to celebrate each 29 May, he feared that the mood would escape public control.[143] He himself liked to draw public attention to the two anniversaries, but in an opposite spirit: 30 January was for him a day for reverential memory, 29 May one for national shame.[144] His view of the Restoration commanded a wider potential appeal than his admiration for the regicide, for since 1688 the ruling order had hesitated or declined to defend the reign of Charles II, when corruption, degeneracy, and arbitrary tendencies in government were held to have prevailed. Likewise there were many readers who, while they might have been horrified to remember the killing of Charles I,

139. Blackburne, p. 61.

140. Baron was ready to defend Buckingham's assassination by John Felton in 1628. Neville, *Diary*, p. 23. A similar enthusiasm was professed in *The Political Register* (July 1767, p. 138), a periodical in which Hollis arranged the publication of "pieces in favour of public liberty." HD, 10 April, 2 May 1769; 1 May 1770.

141. *Political Register*, September 1769, p. 145; May 1770, p. 270; June 1770, pp. 320, 324–25.

142. Ibid., April 1770, p. 226; compare Neville, *Diary*, p. 23.

143. HD, 29 May 1766; compare *Collection of Letters and Essays in Favour*, 1:33–36, 232–41, 2:140; Sidney, *Discourses* (1763 ed.), p. 10.

144. HD, 6 February, 4 June 1769. For celebrations on 30 January see, too, Neville, *Diary*, pp. 90, 91, 149, 301.

would have taken no pleasure in the royalist response to it, *Eikon Basilike* (1649), an advertisement for the divine authority of kingship that, as Hollis liked to remember, John Toland had effectively attacked.[145] Toland had also exploited the embarrassment within conventional opinion at the memory of the hideous executions of the regicides in 1660–62. Hollis played on the same sentiment by placing on the title page of his edition of Sidney's *Discourses* the line of *Samson Agonistes* in which Milton had alluded to those "unjust tribunals under change of times."

Like Baron's, Hollis's republication of seventeenth-century writings was designed to instruct and animate the eighteenth. As his memorialist Francis Blackburne would recall in 1780, Hollis aimed "to stem the pernicious current and apprise the men of England of their danger, by referring them to those immortal geniuses Milton, Sidney, Locke, &c. for instruction upon what only solid foundation the preservation of their rights and liberties depends." "It never was more necessary," added Blackburne, "than it has been" in the seventeen years since the republication of Sidney's *Discourses* in 1763 "to let such men as Sydney speak for themselves."[146] Against the background of the Tory reaction of the 1760s, Hollis viewed the prospects of his edition of Sidney with pessimism.[147] It had been planned in the last years of George II,[148] but it was published, as Blackburne would recall, "at that critical period when it began to be visible that the management of our public affairs was consigned into the hands of men known to have entertained principles notoriously unfavourable to liberty," principles "upon which those men acted who sacrificed Sydney without law or justice, to the tyranny of a profligate and licentious court and ministry."[149] Tories struck heavy blows at Sidney's reputation, and at those

145. Blackburne, p. 237; compare HD, 25 July 1761; *Collection of Letters and Essays*, 1:33–36, 234–35.

146. Blackburne, pp. 148, 188. Compare *Political Register,* November 1768, p. 280.

147. HD, 25 April 1763.

148. Blackburne, p. 97.

149. Ibid., pp. 186–87; compare Peter Karsten, *Patriot-Heroes in England and America* (Madison, Wisc.: University of Wisconsin Press, 1978), p. 49.

of other members of the canon, in the years and decades following the appearance of Hollis's edition.[150] John Adams, the future president of the United States, recorded in his *Thoughts on Government* in 1776 that "a man must be indifferent to the sneers of modern Englishmen, to mention in their company the names of Sidney, Harrington, Locke, Milton, Nedham, Neville, [Gilbert] Burnet, and [Benjamin] Hoadly. No small fortitude is necessary to confess that one has read them."[151]

That, however, depended on the company one kept. The Tory revival of the 1760s provoked its own reaction, which succored Hollis's projects. He was ready to brave Tory jibes. In 1763 a newspaper article, probably written by him,[152] asked "Men of England . . . what is become of the noble spirit of your ancestors! Where are your Pyms, your Hampdens, your Ludlows, your Sydneys, and all the illustrious spirits of forty-one [1641]! Suffer not the noble memorials of them longer to be defaced by moths and cobwebs in your libraries. Bring them forth to action. . . ."[153] In 1768 he caused extracts from Harrington's *Oceana* to be printed in the gazettes so as to bring its "exciting, just and valuable ideas" into current political debate.[154] But it was the beliefs and characters of "the divine Milton"[155] and Algernon Sidney, the two seventeenth-century authors whom he most intensely admired, that he, like Baron, most zealously promoted. "All antiquity," proclaimed Baron's preface to *Eikonoklastes,* "cannot shew two writers equal to these." Hollis reproduced that statement in his edition of Sidney's *Discourses* and, with it, the observation in the same preface that "Many circumstances at present loudly call upon us to exert ourselves.

150. See Blair Worden, "The Commonwealth Kidney of Algernon Sidney," *Journal of British Studies* 24 (1995): 1–40, at pp. 32, 35.

151. Charles S. Hyneman and Daniel S. Lutz, eds., *American Political Writing During the Founding Era, 1760–1805,* 2 vols. (Indianapolis: Liberty Press, 1983), 1:403.

152. Compare it with the injunction by Hollis to "Men of New England" quoted in Akers, *Called unto Liberty,* p. 145.

153. Blackburne, p. 318.

154. HD, 8 June 1768, 18 February 1769.

155. Blackburne, pp. 60, 93. Hollis was echoing, as many others did, a phrase of the poet James Thompson.

Venality and corruption have well nigh extinguished all principles of liberty."[156] Though the Sidney edition was the product, as Hollis recalled, of "considerable expense" and "*great* and continued labor,"[157] he readily acknowledged its limitations. In light of them he commissioned a revised version, which was published in 1772 by a new editor whose improvements he handsomely acknowledged.[158]

Despite their shared commitments, the friendship of Hollis and Baron withered and died. By the autumn of 1760 Baron's behavior to Hollis, as Hollis reported it, was becoming "shameful" and "most strange, extravagant, and ungrateful."[159] Perhaps two men so readily hurt by disagreement were bound to fall out. Still, Hollis knew the ability and usefulness of Baron, that "thorough friend to liberty," and was anxious not to alienate him.[160] Baron for his part depended desperately on Hollis's largesse and on payment by him for editorial work. So the working partnership survived the friendship. In 1763, following Hollis's republication of Sidney's *Discourses,* he and Baron worked closely together on a new edition of John Locke's *Two Treatises of Government,* which would be published the following year. Hollis had acquired, and Baron prepared for publication, a copy of the text that contains manuscript corrections in the hand of Locke's amanuensis Pierre Coste.[161] On its publication in 1764 Hollis presented the text to Christ's College Cambridge, where it would attract modern scholarship that has revolutionized the study of Locke's political thought.[162] In 1764 Baron and Hollis collaborated again, now on an edition of Locke's *Letters on*

---

156. Sidney, *Discourses* (1763 ed.), p. 45.
157. HD, 31 March 1763; compare ibid., 27 October 1761; Blackburne, p. 186.
158. Blackburne, pp. 447–49.
159. HD, 8 October, 1 December 1760; compare 11 July, 2 September 1767.
160. Ibid., 26 October 1763.
161. Ibid., 26 October, 9 November 1763; 17 April, 2 May 1764; John Locke, *Two Treatises of Government* (London, 1764); John Locke, *Two Treatises of Government,* ed. Peter Laslett (Cambridge, U.K.: Cambridge University Press, 1960), p. 23.
162. HD, 20 April 1764; Locke, *Two Treatises,* ed. Laslett. There is another Hollis presentation copy in the Bodleian Library, Radcliffe e.271. For other donations by Hollis to Christ's see HD, 7 April 1762, 28 May 1765.

*Toleration,* which would be published in 1765. Baron, having compiled the text, wrote the preface, which he and Hollis "revised" and "altered" during long discussions.[163]

The preparation of *The Excellencie* for the press followed the same pattern. We cannot say whether it was Baron or Hollis who discovered the tract or first mooted its republication. But again it was Baron who did the donkeywork. The text was ready by the close of 1766, when its forthcoming publication was announced in the press.[164] Baron had drafted the preface by 1 January, the date given to it in the publication. But the next day it was "altered" and "settled" in a discussion between him and Hollis that lasted nearly four hours. They discussed it again on 13 January, and again the next day, when, recorded Hollis, it was "altered in several respects, much I think for the better, and finally settled for the press."[165] As in the case of the preface to the edition of Locke, the reader may wonder that so brief a document called for such prolonged conversation. (The preface is printed in appendix B.) The book was published on or around 19 February.[166]

Though Hollis, who liked his exertions on liberty's behalf to be anonymous, was happy to see the preface, and thus the edition, carry Baron's name alone, he had his own interest in Nedham. He possessed at least some issues of *Mercurius Politicus,* that "celebrated journal," "that remarkable State newspaper in favour of the Commonwealth," as he called it.[167] He transcribed an extract from one issue of the newsbook (no. 56, 26 June–3 July 1651) into a copy of Baron's edition of *Eikonoklastes,* as he did a passage from an issue of Nedham's *Mercurius*

163. HD, 8 May, 26 June, 21, 30 October, 6, 9, 10, 16 November 1764.

164. *London Chronicle,* 30 December 1766; compare *Lloyd's Evening Post,* 2 January 1767; *Public Advertiser,* 22, 29 January 1767. For Hollis and the *London Chronicle* see also HD, 14 April 1769.

165. HD, 2, 13, 14 January 1767; compare 12, 13 December 1766.

166. *London Chronicle,* 19 February 1767; *Public Advertiser,* 20 February 1767.

167. Hollis's notes on the copy of Nedham's edition of John Selden's *The Dominion of the Seas* in the Houghton Library, EC65. H7267. Zz6525 (hereafter "Houghton Selden"); *London Chronicle,* 6 October 1772. *Politicus* is described as "that celebrated state-paper" in the preface to the 1767 edition of *The Excellencie,* a phrase we can ascribe to Hollis.

*Pragmaticus.*[168] Hollis's interest in Nedham took other directions too. He tried to arrange the republication of a tract of his of 1649, a plea to the Rump's council of state to tolerate the printing of dissenting political opinion.[169] Though written in the royalist cause, the pamphlet seemed to Hollis a kindred spirit of Milton's *Areopagitica.* Hollis delighted to discover Nedham's translation and edition of John Selden's *Of the Dominion of the Seas,* which had been published in 1652.[170] In it he found testimony to the assertion of England's might in the 1650s, an achievement that again shamed the present, and that inspired him to applaud the naval and foreign exploits of the Rump,[171] the government under which Nedham's edition of Selden was compiled. He cited Nedham's description of that regime as "the most famous and potent republic this day in the world." [172]

168. Blackburne, pp. 760, 773. At a few points the text of *The Excellencie* of 1767, which is otherwise mostly faithful to the version of 1656, effects slight alterations that bring the wording into line with the passages of *Politicus* from which Nedham had reproduced it in 1656 (pp. 130–31). Most of these changes correct obvious misprints and would likely have been made whether or not Baron or Hollis had access to the corresponding issues of the newsbook. It is, however, hard to decide whether that explanation can be extended to the other alterations. Various runs and separate issues of the newsbook survive. I owe to Moses Tannenbaum the information that a run of *Politicus* from 1650 to 1655 in the Cambridge University Library belonged to John Moore (1646–1714). The same library has a run from August 1651 to September 1652, roughly the period of the sequence of editorials reproduced in *The Excellencie.* Copies of *Politicus* travelled to America, where in 1799 Noah Webster's *A Brief History of Epidemic and Pestilential Diseases* (Hartford, Conn.; pp. 189–90) drew on what looks to have been a run of the newsbook at least from 1652 to 1656.

169. Blackburne, pp. 269, 358; *Certain Considerations tendered in all humility, to an Honorable Member of the Council of State* (London, 1649).

170. Blackburne, p. 357; Sidney, *Discourses* (1763 ed.), p. 14; Houghton Selden.

171. Sidney, *Discourses* (1763 ed.), pp. 17–21.

172. Ibid., pp. 12–13. Hollis likewise commended the foreign exploits of Cromwell, whose "spirit" in war and diplomacy he admired even as he denounced what he thought of as the protector's "shocking usurpation." Ibid., pp. 43–44; Blackburne, pp. 92–93; Houghton *Eikonoklastes,* pp. vi, vii; Toland, *Life of John Milton,* ed. Hollis, p. 98; HD, 30 September 1759, 29 December 1763. Compare *Political Register,* November 1767, p. 45; *London Chronicle,* 9 June 1768, p. 551; 30 June 1768, p. 620.

In the spring of 1767 Hollis was planning fresh editions of works by Milton, Marvell, and Locke. He hoped that Milton's prose works would appear in a version superior to Baron's hastily compiled edition of 1753, and would be adorned, like Hollis's editions of Sidney and of Toland's life of Milton, with extensive annotations and quotations. Nedham would have been one of the authors cited.[173] Hollis wanted Baron to compile the texts of the Marvell and Milton editions, but after "much discourse" Baron judged himself "not equal to the task, for want of anecdotes, [and] did not seem inclined to undertake" the Marvell project, while the plan for a new edition of Milton's prose works foundered after a quarrel, involving both Hollis and Baron, with the prospective publisher, Andrew Millar.[174] It was Millar who, alone or with others, had published the eighteenth-century editions of Baron and Hollis—that is, Baron's editions of Ludlow and Milton in the 1750s, Hollis's editions of Milton and Sidney in the early 1760s, and *The Excellencie* in 1767.

In January 1768, a year after the preparation of *The Excellencie* for the press, Baron died. *The Excellencie* seems to have been his last production. Hollis, deprived of his assistance, was dismayed by the demise of "an old acquaintance, once a friend, of great genius and infirmities."[175] He assisted Baron's distressed family and, "from regard to his memory," supported his wife "although, as often informed, a drunken, bad hussey."[176] Hollis's own labors were beginning to wilt. In 1770 he would retire to his Dorset estates,[177] where he now named farms or fields after friends of liberty, Nedham among them.[178]

The preface of 1767 concedes the inferiority of *The Excellencie* to the "incomparable writings" of Milton, Harrington, Sidney, and Locke. It

173. Blackburne, p. 366.
174. Ibid., pp. 356–67.
175. HD, 23 February 1668.
176. Ibid., 2 January 1769.
177. Robbins, "Strenuous Whig," p. 184.
178. Idem, "Thomas Hollis in his Dorsetshire Retirement," in *Absolute Liberty*, p. 244.

nonetheless commends the book as one of "many lesser treatises on the same argument" that "deserve to be read and preserved," and it describes Nedham as "a man, in the judgement of many, inferior only to Milton." It looks forward to the prospect of further republications of second-rank seventeenth-century works if opportunity should arise. Yet no such volumes appeared. In Hollis's publishing activities *The Excellencie* had a low priority. The humble octavo form of the edition of 1767 distinguishes it from the handsome and costly editions, in folio and quarto, of his other republications from the seventeenth century. On only one subject, the commendable practice of classical antiquity in revering the slayers of tyrants, does he ever seem to have quoted *The Excellencie* in writing of his own, and even then not in print.[179] Since he republished the book, we must suppose that he approved the thrust of its arguments, or anyway judged that their reappearance would be of public benefit. The virtues and histories of the classical republics had supplied his earliest lessons in liberty.[180] Of the "lesser" seventeenth-century books that he might have republished, it was *The Excellencie,* that innovative analysis of the Roman republic, that he singled out. Why then did he not promote the publication more widely and more boldly?

Perhaps his admiration for the tract was tempered by unease. For one thing, there were the belligerence and candor of Nedham's republicanism. Francis Blackburne called Richard Baron "a high-spirited republican,"[181] which he likely enough was. The little we know of Baron suggests that he at least is unlikely to have had any qualms about the content of *The Excellencie.* But Blackburne was careful to defend Hollis's memory from the imputation of republicanism, which had fallen on Hollis when he republished Sidney's *Discourses.*[182] Hollis could hardly have complained of the charge, since the edition, as well as commending

179. Blackburne, pp. 772–73.
180. Robbins, "Library of Liberty," p. 212.
181. Blackburne, p. 61; and see Hill, *Republican Virago,* p. 169.
182. Blackburne, pp. iii–iv, 117–18, 186, 210, 449.

the exploits of the English republic abroad, had described Sidney as "both by inclination and principle, a zealous republican" and had invoked the parliamentary declaration that vindicated the abolition of monarchy in March 1649.[183] Hollis loved to remember examples of republican virtue and heroism and courage and to publish the evidence for them.

But there were lines to be drawn. The spirit of past republics, even their forms of rule, could be openly admired across a wide range of eighteenth-century opinion, so long as authors did not call for kingless government in the present day. Nedham's tract is a polemical demand for the elimination of the forms and spirit of monarchy. Hollis did, it is true, feel able to press on the public's attention, in words he took from Toland, the scheme of republican government that had been proposed in Harrington's *Oceana*, which "for practicableness, equality and completeness" was "the most perfect model of a commonwealth that ever was delineated by ancient or modern pen."[184] But Harrington's proposals, which were advanced without the aggression that marked Nedham's writing, had lost their revolutionary sting by the eighteenth century. Writers had learned to detach from his nonmonarchical framework the principle of constitutional balance that he had advanced, and to portray it as the guiding premise of the post-Revolutionary constitution.[185]

When, before the civil wars, authors critical of the conduct or character of monarchical rule had appealed to Roman example, they had done so not in order to propose a republican alternative, but with one or both of two different purposes: to remark on the oppression that follows when single rule degenerates into tyranny, or to commend the examples of courage or probity or prudence of those Romans who had challenged that trend or had found honorable ways of enduring it. Under the English republic, Nedham's candid republicanism had broken with that approach. With the Restoration, monarchical assumptions returned. In

183. Sidney, *Discourses* (1763 ed.), pp. 2, 10–11, 13; but see also ibid., pp. 40–41.
184. Blackburne, p. 306; Darbishire, ed., *Early Lives of Milton*, p. 174.
185. H. F. Russell Smith, *Harrington and His "Oceana": A Study of a Seventeenth-Century Utopia and Its Influence in America* (1914; repr. New York: Octagon, 1971), pp. 145–48.

the later seventeenth century Algernon Sidney, Henry Neville, John Toland, and others, all drawn in their various ways to classical republican practice, found ways of combining that admiration with outward respect for England's monarchical constitution. They won more support by their opposition to tyranny than by their republicanism.[186] The same was still more true of the eighteenth-century impact of the same authors.[187] Nedham's standing suffered from his omission from the canon created by Toland's circle, which had published works that had followed in Nedham's wake. *The Excellencie* had advanced too few arguments that, by the time of its republication, had not become familiar from those other writings, so that what now chiefly distinguished the book was its unpalatable republicanism. In 1697 John Toland and his friends had silently appropriated a passage from Nedham that bore on the evils of standing armies and the virtues of citizen militias. That remained a live issue in the later 1760s.[188] Hollis, to whom "our trained bands are the truest and most proper strength of a free nation," reminded readers of the pertinence of other seventeenth-century writings to the subject.[189] In one of the two copies of *The Excellencie* that he sent to Harvard he marked (as well as other passages) Nedham's praise of citizen militias.[190] Yet he did nothing else to exploit Nedham's discussion of the topic, which by 1767 had little to add to public thinking. It could scarcely have competed with the autobiography of Edmund Ludlow,

186. Wootton, *Republicanism,* chap. 4.

187. Worden, *Roundhead Reputations,* chaps. 5, 6.

188. See, for example, *Political Register,* May 1768, p. 326; July 1768, pp. 6–18; Neville, *Diary,* p. 55.

189. Blackburne, pp. 660, 799; Sidney, *Discourses* (1763 ed.), pp. 13, 30; Houghton *Eikonoklastes,* p. 440; Toland, *Life of John Milton* (ed. Hollis), p. 104; HD, 5 June 1768, 10 April 1769; compare Andrew Eliot to Thomas Hollis, 29 September 1768, MS Am. 882.5F, Houghton Library. Hollis's alertness to the topic complicated his perception of the civil wars, for his admiration for the regicide was accompanied by a dislike of the new model army as a standing force, which had carried it out in so unconstitutional a manner. Houghton *Eikonoklastes,* p. [vi]; Blackburne, pp. 92–93. Jonathan Mayhew had the same difficulty with the regicide: see his *A Discourse concerning Unlimited Submission and Non-Resistance to the Higher Powers* (Boston, 1750), pp. 44–48.

190. EC75. N2845 656eb, pp. 114–15, Houghton Library.

which Toland's editorial exertions had turned into a vivid warning against standing armies, and which had a wide and deep influence on eighteenth-century thinking on the subject, both through the circulation of Toland's text and through excerpts from it in pamphlets.[191]

Hollis consistently portrayed himself as a champion of "the most noble, the most happy Revolution," the "ever-glorious Revolution," of 1688. He thrilled to remember the "glorious struggles" that had "obtained" the Revolution and had produced the Act of Settlement in 1701.[192] He was distressed by the "subversion" of "Revolution principles,"[193] which by George III's reign, as he often remarked in exclamatory style or punctuation, were "waning" or "ruining" fast.[194] Not only had they been threatened from the outset by the prospect of invasion and rebellion and conspiracy in the Jacobite and popish causes,[195] they had been undermined by the corruption of ministries and of public spirit and by the unconstitutional aspirations that such corruption had fostered. Even so, he remained pledged to "the rights of the House of Hanover," to "the Protestant Revolution family," and to "liberty and King George the Third." He longed for George to become a second King Alfred or a patriot king.[196] Hollis's perception of the Revolution of 1688, it is true, was not a mainstream one. Like Toland before him, he saw it as a continuation of the valiant cause of 1649. It was the radical Whigs of the decades after the overthrow of James II whose memory he honored: Toland himself, "a man of great

191. Worden, *Roundhead Reputations*, s.v. "standing armies"; Robbins, *Eighteenth-Century Commonwealthman*, p. 48. See, too, the annotations in the copy of the edition, sponsored by Hollis, of Ludlow's *Memoirs* of 1771 in the Elham collection of publications in Canterbury Cathedral Library; and *Critical Memoirs of the Times*, 10 Febuary 1769, p. 125. This was another periodical in which Hollis involved himself (e.g., HD, 14 April 1769).

192. HD, 15 September 1768; Sainsbury, *Disaffected Patriots*, pp. 8–9.

193. HD, 6 March 1769.

194. Ibid., 24 November 1767; 15 April, 7 October, 19 December 1768; 2 January, 4 February, 14 April, 20 October 1769; 18 January, 14 April 1770.

195. Bond, *Thomas Hollis*, p. 9.

196. HD, 25 October 1760; 24 October, 3 November 1763; 24 November 1767; 19 December 1768; 4 March 1769; 2 May 1770; compare Sidney, *Discourses* (1763 ed.), pp. 31–32.

genius and learning, a staunch asserter of liberty";[197] Toland's close and incendiary political ally the clergyman William Stephens, whom Hollis associated with the "OLD WHIG" cause;[198] Lord Molesworth, to whose "political creed" Hollis was "a subscriber";[199] John Trenchard, "that magnanimous gentleman," "the last great Englishman!"[200] Those writers, heirs to the republican thinkers of the civil wars and the Restoration, had constituted a second wave, even stronger than the first, of the "ideological origins of the American Revolution."[201] Some of them had given hints of pure republicanism, yet they had been careful never to embrace it openly, at least not without qualification. They had tended to use the term "free government" rather than "free state" and had remembered to equate free government with "the constitution of the English monarchy."[202] Their caution was heightened as the Tory reaction of the beginning of the eighteenth century advanced.

Hollis took the same path. He was an adversary of tyranny, but not, as Nedham had been, of kingship. What he applauded about the execution of Charles I was not that it prepared the way for republican government but that it asserted the principle, of which he saw Milton and Sidney as heroic exponents, of the right or duty of resistance to tyrants. He likewise revered the sixteenth-century thinkers who had proclaimed the same tenet: Christopher Goodman, John Ponet, François Hotman, Hubert Languet, and the "master-patriot" George Buchanan.[203] The Excellencie vindicated the principle too, but that was not

197. Blackburne, p. 236.

198. HD, 18 February 1770; Sidney, Discourses (1763 ed.), p. 40.

199. Blackburne, p. iii. Compare Blackburne, pp. 236–37, 659; Toland, Life of John Milton, ed. Hollis, p. 248; HD, 28 September 1760.

200. HD, 24 February 1769. Anthony Collins was another figure from the period who attracted Hollis. HD, 26 June 1764; Blackburne, p. 660; Toland, Life of John Milton, ed. Hollis, p. 255. Henry Booth, Lord Delamere and Earl of Warrington, was one more radical Whig admiringly remembered in Hollis's time. Political Register, December 1768, pp. 352–54.

201. Bailyn, Ideological Origins, pp. 35–40.

202. Thus see An Argument, Shewing, title page.

203. Robbins, "Library of Liberty," pp. 223–26; Blackburne, pp. 659, 750–51, 771; HD, 27 December 1764, 4 January 1765, 29 June 1768, 7 June 1770; compare Collection of Letters and Essays, 1:115–16.

the main concern of the tract, which added nothing of substance or eloquence to other vindications. Echoing some earlier critics of the Stuart monarchy, Hollis insisted that it was only because Charles I had destroyed "the ancient form" of the English government that men such as Milton, who as Hollis says elsewhere "commends" it, were driven to replace it.[204] When Hollis sent copies of his publications of Sidney and Milton to Harvard he was glad to inscribe them with descriptions of himself as a "lover of liberty, his country and its excellent constitution, so nobly restored at the happy Revolution" of 1688.[205] The streak of ancient constitutionalism discernible in both writers may have seemed to Hollis to lend aptness to the sentiment. He informed prospective readers of Milton in America that "we owe the most noble, the most happy Revolution to his principles."[206] But the animating theme of Nedham's *The Excellencie* is the need to renounce the ancient constitution and to create anew. Can Hollis, in a copy of the tract that he sent to Harvard, have inscribed the tribute he there pays to "the wonderful restoration of the constitution" in 1688[207] without a sense of discordance?

In Hollis's eyes what properly characterized that constitution was "the harmony of the three estates."[208] Nedham's apologia for the unicameral Rump was remote from that ideal. Hollis was equally far from sharing Nedham's aggressive populism, which, like the belligerence of his republicanism, distinguished his writing from the canonical publications of 1698–1700. There were, it is true, writers in the canon, higher in Hollis's esteem, who believed that constitutions should have democratic components. Harrington and Sidney and Neville were at their fore. Their writing, however, was more accommodating toward aristocratic or gentle outlooks and interests. The eighteenth century looked for gentility, or anyway for respect for it, in political thinkers.

204. Blackburne, pp. 92–93. Milton's state letters, which Hollis admired, provided support for that view. *LP*, p. 230.

205. EC75. H7267. Zz763s2 (Sidney), EC65. M6427. 3753wa (Milton), Houghton Library.

206. Blackburne, p. 93.

207. EC65 N2845 656eb, Houghton Library.

208. Toland, *Life of John Milton*, ed. Hollis, p. 248.

Baron's hero Thomas Gordon, in translating Tacitus, commended the Roman historian for having "the good sense and breeding of a gentleman."[209] Hollis liked to invoke James Harrington's observation that in the leadership of a commonwealth "there is something" that "seems to be peculiar unto the genius of a gentleman."[210] Nedham was no gentleman.

Perhaps there was a further question mark in Hollis's mind about *The Excellencie,* one that Toland and his circle would have understood. An approving but lukewarm reviewer (apparently the only reviewer) of the republication declared that "the rights of the people are well explained and vindicated" by the book, but complained that "the strongest argument . . . in favour of national freedom, is not sufficiently enforced, which is the tendency it has to promote the happiness in society upon moral principles."[211] In conventional thinking of the later eighteenth century, political thought was morally improving or it was nothing. If there is a single moral quality for which the eighteenth century looked to political heroes it was "disinterestedness": an impregnable immunity to the claims of reward, faction, and corruption. In accord with the spirit of the age, Hollis liked his heroes to be "inflexible."[212] It was for their sturdy and stoical refusal to compromise with power or corruption that Sidney and Ludlow won admiration from eighteenth-century readers who would never have endorsed their revolutionary political deeds. Like Toland, Hollis dwelled as much on the characters as on the opinions of the seventeenth century's republicans. A favorite adjective of his was "honest." His own "honest views" were fortified by the examples of "honest Ludlow" and "honest Andrew Marvell" in England, or by "honest Lucan" in ancient Rome.[213] "Sidney, Milton and honest

---

209. *The Works of Tacitus,* 2 vols., trans. and ed. Thomas Gordon (Dublin, 1728–32), 1:27.

210. HD, 8 June 1768 (compare ibid., 18 February 1769); *London Chronicle,* 11, 14 June 1768; Toland, *Life of John Milton,* ed. Hollis, p. 243.

211. *Monthly Review,* January 1767, p. 39.

212. Worden, *Roundhead Reputations,* especially chap. 6; compare Blackburne, pp. 118, 144.

213. Blackburne, pp. 66, 188; HD, 8 September 1760; 18 April, 25 July 1761; 19, 23 February 1768; Sidney, *Discourses* (1763 ed.), p. 33.

Ludlow are my heroes," he told Jonathan Mayhew in 1769.[214] By commissioning engravings and wax impressions he made such men into figures of immovable Roman integrity. They became the modern counterparts to Brutus and Cassius, with whose nobility of spirit Hollis also liked to associate his own character.[215] But how could he have made a stoical or incorruptible Roman of the venal Nedham? Hollis searched assiduously for biographical information about Milton and Sidney and eagerly communicated it to the public. By contrast the preface to *The Excellencie* gives no account of Nedham's life and no sense of his personality, save to remark defensively that Wood's sketch of his character, which still pursued Nedham, was "drawn in bitterness of wrath and anger."[216] Even if paintings or drawings of Nedham had survived, would Hollis have reproduced them? Francis Blackburne, writing in 1780, judged the impact of Hollis's republication of *The Excellencie* to have been limited, and related its failure to the moral reputation of its author. The book, he pronounced,

> is well written, and upon sound principles; but was attended with the common fate of the works of all such writers as Nedham, who had been a sort of periodical hackney to different parties; and when a man has lost his reputation for steadiness and consistency, let him write and speak like an angel, he reaps no other reputation from his abilities but that of being a graceful actor on the political stage; an useful admonition to some of our modern renegado patriots, and others who have changed their party through disgust and disappointment.[217]

Nedham's ill reputation persisted.[218] It undermined the republished version of *The Excellencie* and mocked Hollis's publication of him.

214. Knollenberg, "Thomas Hollis and Jonathan Mayhew," p. 116.
215. Bond, *Thomas Hollis,* pp. 23, 33; HD, 30 August 1765; Hollis to Timothy Hollis, 20 May 1771, MS 1191.1/2, Houghton Library; Worden, "Commonwealth Kidney," p. 31.
216. Houghton Selden, sig. G2v.
217. Blackburne, p. 357.
218. Horace Walpole, *The Yale Edition of Horace Walpole's Correspondence,* 48 vols., ed. W. S. Lewis et al. (New Haven: Yale University Press, 1937–83), 16:5. An earlier condemnation of his character is found in *Daily Gazetteer,* 5 May 1737.

Hollis was wont to proclaim selfishness, or "self," to be the underlying evil of the times. When, in 1784, some words from Nedham's preface to his translation of Selden were delivered as the "Invocation" in a public concert, a reporter of the event remarked that Nedham had been "driven by the abject selfishness of his principles" to his changes of side. "The treachery of such miscreants," added the reporter, "creates apprehensions even against fidelity, and hinders the deceived from trusting those who merit truth."[219]

## The Reception of the Republication

Caroline Robbins included *The Excellencie* among the eighteenth century's "sacred canon" of "Real Whig" writing.[220] Yet how wide was its readership? Most of the known admirers of the work were people who are known, or are likely, to have been introduced to it by Hollis or by his friends. Nedham did have his open enthusiasts in England. In 1762, five years before the publication of *The Excellencie,* William Harris's biography of Cromwell, in which Hollis had had "some share,"[221] named Nedham alongside Milton to illustrate his claim that "the best pens" had been "sought out and recommended by the parliament for writing in behalf of civil and religious liberty." Harris published long excerpts from two consecutive editorials of *Politicus* (nos. 98–99, 15–29 April 1652), the first showing that "the original of all just power is in the people," the second attacking "the corrupt division of a state into ecclesiastical and civil."[222] He had evidently acquired them from Hollis, for his text repeats errors that appear in a transcription of Hollis's own.[223] Harris hailed Nedham's repudiation of "reason of state" as a "beautiful piece of satire." In 1771 another beneficiary of Hollis's assistance,

---

219. *Public Advertiser,* 20 May 1784; compare *Diary or Woodfall's Register,* 16 May 1792.

220. Robbins, *Eighteenth-Century Commonwealthman,* pp. 4–5.

221. HD, 2 July 1761.

222. William Harris, *An Historical and Critical Account of the Life of Oliver Cromwell* (1672), pp. 295–305.

223. Blackburne, p. 660. I owe this observation to Moses Tannenbaum.

Catharine Macaulay, concluded her *History of England,* which at that time ended at the Restoration, with a paean to "the illustrious champions of the public cause" during the civil wars. She was glad to observe that, now that "time and experience" had "abated the violence" of feeling aroused by the conflict, the greatness of the "champions" had become "a theme of delight among the few enlightened citizens." Immortal qualities, she ruled, were to be found above all in Sidney and Ludlow and Harrington and Neville, authors whose works "excel even the ancient classics." But she also had warm words for Nedham. The fact that he was now read "with pleasure and applause," she proclaimed in the last words of the book, was evidence of "the recovered sense and taste of the nation." In the following year another edition of her *History* added the information that he had "the keenest pen that the age or any other ever produced." With Harris, Macaulay savored what she called the "keen satire" that accompanied Nedham's "judicious reflections."²²⁴

How many people shared Harris's and Macaulay's admiration? Other evidence of the reading of *The Excellencie* in England of the later eighteenth century is hard to come by. His populism might be expected to have appealed to advocates of radical reform of Parliament and society, in whose writings Sidney, Harrington, and Milton were often invoked.²²⁵ Should not the radicals have taken inspiration from Nedham's predominant unicameralism, a position that accorded with the hostility of Tom Paine and his fellow sympathizers to the principle

---

224. Catharine Macaulay, *The History of England from the Accession of James I to the Elevation of the House of Hanover,* 5 vols. (Dublin, 1764–71), 5:361; 5 vols. (London, 1763–83), 5:383; 5 vols. (London, 1769–72), 5:305n, 363, 370. (Although Hollis himself can seem a humorless figure, he enjoyed satire when it was deployed in liberty's cause. He had Henry Neville's "very scarce" satirical work *The Isle of Pines* republished in 1768. HD, 7 September 1765; 23 June 1768.) Harris knew two other tracts by Nedham. Harris, *An Historical and Critical Account of the Life of Charles the Second,* 2 vols. (London, 1766), 1:47ff., 287–94. One of these tracts, *Interest Will Not Lie* (London, 1659), was also cited by Macaulay (Dublin ed., 5:331; London ed., 1772, 5:358) and had other currency in the eighteenth century. Another work of Nedham, his anonymous verse attack on the Presbyterians in 1661, *A Short History of the English Rebellion* (London, 1661), was reprinted in the *Harleian Miscellany* in the mid-1740s, as were two prose tracts of his, also anonymous: *Christianissimus Christianandus* and *The Pacquet-Boat Advice* (London, 1678).

225. See, for example, Worden, "Commonwealth Kidney," pp. 32–33.

of constitutional balance, which they interpreted as an aristocratic pretext for thwarting popular sovereignty? Yet the only one of the radical reformers who appears—alone or with his immediate allies—to have made explicit use of Nedham is John Cartwright. In 1777 he cited Nedham's admonitions against aristocrats who contend against regal power only to appropriate it for themselves. He also (following William Harris) endorsed Nedham's attack on the unscrupulous deployment of the language of "reason of state."[226] Here at least the later eighteenth century could find an unambiguously edifying moral sentiment in Nedham. Five years later Cartwright's Society for Constitutional Information published a series of snippets from *The Excellencie* in support of popular freedom.[227] It may be that Nedham's arguments were also used, as they had been in 1697, by men who prudently concealed their source. Perhaps one writer had Nedham in mind in arguing, in a periodical of June 1767, five months after the publication of *The Excellencie,* that English politics and society were undergoing a movement parallel to one emphasized by Nedham in Roman history: a drift toward aristocracy and thus toward conditions from which a monarchical tyranny might emerge.[228] Four months later a writer in the same periodical recalled, in language that echoes Nedham's (p. 32), the baneful effect of luxury in ancient Greece, which had preserved its freedom "so long as virtue walked hand in hand with liberty."[229] In 1776 we find John Wilkes, in a speech in the Commons on parliamentary representation, offering a warning against the prolongation of political power that is suggestively close to one of Nedham's.[230] In none of those cases, however, is a debt to him

226. John Cartwright, *The Legislative Rights of the Commonalty Vindicated* (London, 1777), pp. 70–71, 75.

227. *Parker's General Advertiser and Morning Intelligencer,* 11 November 1782; Robbins, *Eighteenth-Century Commonwealthman,* p. 375 and n. 82.

228. *Political Register,* June 1767, pp. 143–46; cf. ibid., January 1768, pp. 144–45; August 1770, pp. 140–41.

229. Ibid., October 1770, pp. 203–4. But Hollis, at least, did not need lessons from Nedham on the preservation of Greek liberty. Toland, *Life of John Milton,* ed. Hollis, p. 254.

230. Compare John Wilkes, *The Speeches of John Wilkes,* 3 vols. (London, 1777–78), 1:87 with p. 115. Wilkes maintains that "the leaving power too long in the hands of the same persons, by which the armies of the republic became the

certain. It does not look as if *The Excellencie* exerted any great popular appeal.[231] By 1815 Cartwright himself had moved on from Nedham, and was ready to mock *The Excellencie* for its failure to demand annual parliamentary elections.[232]

If the influence of *The Excellencie* in England in the decades after its publication was restricted, one American writer, who noticed its neglect in its native land, claimed that it had had a much greater impact abroad. This was John Adams. Adams claimed, in statements made in distant retrospect, to have studied Nedham in his youth. In 1807 he recalled that he had read Nedham "long before" the Stamp Act crisis—that is, some years before Hollis's republication of *The Excellencie*.[233] It is likely that his memory deceived him. In 1765 he did include Nedham's name in a list of other civil-war Englishmen who "are all said to have owed their eminence in political knowledge" to the experience of the tyrannies of James I and Charles I. The others were Lord Brooke, John Hampden, Sir Henry Vane, John Selden, Milton, Harrington, Neville, Sidney, and Locke. Adams's pronouncement appeared in one of a series

---

armies of Sylla, Pompey, and Caesar," helped to "enslave" Rome. Nedham's point itself draws on Machiavelli's *Discourses,* bk. 3, chap. 24, which argues that "the continuation of governments brought Rome into thraldom," and which one might therefore suppose to be Wilkes's source. But Machiavelli cites the power only of Sylla, Marius, and Caesar, whereas Nedham and Wilkes add the name of Pompey. Hollis, who had a mixed but generally approving view of Wilkes, pressed the virtues of Algernon Sidney on him. HD, 19 January 1765; compare *Political Register,* June 1768, p. 412.

231. Even the populist annotations, which presumably were not for public consumption, in the copy in the British Library (reproduced in "Eighteenth-Century Collections Online," http://www.gale.cengage.com/DigitalCollections/products/ecco/index.htm) of John Thelwall's abbreviated version of Walter Moyle's essay on Roman history, *Democracy Vindicated* (Norwich, 1796), do not refer to Nedham, even though both Thelwall and the annotator would have concurred with much in Nedham's work. For Moyle's own silent debt to Nedham see p. lviii.

232. Cartwright, *Letter, &c. [to Sir Francis Burdett, 12 December 1815]* (London, 1815), p. 9 (2274 d. 11, Bodleian Library).

233. John Adams, *Diary and Autobiography of John Adams,* 4 vols., ed. L. H. Butterfield (Cambridge, Mass.: Harvard University Press, 1961), 3:358; "Correspondence Between John Adams and Mercy Warren," *Collections of the Massachusetts Historical Society* 44 (1878): 324.

of articles by him in the *Boston Gazette* which Hollis, who took a keen interest in Adams and shared American contacts with him,[234] published in book form in 1768.[235] There is no indication in his statement, however, that Adams has read Nedham. In 1776 Adams included Nedham in another list of seventeenth-century English names, the ones at whom the "sneers" of Englishmen were directed. A "reading" of them, he there claimed, would "convince any candid mind, that there is no good government but what is republican." [236]

But how considered had Adams's own "reading" of Nedham's tract been? It seems not to have been until 1787, thirteen years after Hollis's death, that he paid close attention to *The Excellencie.* He was then living in London as ambassador for the American republic and longing to return to his homeland from "a life so useless to the public and so insipid to myself, as mine is in Europe." [237] In January of that year Thomas Brand, Hollis's heir, who had lengthened his own name to Thomas Brand Hollis, sent a copy of the edition of 1767 to his own "friend" Adams, "to be deposited among his republican tracts." [238] Adams had recently completed the first of the three volumes of his *Defence of the Constitutions of America.* It appeared in February 1787. The *Defence* is a series of hastily written essays on historical and political writers whom Adams judged to be of present political relevance. In the first volume Adams made no mention of Nedham, but

234. Bond, *Thomas Hollis,* pp. 120–21; HD, 21 June 1768; and see Andrew Eliot's letters to Hollis, MS Am. 882.5F, Houghton Library.

235. HD, 4, 21 June, 15 July 1768; 24 April 1769; *The True Sentiments of America* (London, 1768), p. 141. Perhaps Adams (who did not know Hollis when the articles in the *Boston Gazette* appeared) had learned of Nedham, directly or indirectly, from the quotations from *Politicus* in William Harris's life of Cromwell in 1762. A copy of Harris's book, annotated by Hollis, is in the Adams National Park and Museum.

236. Hyneman and Lutz, *American Political Writing,* 1:403.

237. John R. Howe, Jr., *The Changing Political Thought of John Adams* (Princeton: Princeton University Press, 1966), p. 129.

238. Zoltán Haraszti, *John Adams and the Prophets of Progress* (Cambridge, Mass.: Harvard University Press, 1952), p. 162. A letter of Adams to Brand Hollis about the Cromwellian times is found in John Disney, *Memoirs of Thomas Brand-Hollis* (London, 1808), pp. 32–33.

the receipt of the copy from Brand Hollis brought him forcefully back into his mind. The second volume, which had appeared by August 1787, and the third, which appeared in 1788, contained a very long commentary on *The Excellencie,* far longer than Nedham's text itself, and far longer than the observations offered by the *Defence* on the writings of other authors.

*The Excellencie* merited so much attention, explained Adams, because it "is a valuable morsel of antiquity well known in America, where it has many partisans"; because "it contains every semblance of argument which can possibly be urged in favour of" the system of government that it advocates; because it provides "the popular idea of a republic in England and France";[239] and because it was "a valuable monument of the early period in which the true principles of liberty began to be adopted and avowed in" England.[240] Adams viewed Nedham with a divided mind. He found much to applaud in his book, which "abounds with sense and learning" and demonstrated "profound judgement."[241] Yet he found more, often much more, to distress him. With one part of himself Adams liked to believe that "conscience was always uppermost" in Nedham's arguments.[242] Yet he simultaneously doubted whether he was "sincere" or "honest."[243] He charged him with "specious" or "absurd" or "very ridiculous" reasoning;[244] with "declamatory flourishes" fit only for "a fugitive pamphlet," not for a work of serious thought;[245] with manipulating the evidence of Roman history to support "popular sophisms"; and with "miserably pervert[ing]" his learning to "answer a present purpose."[246] Analyzing Nedham's text page by page, he concludes that his "system" is uniformly disproved by the very historical examples he cites on its behalf.[247]

239. John Adams, *A Defence of the Constitutions of Government of the United States of America,* 3 vols. (London, 1794), 3:213.
   240. Ibid., 3:400.
   241. Ibid., 3:400, 410; compare 3:288, 398.
   242. Ibid., 3:407.
   243. Ibid., 2:224, 3:472.
   244. Ibid., 3:270, 287.
   245. Ibid., 3:213, 219.
   246. Ibid., 3:400
   247. Ibid., 3:232, 267, 279, 410.

Though Adams referred to "the Proteus Nedham" and to his changes of side,[248] it was not the inconsistencies of Nedham's career that troubled him. It was his arguments. For on both sides of the Atlantic, Adams insisted, there was a choice to be made. The fundamental principle of political health, one not only taught by history but discernible in nature itself, was the balancing of powers. It had been at work in Roman history and was embodied in the British constitution, which modern ministries had betrayed. It turned on the separation of legislative, executive, and judicial power, and on a division of the legislature itself. "The fundamental article of my political creed," he declared in 1785, "is that despotism, or unlimited sovereignty, or absolute power, is the same in a majority of a popular assembly, an aristocratic council, an oligarchical junto, and a single emperor. Equally arbitrary, cruel, bloody, and in every respect diabolical."[249] In the United States he had observed the contentious establishment of unicameral rule in Pennsylvania and other states.[250] His commentary on Nedham contains a series of anxious glances, indicative of a deepening pessimism and conservatism in Adams's political thinking around this time,[251] at the "hazardous experiment" of the American constitution in providing, as Nedham urged nations to do, for frequent elections to office.[252] Perhaps Shays's Rebellion in Massachusetts in 1787 had intensified the horror of populism that informs Adams's reading of Nedham's book.[253] *The Excellencie*, as Adams read it, advocated pure democracy. In charitable moments he suggested that Nedham did not really subscribe to the "crude conceptions" he advanced on behalf of "the people" and that only the particular circumstances in which he had written, when the exiled Stuart monarch, and most of the peers,

---

248. Haraszti, *John Adams*, p. 209.

249. Ibid., p. 26.

250. Gordon S. Wood, *The Creation of the American Republic, 1776–1787* (Chapel Hill: University of North Carolina Press, 1969), pp. 163, 441.

251. Howe, *Changing Political Thought*, pp. 130–31, 170–71, 173–74.

252. Adams, *Defence*, 3:239, 296, 373.

253. Haraszti, *John Adams*, p. 35; John Adams, *The Adams-Jefferson Letters*, ed. Lester J. Cappon (Chapel Hill: University of North Carolina Press, 1959; repr. New York: Simon and Schuster, 1971), p. 166.

sought the destruction of the Commonwealth, had obliged him to turn against two of the three estates.[254] But in Adams's own time, he warned, those "conceptions" had a dangerous potential. One by one he seeks to take apart Nedham's claims: that the people are the best keepers of their own liberty; that popular rule is the form of government best equipped to withstand tyranny, defy faction, and prevent corruption; that it alone ensures the promotion of merit; and so on.[255]

Adams's presentation of Nedham as a writer committed to the concentration of all power in a single assembly is compatible with most of the content of *The Excellencie,* but not with all of it. It does not square with Nedham's proposal for the creation of tribunes and popular assemblies to counter or restrict the weight of the senate. Then there is Nedham's insistence on the separation of executive and legislative power. "In the keeping of these two powers distinct, flowing in distinct channels," he writes, "consists the safety of the state" (p. 109). Adams, introducing his readers to that passage, invites them "to pause here with astonishment" at an argument that, he alleges, contradicts the whole trend of its author's thought.[256] He might have added that in any case the executive and legislature envisaged in *The Excellencie* do not "flow in distinct channels." Rather, the power of the executive is "transferred" by the legislature and is thus "derived from" it (p. 109). Just so did the Rump's executive body, the council of state, the body to which Nedham was directly answerable for *Politicus,* report to the legislature, the Parliament, which appointed it and defined its powers. Adams had been alarmed to find how many of the leaders of the American Revolution had had something similar in mind for their own country's future: they had "no other idea of any other government but a contemptible legislature, in one assembly, with committees of executive magistrates. . . ."[257]

254. Adams, *Defence,* 3:211–12.
255. C. Bradley Thompson, *John Adams and the Spirit of Liberty* (Lawrence: University Press of Kansas, 1998), pp. 128–30.
256. Adams, *Defence,* 3:418.
257. Adams, *Diary and Autobiography,* 3:358.

Yet it looks as if Nedham's own thoughts were closer to those of Adams than the American realized.[258] As in his suggestions for the creation of tribunes and representative assemblies, Nedham may have been looking toward constitutional machinery that would have been incompatible with the undivided sovereignty that was claimed by the Commons, and that he outwardly endorsed, in 1649–53. In 1654 the passage advocating "distinct channels," which had been printed in *Politicus* in 1652, reappeared in *A True State of the Case of the Commonwealth*, the tract Nedham wrote in vindication of the Instrument of Government. The Instrument envisaged a new relationship between executive and legislature. The two would assist and complement each other, but would also be balanced against each other. In *A True State* the wording of *Politicus*, now lengthened and strengthened, was directed against the memory of the Rump, precisely on the ground that the parliament had sought to preserve the "placing the legislative and executive powers in the same persons," a practice that "is a marvellous in-let of corruption and tyranny." The Rump, Nedham now complains, made provision for "no manner of check or balance" to be "reserved upon" the power of the Commons.[259]

258. Haraszti, *John Adams*, p. 163; W. B. Gwyn, *The Meaning of the Separation of Powers*, Tulane Studies in Political Science, vol. 9 (New Orleans: Tulane University, 1965), pp. 118–21. Adams's interpretation was distorted by his conflation of the two issues of constitutional balance and the separation of powers.

259. *A True State of the Case of the Commonwealth* (London, 1654), p. 10. It seems that Nedham, a pioneer here as elsewhere, may have introduced the language of constitutional "checks," which in the eighteenth century would be so frequent and potent to political thought. At least, it is fair to speculate that he was responsible for two known uses of the term during the Puritan Revolution. The term *checks* appeared in a declaration of the new model army in August 1647 in which he seems likely to have had a hand (*LP*, p. 183), and in 1657 it was used in a speech by Cromwell, who depended on Nedham for the articulation of political concepts (*LP*, p. 141). For those instances and the early history of the term *checks*, see David Wootton, "Liberty, Metaphor, and Mechanism: 'Checks and Balances' and the Origin of Modern Constitutionalism," in *Liberty and American Experience in the Eighteenth Century*, ed. David Womersley (Indianapolis: Liberty Fund, 2006), pp. 209–74, especially pp. 216–17, 221, 237–38. To those two uses we may add Cromwell's insistence on the need for "a check" and for "a balance" in his speech to Parliament of 12 September 1654 (*Writings and Speeches*, ed. Abbott, 3:459–60) and the pleas by his supporters in the Commons, during the previous days, for a "check"

It was as an enemy of the division of powers, not as its friend, that Adams assailed Nedham. Why did he assail him at such length? Adams became obsessed by the dangers inherent in the arguments of *The Excellencie.* The book had gotten under his skin. He discerned, or imagined, its malign influence in places where it never reached. It is scarcely an exaggeration to say that whenever he encountered unicameralist arguments he blamed them on Nedham. What he called the "democratical hurricane"[260] of the French Revolution heightened that tendency. "Nedham's perfect commonwealth," he told Thomas Jefferson in 1796, was spreading everywhere. It had been implemented in France and America, was winning support in Holland, and threatened to extend to England.[261] Adams unwarrantably discerned an allusion to *The Excellencie* in Mary Wollstonecraft's *An Historical and Moral View of the Origin and Progress of the French Revolution* (1794).[262] The only particularization Adams ever offered of his claim that *The Excellencie* had "many partisans" in America and was "well known" there is to be

---

on Parliament's authority: Thomas Burton, *Diary of Thomas Burton,* 4 vols., ed. J. T. Rutt (London, 1828), 1:xxviii, xxii. In Wootton's account the term went into abeyance after Nedham's use of it and was revived at the end of the century by John Trenchard, Walter Moyle, and John Toland, whom Wootton portrays as "key figures" in the evolution of the language. Did those writers, owing an unacknowledged debt to Nedham on the subject of standing armies, also draw on him—this time on *A True State*—here? Elsewhere, too, Nedham as an innovator awaits proper recognition. He helped to bring to domestic politics (as distinct from international relations, where it had already been applied) the notion, which would gather a widening following in the later seventeenth century, that the key to political health and stability is the identification and balancing of competing interest groups of society. J. A. W. Gunn, *Politics and the Public Interest in the Seventeenth Century* (London: Routledge and K. Paul, 1969); Worden, "'Wit in a Roundhead,'" pp. 317–18. I hope to show elsewhere that he had a pioneering role in the shaping of a new vocabulary that brought the causes of civil and religious liberty together. Moreover, his obituary of his friend John Bradshaw in 1659 (*LP,* p. 47) was, in its scope and character, a literary departure.

260. Howe, *Changing Political Thought,* p. 171.

261. Adams, *Adams-Jefferson Letters,* p. 261

262. Mary Wollstonecraft, *An Historical and Moral View of the Origin and Progress of the French Revolution* (London, 1794), p. 356; Haraszti, *John Adams,* p. 213.

found in his groundless allegation that Benjamin Franklin was "the weak disciple of Nedham."[263]

How many American "partisans" did the book in fact have? The one conspicuous judgment passed in its favor was delivered by the New England clergyman Andrew Eliot, Hollis's ally in the publicizing of the colonists' cause. Eliot wrote to Hollis in May 1767, three months after the publication of *The Excellencie,* to thank him for a copy of it: "I was so particularly pleased with *The Excellencie of a Free State.* I wonder so valuable a performance has been so long hid. The style and manner are far beyond the writers of that day, and the treatise justly gives the author a place among the most noble writers of government." Eliot's single regret was that when Baron, in his preface, described Nedham "as inferior only to Milton" he had not added alongside Milton's name that of Algernon Sidney, "'that', as you justly style him, 'Martyr to Civil Liberty.'"[264] Another evident admirer of Nedham was Josiah Quincy Jr., who acted as counsel for Adams in the trial of Captain Preston in 1770. In pseudonymous articles in the *Boston Gazette* in 1772–74 he used "Marchamont Nedham" as one of his pseudonyms (another being the Leveller Edward Sexby). Quincy did not, however, mention *The Excellencie.* His interest in Nedham may have derived not from the tract but from *Mercurius Politicus,* of which Quincy knew at second hand. In his commonplace book, sometime between 1770 and 1774, he transcribed the inaccurate copy of an issue of *Mercurius Politicus* that William Harris, who in turn had received it from Hollis, had included in his life of Cromwell.[265] Presumably

263. Haraszti, *John Adams,* p. 203.

264. Richard Fotheringham, ed., "Letters from Andrew Eliot to Thomas Hollis," *Collections of the Massachusetts Historical Society,* 4th ser., 4 (1858): 403. For Eliot and Nedham see, too, Alice M. Baldwin, *The New England Clergy and the American Revolution* (Durham, N.C.: Duke University Press, 1928), pp. 9n, 11. Eliot repeated the phrase about Sidney (H. Trevor Colbourn, *The Lamp of Experience: Whig History and the Intellectual Origins of the American Revolution* [Chapel Hill: University of North Carolina Press, 1965], p. 60).

265. Josiah Quincy Jr., *Portrait of a Patriot: The Major Political and Legal Papers of Josiah Quincy Junior,* ed. Daniel R. Coquillette and Neil Longley York (Boston: Colonial Society of Massachusetts, 2005–), 1:68–70, 85, 178. I am indebted to Moses Tannenbaum for guidance on Eliot and Quincy, as on much else.

Harris's book, or else Hollis himself, was Quincy's source. *The Excellencie* itself was rarely named, at least in print, by Eliot's and Quincy's American contemporaries.[266] Even in the replies to Adams's *Defence* the book is hardly mentioned, though one pamphlet of 1796 did take Nedham's side, replying to Adams that Nedham's views on the rotation of power "perfectly" and "calmly accord[ed] with the spirit and nature of the United States" and with "the provisions of its federal constitution."[267]

It may of course be that, in America as in England, there were writers ready to use Nedham's writing but not to acknowledge their source. Yet any unacknowledged debts are hard to pin down. Late eighteenth-century American political literature contains various echoes of Nedham's assertions (which themselves derived from Machiavelli) that "the people are the best keepers of their own liberties."[268] He made the claim alongside the statement that the people's liberties are most "safe" in their own "hands" (p.20). Nedham perhaps influenced a sermon delivered in Boston on the occasion of the "Commencement" of John Adams's Constitution of Massachusetts, when the preacher, having praised "the immortal writings of Sidney and Locke," noted how "effectually" the Constitution "makes the people the keepers of their own liberties, with whom they are certainly safest."[269] Likewise

266. It is no surprise to find that Nedham does not figure among the well-known authors mentioned by Donald S. Lutz, "The Relative Influence of European Writers on Late Eighteenth-Century Political Thought," *American Political Science Review* 78 (1984): 189–97. *The Excellencie* was included in a very long list of the books "more frequently used" by "undergraduate sophisters" at Harvard in a catalogue of the library there in 1773, but the description is doubtful: see W. H. Bond and Hugh Amory, eds., *The Printed Catalogues of the Harvard College Library, 1723–1790* (Boston: Colonial Society of Massachusetts, 1996), pp. xxxv, 186, 254.

267. [Trench Coxe], *The Federalist: containing some Strictures upon a Pamphlet, entitled "The Pretensions of Thomas Jefferson. . . ."* (Philadelphia, 1796), pp. 20–24. See too [William Griffin], *Eumenes* (1799), p. 123. In England a reviewer of the third volume of Adams's *Defence* described *The Excellencie* as an "able" work, but gave no indication of having read it. The reviewer took it on trust from Adams that the tract was "a favourite book in America." *Monthly Review*, October 1788, pp. 289–97.

268. Here as elsewhere in this paragraph I am indebted to Mr. Tannenbaum.

269. Samuel Cooper, *A Sermon Preached before his Excellency John Hancock* (Boston, 1780), p. 28.

in December 1792 James Madison asked, "Who are the best keepers of the people's liberties," and answered, "the people themselves," for nowhere can the trust of government be so "safe" as in their "hands."[270] Yet we could not be confident in attributing such language to Nedham's influence.

Modern tributes to the eighteenth-century impact of *The Excellencie*, and the allocation to it of a place in the "sacred canon," seem to derive from Adams's assertions. Even on the most generous estimate, the book commanded nothing like the influence, on either side of the Atlantic, of the writings of the figures whose place in the canon is incontestable.[271] On the whole the canon, and Hollis's promotion of it, had considerably more success in America than in his native land. In England, where Hollis was accused of misspending his fortune "in paving the way for sedition,"[272] the tradition of resistance to tyranny that he championed was widely feared and widely derided. In America it chimed with an emerging political culture and helped to shape it. But Nedham's part in that process was far smaller than that of the canonical works that Toland had put into circulation. Adams himself, who contended so strenuously against Nedham's unicameralism, relished the arguments for mixed or balanced constitutions that he found in Harrington and Sidney.[273] Other Americans savored them too. As in England itself, the mixed or balanced English constitution—as distinct from the modern ministries that abused or perverted it—was judged to be perfect.[274] Besides, Americans, no less than Englishmen, liked to find high morality and virtue in political thinkers. Adams, who believed "pure virtue" to be "the only foundation of a free constitution,"[275] was enraptured by the courage and incorruptibility of

---

270. *National Gazette*, 20 December 1792. Conceivably, too, Nedham's influence is present in the passage of a pamphlet of 1776 which maintained that "the people know best their own wants and necessities, and therefore are best able to rule themselves" (quoted by Bailyn, *Ideological Origins*, p. 294).

271. A copy of the book did make its way to Monticello. Colbourn, *Lamp of Experience*, p. 220.

272. Robbins, "Library of Liberty," p. 208.

273. Adams, *Defence*, 1:148–52, 158–61; Haraszti, *John Adams*, pp. 34–35.

274. Bailyn, *Ideological Origins*, p. 67.

275. Howe, *Changing Political Thought*, p. 88.

Sidney, that "martyr to liberty,"[276] the example of whose courage in vindicating armed resistance was urged on him by Hollis or through his influence.[277] Andrew Eliot remembered that it was Sidney who had "taught him any just sentiments of government."[278] Jonathan Mayhew, another figure whom Hollis introduced to Sidney's merits,[279] thought "virtue inseparable from civil liberty" and acknowledged the debt of his own understanding of "civil liberty" to the teaching of Sidney, as of Milton.[280] Peter Karsten's study of *Patriot-Heroes in England and America* illustrates the lasting and widespread reverence that the characters and deeds of Sidney, Milton, and John Hampden won for their names. Karsten has no occasion to mention Nedham.

Yet it was not in the English-speaking world that Adams believed Nedham's book to have had its most pernicious effect. It was in France. The works published by Toland's circle at the end of the seventeenth century had won a following there. Thus the *Memoirs of Edmund Ludlow* were quickly translated into French, as were Sidney's *Discourses,* in an edition that would be reprinted in 1755. Sidney, Ludlow, Milton, and Harrington would be influential writers or role models in the era of the Revolution. In France, and in France alone, can Nedham claim an influence comparable to theirs, albeit hardly an equal one. The English text of 1767 was translated into French by the Chevalier d'Eon de Beaumont, a French diplomat who had arrived in England in 1762, and whose colorful and sometimes scandalous sojourn there, which lasted fifteen years, may have involved him in dealings, treasonous to his own masters, with opposition politicians.[281] The translation was included in

276. See, for example, Colbourn, *Lamp of Experience,* pp. 91–92; Worden, *Roundhead Reputations,* p. 157.

277. Bond, *Thomas Hollis,* pp. 120–21; compare *Political Register,* June 1767, pp. 136–37.

278. Colbourn, *Lamp of Experience,* p. 60.

279. Knollenberg, "Thomas Hollis and Jonathan Mayhew," p. 102.

280. Jonathan Mayhew, *The Snare Broken* (Boston, 1766), p. 43; Colbourn, *Lamp of Experience,* p. 65.

281. D'Eon would return to England in 1785 and remain until his death in 1810. For d'Eon and Nedham see Rachel Hammersley, *French Revolutionaries and English Republicans: The Cordeliers Club, 1790–1794* (Woodbridge, U.K.: Boydell Press, 2005), pp. 58–60. For a fuller exploration of the subject, see Hammersley,

1774 in his eight-volume compilation, *Les Loisirs du Chevalier d'Eon,* a copy of which Hollis apparently sent to America.[282] Perhaps d'Eon learned of *The Excellencie* through his friends, and Hollis's associates, John Wilkes and Catharine Macaulay. D'Eon remarked on the "boldness" of *The Excellencie,* as well as its "profundity and solidity." [283] But he did not dwell on the distance between its recommendations and England's eighteenth-century constitution, which, like other Frenchmen of the century, he presented as a healthy contrast to the French one. He portrayed the book as a characteristically English work that testified to the spirit of freedom in that "island of philosophy and liberty."

D'Eon noticed how little known *The Excellencie* was in England.[284] His own translation may not have done much for it in France. In 1790 there would be a second translation, whose author, Théophile Mandar, did not know (or anyway did not tell his readers) of d'Eon's version.[285] Mandar, who was reportedly one of the inciters of popular insurrection in July 1789, thereafter "devoted myself more than ever to the reading of works that have contributed towards enlightening men on their interests. The first to which I gave my attention was that of Needham." The author of *The Excellencie,* claimed Mandar, was regarded by the English "as one of the most daring geniuses who had written on the liberty of the people,"[286] and his writing entitled him to "a reputation as a

*The English Republican Tradition and Eighteenth-Century France: Between the Ancients and the Moderns* (Manchester, U.K.: Manchester University Press, 2010). My account of the French reception of *The Excellencie* is almost entirely indebted to her pioneering studies (though I must not implicate her in my inferences from them).

282. Robbins, "Strenuous Whig," p. 219n18.

283. Charles d'Eon de Beaumont, *Les Loisirs du Chevalier d'Eon de Beaumont,* 8 vols. (Amsterdam, 1774), 5:137. Caroline Robbins's reference to "an Amsterdam reprint" of *The Excellencie* in 1774 (*Eighteenth-Century Commonwealthman,* p. 49) has misled some readers by implying that there was a second edition of the Hollis-Baron publication. She was presumably thinking of d'Eon's publication. The edition of 1767 was re-advertised in 1771. *Public Advertiser,* 11 September 1771; see, too, *St. James's Chronicle,* 4 August 1767, and *Public Advertiser,* 29 October 1768.

284. Hammersley, *French Revolutionaries,* p. 60.

285. For Mandar's translation see ibid., chap. 2.

286. Ibid., pp. 56, 65.

profound political thinker, if one considers the time in which he wrote."
Mandar, who dedicated his translation to "my brothers in arms,"[287]
became an active member of the Cordeliers Club, on which much of
the French interest in English republicanism centered. Like d'Eon before him, Mandar had little idea about the circumstances from which
*The Excellencie* had emerged. At one point he suggests that "this immortal work" had appeared in the reign of Charles II.[288] Little if any-
thing seems to have been known in France about Nedham's character
and career, those obstacles to his acceptance in the English-speaking
world. Mandar's translation appeared in two volumes, under the title
*De la Souveraineté du Peuple, et de l'excellence d'un état libre* (Paris: La-
villette, 1790). Perhaps in imitation of Hollis's editions of Sidney and
of Toland's life of Milton, Mandar supplies an apparatus of extensive
commentary and quotation that relates the arguments of the text to
the concerns of all ages and especially of the present one.[289] Mandar
was particularly eager to link Nedham's reasoning to that of Rousseau.
He also portrayed Nedham as a kindred spirit of Sidney, a writer who
meant more to Mandar than did Nedham, and whose *Discourses* he
revered.[290] Occasionally Mandar adjusted Nedham's text. Its populism,
which alarmed Adams and may have inhibited admiration among
other English-speaking readers, had a ready appeal to the Cordeliers. It
was heightened by Mandar, whose translation eliminated the hesitancy
and the qualifications that had accompanied Nedham's endorsement
of the principle of political equality. Mandar's version was favorably
noticed by the daily newspaper *Le Moniteur*, which commanded a wide
circulation. The reviewer welcomed Nedham's ripostes to "the partisans
of tyranny" and endorsed Mandar's claims for the present relevance of
the work and for its affinity to Rousseau.[291]

287. Ibid., p. 62.
288. Ibid., p. 79. The preface, however, states that the book was published
under the protectorate.
289. Despite his "immense prejudice" against the French, Hollis sent books
to France, though not on the scale of his dissemination of literature elsewhere.
Robbins, "Library of Liberty," pp. 213–14.
290. Hammersley, *French Revolutionaries*, pp. 80–81.
291. Ibid., pp. 272–75.

There is, however, no sign that Adams knew of the French translations, which would have been grist to his mill. It was other French writings that troubled him. In 1778 the politician and economist Anne Robert Jacques Turgot, whom Adams met in that year, wrote a letter to the English reformer Richard Price, which Price published in his own commentary on the American Revolution in 1784.[292] Turgot complained that the American republic, instead of introducing a pure democracy, had emulated the English principle of mixed government. Turgot's argument would be supported by Antoine-Nicolas de Condorcet, who in a posthumously published work of 1795 fleetingly commended Nedham, alongside Harrington, as an advocate of resistance to tyranny.[293] That was hardly Nedham's prime claim to notice, and was still less Harrington's. Condorcet apparently lacked firsthand knowledge of either author. Equally there seems to be no indication that Turgot himself had read Nedham. Adams nonetheless declared that Turgot's "idea of a commonwealth, in which all authority is to be collected in one centre, and that centre the nation, is supposed [by Adams] to be precisely the project of Marchamont Nedham, and [was] probably derived from" *The Excellencie.* Adams's *Defence* thus becomes an attack on the political scheme of "Mr. Turgot and Marchamont Nedham."[294] Later Adams would assert, implausibly, that the whole "system" of the French revolutionaries was "a servile imitation of Nedham's."[295]

In the nineteenth century *The Excellencie* had no discernible reputation in France, America, or England. Nedham's friendship with Milton did keep his name alive. In his *History of the Commonwealth* (1824–28), the republican William Godwin, struck by the friendship, considered Nedham "too extraordinary a man . . . not to make it proper that we should

292. Paul Rahe, *Republics Ancient and Modern: Classical Republicanism and the American Revolution* (Chapel Hill: University of North Carolina Press, 1992), p. 254.

293. Jean-Antoine-Nicolas de Caritat, Marquis de Condorcet, *Outlines of an Historical View of the Progress of the Human Mind* (London, 1795), p. 201.

294. Adams, *Defence,* 2:13, 236; Thompson, *John Adams,* pp. 129–30.

295. Haraszti, *John Adams,* p. 209.

pause for a moment to enter his history," though Godwin, within whose radicalism an eighteenth-century country-party philosophy lived on,[296] did wonder that so austere and sublime a poet should have chosen as a close companion a figure so unrepresentative of what Goodwin judged to have been "an age of principle in England." Like so many before him, Godwin was more drawn to Milton, Ludlow, and Sidney, "men," he recalled, "far beyond the imputation of interested views."[297] By Godwin's time, however, seventeenth-century republicanism, and appeals to Roman republican example, had a declining prestige among radicals, not least because of a growing readiness, as the Industrial Revolution advanced, to equate "Roman" with aristocratic morality, and of growing indignation at the Roman practice of slavery.[298] Among mainstream opinion, Victorian censoriousness was no friendlier to Nedham than Hanoverian country-party sentiment had been. Those great Victorian historians David Masson and S. R. Gardiner were led to Nedham by Milton's involvement in the production of *Mercurius Politicus,* but Masson could not warm to the "dull drollery," "scurrility," and "ribaldry" of the editorials,[299] while Gardiner lamented not only the "scurrility" but the "wearisome monotony" of Nedham's prose.[300] It was left to Gardiner's disciple C. H. Firth in 1909 to recognize in Nedham not only

296. Worden, *Roundhead Reputations,* s.v. "Godwin."

297. William Godwin, *History of the Commonwealth of England,* 4 vols. (London, 1824–28), 2:24, 31, 3:343–47. In 1854 brief excerpts from issues of *Mercurius Politicus* published around the time of Oliver Cromwell's death were reprinted, without explanation, in a curious publication, *The Commonwealth Mercury.*

298. Worden, *Roundhead Reputations,* p. 284. The authority of Roman history on English political thinking at large was challenged by two other developments: a confidence that the modern world, and modern England, were at least as well equipped as the inhabitants of classical antiquity to discover the rules of political prudence; and a growing emphasis on the turbulence and instability of the classical republics. Ibid., p. 161; and see *Political Register,* 25 February 1769, pp. 187–88.

299. David Masson, *The Life of John Milton,* 7 vols. (London: Macmillan, 1859–94), 4:335.

300. S. R. Gardiner, *History of the Commonwealth and Protectorate, 1649–1660,* 4 vols. (1894–1903; repr. New York: AMS, 1965), 1:255, 2:18.

"a journalist of great ability and versatility" but a writer, in his political tracts of 1650–56, of "serious works."[301] Yet no one followed Firth's lead.

Recent interest in Nedham arises from developments in the professional study of the history of political thought, whose practitioners have become readier both to extend their enquiries beyond the more famous writers and to relate historical ideas to political contexts such as that from which Nedham's writings emerged. The rediscovery of Nedham is indebted to Perez Zagorin, who briefly discussed his political ideas in 1954,[302] and to the edition of *The Case of the Commonwealth* produced by Philip Knachel in 1969. The principal stimulus has been the work of J. G. A. Pocock, who in 1975 pointed to Nedham's role in the emergence of English republican thinking in the 1650s, a development that Pocock in turn placed within a long movement of republican ideas from the Italian Renaissance to the American Revolution.[303] Even when we have acknowledged the shallowness and slipperiness

301. C. H. Firth, *The Last Years of the Protectorate*, 2 vols. (London: Longmans, Green, 1909), 1:156. Firth seems to have been the first to notice the disparities between the editorials and the corresponding passages of *The Excellencie*, though he apparently did not explore them. Firth e. 147, Bodleian Library pamphlets.

302. Perez Zagorin, *A History of Political Thought in the English Revolution* (London: Routledge and Paul, 1954), chap. 10.

303. J. G. A. Pocock, *The Machiavellian Moment: Florentine Political Thought and the American Republican Tradition* (Princeton: Princeton University Press, 1975), pp. 382–84, 508. Nedham's observations about militias and standing armies, which were selected for covert polemical use in the late seventeenth century, have attracted modern attention too. Pocock was especially interested in Nedham's espousal of what Pocock took to be Machiavelli's "ideal of the armed and militant people" and of the *"vivere civile e popolare"* that derived from "the classical ideal of the armed citizen." Paul Rahe, however, maintains that Machiavelli "never contended that arms-bearing should depend on citizenship or vice-versa" and portrays Nedham himself as "the first modern political theorist to insist, as [Aristotle and] the ancients had done," on that equation (*Against Throne and Altar* [New York: Cambridge University Press, 2008], pp. 239–40). Nedham is a substantial figure in Rahe's book. He figures prominently too in Jonathan Scott, *Commonwealth Principles: Republican Writing of the English Revolution* (Cambridge, U.K.: Cambridge University Press, 2004).

that can characterize Nedham's writing, and even when we have recognized the exaggerations in the claims that have been made for his
posthumous readership, he remains a critical figure in English political
thought. His assault on ancient constitutionalism, and his advocacy of
an Italianate republican alternative to it, opened a door through which
Harrington and Sidney and their republican or Whig successors, in
England and America, would pass. In the story that leads from Machiavelli to the revolutionary thinking of the later eighteenth century, the
editorials that Nedham republished in *The Excellencie of a Free-State*
are a decisive moment.[304]

304. As this volume goes to press I can add that the Dutch 'Patriot' movement of the late eighteenth century produced two native-language versions of
*The Excellencie.* In the first, *De Voortreflykheid van een Vryen Staat* (Amsterdam,
1783), the portion to be found on pp. 8–46 below is reproduced, without any
indication of the origins or authorship of the work. The publication was dedicated to George Washington. Ten years later Théophile Mandar's French translation was converted into Dutch as *De Oppermagt des Volks, of de Voortrefelijkheid
van eenen Vrijen Staat* (Amsterdam, 1793). There is now a modern edition of
Mandar's translation: Marchamont Nedham, *De la Souveraineté du Peuple, et de
l'Excellence d'un État Libre,* ed. Raymonde Monnier (*Comité des Travaux Histo-
riques et Scientifiques,* Paris, 2010). I am most grateful to Rachel Hammersley,
Wyger Velema, and Arthur Weinsteijn for their help in these matters.

# NEDHAM AND HIS
# CLASSICAL SOURCES

Nedham's argument proceeds by the invocation and accumulation of historical examples. He does not deploy or cite them in a fastidious spirit. His historical illustrations, sometimes evidently taken from memory, are frequently characterized by liberal paraphrase or loose quotation or misleading abbreviation. The writers to whose authority he appeals would have been surprised by some of the uses to which, through either overeagerness or deliberate distortion, he puts them.[305] Because of his habits of imprecision, the identification of his sources for particular statements can, as Philip Knachel remarked in the preface to his admirable edition of Nedham's *The Case of the Commonwealth of England, Stated,* be "a difficult and occasionally impossible task."

The same habits preclude confident assessments of the extent of his reading. He used the conventional range of histories by classical writers, but did he go further? His literary associate Bulstrode Whitelocke,

---

305. One passage (pp. 48–52) carries the tendency to extremes. In it Nedham, denying that republican rule leads to "levelling," claims that Spartan and Roman history show that the true "Levellers" are kings. His manipulation of evidence at that point was accounted "wit and burlesque" by John Adams (*Defence,* 3:395–96) and has been independently characterized by a modern authority as "truly contorted, nearly comical" (Eric Nelson, *The Greek Tradition in Republican Thought* [Cambridge, U.K.: Cambridge University Press, 2004], p. 92).

in passages on Roman history that draw extensively on Nedham's writings (p. xlv*n*71), employed Renaissance commentaries by Carolus Sigonius, Pedro Mexia, Johannes Rosinus, and Jean Bodin. It seems impossible to say whether Nedham did the same. He may, but may not, have used such compendia as Sir Robert Dallington's *Aphorismes Civill and Militarie* (London, 1613), which conveniently reproduced, in English, extracts from Francesco Guicciardini. Nedham was not above appropriating English translations of classical historians, but does not seem to have been generally dependent on them.

In most cases Nedham turns to historians of antiquity merely for historical examples to support his own thesis. There are, however, three preeminent classical writers to whom his debt goes further, and whose political philosophies can be said to inform the editorials: Aristotle, Cicero, and Livy. Enterprising as his use of them is, he never quite integrates the varying perspectives with which they supply him. To Aristotle's *Politics* he owes not only general debts—to its historical content and to accounts of the characteristics and tendencies of the various forms of government—but insights into the means by which governments, especially new ones, maintain power. He finds evidence of the importance of a public militia (*Politics* IV.13.1; p. 89) and of educating young people in the principles of government (V.9; p. 92) to the preservation of a free state. In the earlier part of *The Excellencie* Nedham makes use of Cicero's *De Officiis* to argue that a free state is the form of government best suited to human nature. Later he turns to the same work to demonstrate Cicero's own hostility to tyranny and preference for a republic.

Nedham's use of Livy's *Ab Urbe Condita*, which in the earlier stages of *The Excellencie* is largely restricted to the depiction of exemplary republican figures, grows much more extensive nearly halfway through, when it becomes the basis of Nedham's analysis of the survival of "kingly power" in senatorial or consular hands. Livy's own views are subtly, and sometimes not so subtly, transformed. References by the Roman historian to specific abuses of government are presented as general condemnations of the system of rule. His equivocal presentation of the Decemviri (III.9.4) is turned by Nedham into an unequivocally hostile one (p. 81). A view of kingly power ascribed by Livy to one of his characters (IX.34.16) is implicitly attributed to Livy himself (p. 85). To a large extent Nedham's reading of Livy is shaped by Machiavelli, whose influence on Nedham has already been described. *The Excellencie* could almost be described as discourses on Machiavelli's *Discourses on Livy*.

# THE TEXT AND THE NOTES

The text reproduced in this volume is that of 1656.[306] The spelling of the original is retained (whereas in my introduction I have modernized the spelling of quotations, though not of titles of books). Except in reproducing proper names I have corrected obvious misprints, which are listed in Appendix A. I have not reproduced the occasional gaps to be found between paragraphs, some of which seem to have been inadvertent. The page numbers in the text that are reproduced within square brackets are those of the 1656 edition, except that I have supplied the page numbers of the preface. I have silently corrected seven errors of page numbering, though I have left the pagination as it is when the text leaps from p. 136 to p. 145. The bracketed headings, for example, [MP 71, 9–16 Oct. 1651], point to the corresponding issues of *Mercurius Politicus.*

Where italicized words are followed in *E* by punctuation in roman, the punctuation is here italicized. Also, in paragraphs that follow breaks in the text, the indentation of the opening line in *E* has been

---

306. Occasionally, indistinct print leaves a letter or punctuation mark uncertain, and in these cases I have made an educated guess as to Nedham's intent.

eliminated. The format of the headings of the sections or chapters of *E* has been standardized and modernized as well.

The footnotes are explanatory. References to classical texts are to the Loeb Classical Library editions. The endnotes, which can be found in Appendix C, record differences between *The Excellencie* and the corresponding editorials of *Mercurius Politicus*.[307]

307. Other guides to Nedham's reproduction of material from *Politicus* may be found in J. Milton French, "Milton, Needham, and *Mercurius Politicus*," *Studies in Philology* 23 (1936): 236–52; and Ernest A. Beller, "Milton and *Mercurius Politicus*," *Huntington Library Quarterly* 5 (1952): 479–87.

*The Excellencie*
*of a Free-State*

# The
# EXCELLENCIE

OF A

## Free-State:

OR,

## The Right CONSTITUTION

OF A

## Common-wealth.

WHEREIN

All Objections are answered, and
the best way to secure the Peoples
LIBERTIES, discovered:

WITH

*Some Errors of Government,*

AND

*Rules of Policie.*

*Published by a Well-wisher to Posterity.*

LONDON, Printed for *Thomas Brewster,* at the three
Bibles neer the West-end of *Pauls.* 1656.

# To the Reader.

*Taking notice of late with what impudence, and (the more is the pity) con-
fidence, the Enemies of this Commonwealth in their publick Writings and
Discourses labour to undermine the dear-bought Liberties and Freedoms of
the People, in their declared Interest of a Free-State; I thought it high time,
by counter-working them, to crush the Cockatrice in the Egg, that so it might
never grow to be a Bird of prey: in order thereto, I have published this following Discourse to the World; that so the Eyes of the People being opened, they
may see whether those high and ranting Discourses of personal Prerogative
and unbounded Monarchy, (especially One lately published by Mr. Howel,\** Inspections.
*that struts abroad with a brazen Face) or a due and* [ii] *orderly succession of
the Supreme Authority in the hands of the Peoples Representatives, will best
secure the Liberties and Freedoms of the People from the Incroachments and
Usurpations of Tyranny, and answer the true Ends of the late Wars.*

 *This Treatise is not intended for a particular Answer to Mr.* Howel's *said
Book, but yet may obviate that part thereof which he calls,* Some Reflexes
upon Government: *for his main design is not so much, (though that be
part) to asperse the long Parliament, (and so through their sides to wound*

---

 \*James Howell, *Som Sober Inspections made into the Cariage and Consults of the
late-Long Parliament* (London, 1655). The passages of the book cited or quoted in
Nedham's preface are on pp. 19–20, 23–24, 179–82.

*all their Friends and Adherents) as to lay a Foundation for absolute Tyr-*
*anny, upon an unbounded Monarchy: and in order thereunto, he advises his*
*Highness to lay aside Parliaments, (or at best, to make them Cyphers) and to*
*govern the Nation* Vi & Armis: *not out of any Honour or respect he bears*
*to his Person,* but to bring the old Interest and Family into more credit
and esteem with the People.

    *His Principles and Precedents, they are purely his own: for I am confident,*
*that the most considerate part of those that did engage for the late King, are*
*so far from* [iii] *owning his Tenets, that they would rather lay aside the*
*Family and Interest of the* Stuarts, *and declare for a Free-State, than indure*
*to be yoked and enslaved by such an absolute Tyranny as he pleads for. My*
*reason is this: because most of the Nobility and Gentry of this Nation have*
*fair Estates of their own, free, without any dependence upon the Crown; and*
*they would be as unwilling to render up their Estates and Posterities in the*
*paw of the Lion, as the Commoners themselves.*

    *His Precedents are as false as his Principles are bad: for proof hereof, take*
*one (and that a main one) for all: he saith, That* until the Reign of *Henry*
the first, the Commons of *England* were not called to the Parliament at
all, or had so much as a Consent in the making of Laws.

    *To prove that this is false, there is extant an old Latine Copy speaking*
*of a Parliament in the Reign of King* Ethelred; *which telleth us, that in it*
*were* Universi *Anglorum* Optimates *Ethelredi* Regis Edicto: & convo-
cata Plebis multitudine collectae Regis Edicto: *A Writ of Summons for*
*all the Lords, and for choice* [iv] *of the Commons: a full and clear Parlia-*
*ment. My Author saith,* The proofs of Parliaments, in *Canute*'s time, are
so many, and so full, that they tire us altogether. *His remarkable Let-*
*ter from* Rome, *recorded by the Monk of* Malmsbury, *runs thus:* To the
Arch-Bishops, Bishops, *&c.* Primatibus & toti Genti *Anglorum,* tam
Nobilibus, quam Plebeis. Hoveden *is full in this also;* Cujus (*Edmundi*)
post mortem, Rex *Canutus* omnes Episcopos, Duces, nec non & Princi-
pes, cunctosque Optimates Gentis *Angliae, Lundoniae* congregrari jussit.
*A clear summons of Parliament: and the very name of Parliament is found*
*(saith my Author) in his time, in the old Book of* Edmunds-Bury. Rex
Canutus, Anno Regni 5. cunctos Regni sui Praelatos, Proceresque, ac
Magnates, ad suum convocans Parliamentum. *And that it was a full*
*Parliament, we may believe from the persons we finde there, at the Charter*

*Howel* saith
*William* the
Conqueror
first brought
the word
*Parlament.*

*to that* Monastery; *confirmed by* Hardicanute, *but granted by* Canute, in suo Publico Parliamento, praesistentibus personaliter in eodem Archi-Episcopis, Episcopis, Suffraganeis, Ducibus, Comi-[v]tibus, Abbatibus, cum quam plurimis gregariis Militibus (*Knights of shires it seems*) & cum Populi multitudine copiosa (*other Commons also*) Omnibus tum eodem Parliamento personaliter existentibus. Edward *the Confessor refers the repairing of* Westminster *to the Parliament: at length,* cum totius Regni Electione, (*they are his own words*) *he sets upon the decayed* Minster.

*But they that would know more of the Customs and Constitutions of this Nation, let them repair to those large Volumes, that are so frequent in print upon that Subject; especially that excellent Piece,* The Rights of the Kingdom.* *This may suffice to prove that the Commons were called to Parliament long before* Henry *the first.*

*I believe none will be offended with this following Discourse, but those that are Enemies to publick welfare: let such be offended still: it is not for their sakes that I publish this ensuing Treatise; but for your sakes, that have been noble Patriots, fellow-Souldiers; and Sufferers for the Liberties and Freedoms of your Country, that Posterity in after-ages may have something to say and shew to (if God shall permit any)* [vi] *succeeding Tyrants, wherefore their Fathers sacrificed their lives, and all that was dear to them: It was not to destroy Magistracy, but to regulate it; nor to confound Propriety, but to inlarge it: that the Prince as well as the People might be governed by Law; that Justice might be impartially distributed without respect of persons; that* England *might become a quiet Habitation for the Lion and the Lamb to lie down and feed together; and, that none might make the people afraid: it was for these things they fought and died; and that not as private persons neither, but by the publick command and conduct of the Supreme Power of the Nation,* viz. *the peoples Representatives in Parliament: and nothing will satisfie for all the Blood and Treasure that hath been spilt and spent, make* England *a glorious Commonwealth, and stop the mouths of all gainsayers; but a due and orderly succession of the Supreme Authority in the hands of the Peoples Representatives.*

Mr. *Howel* would have his Highness lay a Sesment for the repairing of *Pauls* without consent of Parliament.†

---

* John Sadler, *Rights of the Kingdom* (London, 1649).
† St. Paul's Cathedral, which had been restored under Charles I, had fallen into serious disrepair under Puritan rule.

# An Introduction to the
# Following Discourse.

[1]When the Senators of *Rome,* in their publike Decrees and Orations, began to comply with and court the People, calling them *Lords of the world;* how easie a matter was it then for *Gracchus* to perswade them to un-Lord the Senate? In like manner, when *Athens* was quitted of Kings, the Power was no sooner declared to be in the People, but immediately they took it, and made [2] sure of it in their own hands, by the advice of *Solon,* that excellent Lawgiver: for, as *Cicero* saith, There is a natural desire of Power and Sovereignty in every man: so that if any have once an opportunity to seize, they seldom neglect it; and if they are told it is their due, they venture life and all to attain it.*

If a People once conceive they ought to be free, this conception is immediately put in practice; and they free themselves. Their first care is to see, that their Laws, their Rights, their Deputies, their Officers, and all their Dependents, be setled in a state of freedom. This becoms like the Apple of the eye; the least grain, atome, or touch, will grieve it: it is an espoused virgin; they are extreme jealous over it.

* Cicero, *De Officiis,* I.19.

8

Thus strangely affected were the Roman people, that if any one among them (though ne'er so deserving) were found to aspire, they presently fetch'd him down, as they did the gallant *Maelius* and *Manlius;* yea, their[2] jealousie was so great, that they observ-[3]ed every man's looks, his very nods, his garb, and his gait, whether he walked, conversed, and lived as a friend of Freedom among his neighbours. The supercilious eye, the lofty brow, and the grand paw were accounted Monsters, and no Character[3] of Freedom; so that it was the special care of the wiser Patriots, to keep themselves in a demure and humble posture, for the avoiding of suspicion. Hence it was, that *Collatinus,* one of their Freedoms Founders, and of the first Consuls, living in some more State than ordinary, and keeping at too great a distance from the people, soon taught them to forget his former merits: insomuch, that they not onely turned him out of his Consulship, but quite out of the City into Banishment. But his Colleague *Brutus,* and that wise Man *Valerius Publicola,* by taking a contrary course, preserved themselves and their reputation. For, the one sacrificed his Children, those living Monuments of his House, to make the vulgar amends for an inju-[4]ry: the other courted them with the Title of Majesty, laid the Fasces, the Ensigns of Authority at their Feet, fixt all appeals at their Tribunals, and levelled the lofty Walls of his own stately House, for fear they should mistake it for a Castle. Thus also did *Menenius Agrippa, Camillus,* and other eminent Men in that popular State: so that by these[4] means they made themselves the Darlings of the people, whilst many others of a more Grandee-humor, soon lost their Interest and Reputation.

Thus you see, that[5] when a Peoples Right is once declared to them, it is almost impossible to keep it, or take it from them.

[6]It is pity, that the people of *England,* being born as free as any people in the World, should be of such a supple humor and inclination, to bow under the ignoble pressures of an Arbitrary Tyranny, and so unapt to learn what true Freedom is. It is an inestimable Jewel, of more worth than your Estates, or your Lives: it consists not in a License to do what [5] you list, but in these few particulars: First, in having wholesome Laws suted to every Man's state and condition. Secondly, in a due and easie course of administration, as to Law and Justice, that the Remedies of Evil may

be cheap and speedy. Thirdly, in a power of altering Government and Governours upon occasion. Fourthly, in an uninterrupted course of successive Parliaments, or Assemblies of the People. Fifthly, in a free Election of Members to sit in every Parliament, when Rules of Election are once established. By enjoying these onely, a people are said to enjoy their Rights, and to be truely stated in a condition of safety and Freedom.

### [MP 73, 23–30 Oct. 1651]

Now if Liberty is the most precious Jewel under the Sun, then when[7] it is once in possession, it requires more than an ordinary art and industry to preserve it. But the great question is, Which is the safest way? whether by committing of it into the hands of a standing Power, or by placing the Guardianship in the [6] hands of the People, in a constant succession of their supreme Assemblys. The best way to determine this, is by observation out of Romane[8] Stories; whereby it plainly appears, that people never had any real Liberty, till they were possess'd of the power of calling and dissolving the Supreme Assemblies, changing Governments, enacting and repealing Laws, together with a power of chusing and deputing whom they pleased to this work, as often as they should judge expedient, for their own well-being, and the good of the Publike. This power is said to be the first-born of that Peoples Freedom: and many a shrewd fit, many a pang and throw the Commonwealth had, before it could be brought forth in the world: which (*Gracchus* told them)* was a sore affliction from the gods, that they should suffer so much for the ignorance or negligence of their Ancestors, who when they drave out Kings, forgat to drive out the Mysteries and inconveniences of Kingly power, which were all reserved within the [7] hands[9] of the Senate. By this means the poor people missing the first opportunity of setling their freedom, soon lost it again: they[10] were told they were a Free-state; and why? because (forsooth) they had no King, they had at length never a *Tarquin* to trouble them: but what was that to the purpose, as long as they had a *Caius*, and an *Appius Claudius*,

* Plutarch, *Life of Tiberius Gracchus*, XV.4–6.

and the rest of that gang, who infected the Senators with a[11] humour of Kinging it from generation to generation? Alas, when the *Romans* were at this pass, they were just such another Free-state as was that of *Sparta,* in the days of yore, where they had a Senate too, to pull down the pride of Kings; but the people were left destitute of power and means to pull down the pride of the Senate; by which means indeed they[12] became free to do what they list, whilst the people were confined within straiter bounds[13] than ever. Such another Free-state in these daies is that of *Venice,* where the people are free from the Dominion of their Prince [8] or Duke; but little better than slaves[14] under the power of their Senate: but now in the Common-wealth of *Athens* the case was far otherwise; where it was the care of *Solon,* that famous Law-giver, to place both the exercise & interest of Supremacy in the hands of the people, so that nothing of a publick interest[15] could be imposed, but what passed currant by vertue of their consent and Authority: he instituted that famous Council[16] called the *Areopagus,* for the managing of State-transactions: but left the power of Legislation, or law-making, in a successive course of the peoples Assemblies; so that avoiding Kingly Tyranny on the one side, and Senatical incroachments on the other, he is celebrated by all Posterity, as the man that hath left the onely Patern of a Free-state fit for all the world to follow.

[MP 72, 16–23 Oct. 1651]

It is also to be observed, when[17] Kings were driven out of *Rome,* though they were declared and called a Free-state, yet it was a long time ere they could be free indeed, in [9] regard[18] *Brutus* cheated them with a meer shadow and pretence of liberty: he had indeed an Ambition high enough, and opportunity fair enough to have seized the Crown into his own hands; but there were many considerations that deterr'd him from it; for he well perceived how odious the name of King was grown: Besides, had he sought to Inthrone himself, men would have judged it was not love to his Country made him take up Arms[19], but desire of Dominion; nor could he forget, that serene[20] privacy is to be preferr'd before *Hazardous* Royalty: For what hope could he have to keep the Seat long, who by his own example had taught the people both the Theory and practice of opposing Tyranny? It was necessary therefore that he should think of some other course more plausible, whereby to worke his own ends, and yet preserve the love of the people; who not having been used to liberty, did very little understand it, and therefore were the more easily gul'd out [10] of the substance, and made content with the shadow.

For the carrying on this Design, all the projecting Grandees joyned pates together; wherein, as one observes, *Regnum quidem nomen, sed non Regia potestas Româ fuit expulsa:* Though the Name of King were exploded with alacrity, yet the Kingly power was retained with all Art and subtilty, and shared under another notion among themselves, who were the great ones of the City. For all Authority was confin'd within the walls of a standing Senate, out of which, two Consuls were chosen yeerly; & so by turns they dub'd one another with a new kinde of Regality: the people being no gainers at all by this alteration of Government, save onely, that (like Asses) they were sadled with new Paniers of Slavery.

But what followed? The Senate having got all power into their own hands, in a short time degenerated from their first Virtue and Institution, to the practice[21] of Avarice, [11] Riot, and Luxury; whereby the love of their Country was changed into a Study of Ambition and Faction: so that they fell into divisions among themselves, as well as oppressions over the people; by which divisions, some leading Grandees, more potent than their Fellows, took occasion to wipe their Noses, and to assume the Power into their own hands, to the number of ten persons. This Form of Government was known by the Name of the *Decemvirate;* wherein these new Usurpers, joyning Forces together, made themselves rich with the spoiles of the people, not caring by what unlawful means they purchased either Profit or Pleasure, till that growing every day more insupportable, they were in the end by force cashiered of their Tyranny.

How the Romans obtained their Rights and Priviledges

But what then? The people being flesh'd with this Victory, and calling to minde how gallantly their Ancestors had in like manner banished Kings, began at last to know their own strength; and stomack'd it ex-[12]ceedingly, that themselves, on whose shoulders the frame of State was supported, (and for whose sakes all States are founded) should be so much vassalized at the will of others, that they who were Lords abroad, should be Slaves at home: so that they resolved to be ridden no longer under fair shews of Liberty. They raised a Tumult under the conduct of their Tribune *Canuteius*[22]; nor could they by any perswasion[23] be induced to lay down Arms, till they were put in possession of their Rights and Priviledges.* They were made capable of Offices of the Government,[24] even to the Dictatorship; had Officers of their own, called Tribunes, who were held sacred and inviolable, as *Protectors*† of the Commons, and retained a power of meeting and acting with all Freedom in their great Assemblies. Now, and never till now, could they be called a Free State, and Commonwealth, though long before declared so: for the way being open to all without exception, vertue, learning, and good Parts made as speedy [13] a Ladder to climbe unto Honours, as Nobility of Birth; and a Good Man as much respected as a Great; which was a rare felicity of the Times, not to be expected again, but upon the dawning of another golden Age.

*(margin)* Goodness preferred before Greatness.

The main Observation then arising out of this Discourse, is this: That not onely the Name of King, but the Thing King (whether in the hands of one or of many) was pluck'd up root and branch, before ever the Romans could attain to a full Establishment in their Rights and Freedoms.

## [MP 70, 2–9 Oct. 1651]

Now when *Rome* was thus declared[25] A Free State, the next work was to establish their Freedom in some sure & certain way: & in order to this, the first business they pitch'd upon, was, not onely to ingage the people by an Oath against the return of *Tarquin*'s Family to the Kingdom, but also against the admission of any such Officer as a King, for ever, because those brave men, who glorified themselves in laying the

*(margin)* What they did to preserve their Freedom.

* Livy, *Ab Urbe Condita*, IV.1–6.
† This word is not italicized in *Politicus*.

foundation of a Commonwealth, well knew, that in [14] a short Revolution, others of a less publick Spirit would arise in their places, and gape again after a Kingdom.* And therefore it was the special[26] care of those worthy Patriots, to imprint such Principles in mens mindes, as might actuate them with an irreconcilable enmity to the former Power: insomuch, that the very Name of King became odious to the Roman People; yea, and they were so zealous herein, that in process of time, when *Caesar* took occasion by Civil Discords to assume the Soveraignty into his single Hands, he durst not entertain it under the fatal[27] Name of King, but clothed himself with the more plausible stile of Emperor[28]; which nevertheless could not secure him from the[29] fatal stab that was given him by *Brutus* in revenge, on the behalf of the people. Our Neighbours of *Holland* traced this example at the heels, when upon recovery of their Freedom from *Spain,* they binde[30] themselves by an Oath to abjure the Government, not onely of King *Philip,* but of all Kings for ever.

Oaths in those days were not like an old Almanack.

[15] Kings being cashiered out of *Rome,* then the Right of Liberty, together with the Government, was retained within the hands and bounds of the Patrician or Senatorian Order of Nobility; the people not being admitted into any share, till partly by Mutinies, and partly by Importunities[31], they compell'd the Senate to grant them an Interest in Offices of State, and in the Legislative Power, which were circumscribed before within the bounds of the Senate. Hence arose those Officers called Tribunes, and those Conventions called Assemblies of the People, which were as Bridles to restrain the Power and Ambition of the Senate, or Nobility. Before the erection of those, whilst all was in the hands of the Senate, the Nation was accounted Free, because not subjected to the will of any single person: But afterwards they were Free indeed, when no Laws could be imposed upon them, without a consent first had in the Peoples Assemblies: so

No Laws imposed, but with the Peoples Consent in their Assemblies.

* Nedham's newsbook had warmly supported the Rump's divisive decision of 1649–50 to impose on all adult males an "Engagement," which read: "I do declare and promise, that I will be true and faithful to the Commonwealth of England, as it is now established, without a King or House of Lords." *LP,* pp. 84–85, 188–89.

that the Government in the end [16] came to be setled in an equal mixture of both Interests, Patrician and Popular; under which Form, they attained to the height of all their Glory and Greatness. In this Form of Free-State, we now see the Venetian, where the Patrician is predominant, and the People a little too much kept under. The same Form is imbraced also by our Neighbours the United Provinces; but the best part of their Interest lies deposited in the hands of the people. *Rome* kept up their[32] Senate as their standing Councel, for the managing of State-affairs, which require Wisdom and Experience: but as for making of Laws, and the main Acts of Supremacy, they were reserv'd to the Grand Assemblies; so that the People[33] gave Rules whereby to govern, and the secrets of Government were intrusted in the hands of the Senate. And this Commonwealth ever[34] thriv'd best, when the People had most Power, and used most Moderation: and though they made use of it now and then to fly out into ex-[17]travagant courses, yet they were no lasting fits, like those distempers that brake out through the Ambition of the Senators. Besides, we cannot but take notice, as long as the Popular Interest continued regular, and more predominant than the other, so long the People were secure of their Liberties: which enjoyment, was a good Allay and Recompence, for many harsh inconveniences that brake out when they were unruly and irregular[35]: Whereas, when the Senate afterwards worm'd the People out of Power, as that design went on by degrees, so *Rome* lost her Liberty; the Senate domineering over the People, and particular Factions over the Senate, till those Factions tearing one another to pieces, at length he that was head of the paramount surviving Faction, by name *Caesar,* took occasion to usurp over all, swallowing up the Rights and Liberties of the Romans, in the Gulph of a single Tyranny.

The Romans lose their Rights and Liberties.

## [MP 68, 18–25 Sep. 1651]

It was[36] a Noble saying, (though *Machiavel's*) *Not he that placeth a vertuous Government in his own hands, or family; but he that establisheth a free and lasting* [18] *Form, for the Peoples constant security, is most to be* *commended.** Whosoever hath this oportunity, may improve his actions to a greater height of glory, than ever followed the fame of any ambitious Idol that hath grasp'd a Monarchy: for, as *Cato* saith in *Plutarch, Even the greatest Kings, or Tyrants, are far inferiour to those that are eminent in Free-States and Commonwealths:* Nor were those mighty Monarchs of old, to be compared with *Epimanondas*[37], *Pericles, Themistocles, Marcus Curius, Amilcar, Fabius,* and *Scipio,* and other excellent Captains in Free-States, which purchased themselves a fame, in defence of their Liberties.[†] And though the very name of Liberty was[38] for a time grown odious, or ridiculous among us, having been[39] long a stranger in these and other parts; yet in Ancient time, Nations were wont to reckon themselves so much the more Noble, as they were free from the Regal yoke: which was the cause why then there were so many Free-States in all parts of the world.[40]

Nor is it onely a meer Gallantry of spirit that excites men to the love of [19] Freedom; but experience assures it to be the most commodious and profitable way of Government, conducing every way to the enlarging a people[41] in Wealth and Dominion. *It is incredible to be spoken,* (saith *Salust) how exceedingly the Romane Commonwealth increased in a short time, after they had obtained Liberty.* And *Guicciardine*[42] affirms, That *Free-States must needs be more pleasing to God than any other Form, because in them more regard is to be had to the common good, more care for the impartial distribution of Justice, and the mindes of men are more enflamed thereby to the love of Glory and Vertue, and become much more zealous in the love of Religion, than in any other Government whatsoever.*[‡]

It is wonderful to consider, how mightily the Athenians were augmented in a few years, both in Wealth and Power, after they had freed themselves from the Tyranny of *Pistratus*[43]: but the Romans arrived to such a height, as was beyond all imagination after the expulsion of their

*The Romans flourished most when they were a Free-State.*

---

\* Machiavelli, *Discourses,* I.ii (cf. Knachel, p. 118). Nedham uses Edward Dacres's translation, which was published in 1636 as *Machiavel's Discourses upon the First Decade of T. Livius.*

† Plutarch, *Life of Marcus Cato the Elder,* VIII.7–8.

‡ Sallust, *Bellum Catilinae,* VII.3; Francesco Guicciardini, *Historiarum sui Temporis* (Basel, 1566), X. 352; Knachel, pp. 116–17.

Kings, and Kingly Government. Nor[44] do these things happen without special reason; it being usual[45] [20] in Free-States to be more tender of the Publick in all their Decrees, than of particular Interests: whereas the case is otherwise in a Monarchy, because in this Form the Princes pleasure weighs[46] down all Considerations of the Common good. And hence it is, that a Nation hath no sooner lost its Liberty, and stoop'd under the yoke of a single Tyrant, but it immediately loseth its former lustre, the Body fills with ill humors, and may swell in Titles;[47] but cannot thrive either in Power or Riches, according to that proportion which it formerly enjoyed, because all new Acquisitions are appropriated as the Princes peculiar, and in no wise conduce to the ease and benefit of the Publick.

## [MP 37, 13–20 Feb. 1651]

It was the pride of *Richard Nevil* the great Earl of *Warwick*, and he reckoned it the greatest of earthly glories, to be called, (as indeed he was) a King-maker, in that he made and unmade Kings at his pleasure[48]: for we read in our Chronicles, how that he first pull'd down the House of *Lancaster*, and brought King *Henry* the sixth from a Crown to a Prison; setting up the Title [21] of the House of *York*, in the person of King *Edward* the fourth: afterwards, he deposed[49] this *Edward*, drave him out of *England*, and restored the same *Henry* to the Crown, whom he had before depress'd. But the great Query is, Wherefore, and how this was done? One would have thought, there had been no hope of reconciliation betwixt him and the House of *Lancaster*, having so highly disobliged them, in casting down and imprisoning the person of *Henry*. But yet it is very observable of this man, *Warwick*, being[50] on a sudden discontented with the change that[51] he had made, because he missed of those ends which he aimed at, in bringing it about; and perceived other persons (whom he conceived his inferiours), to partake of the interest and favour of *Edward*; therefore, out of an emulous impatience of Spirit, he presently cast about to undo all that before he had done; he supprest the new Government, to advance[52] the old.

From which piece of Story, we may very well conclude,[53] how unsafe it is in a new alteration, to trust any man with [22] too great a share of Government, or place of Trust; for such[54] persons stand ever ready (like that *Warwick*) upon any occasion of discontent, or of serving their own Interests, to betray and alter the Government; especially if they have *Warwick*'s main Guard, that is, if they can (as he did) bring the Prince whom they formerly disobliged, to come in upon their own terms, and upon such conditions as may bridle him, and secure the Power so in their own Hands, that whilst he King it onely in Title, themselves may be Kings *de facto*, and leave their old Friends in the lurch, or yeeld them up at Mercy, (as *Warwick* did) to gratifie the Tyrant[55], and their own Tyrannical ambition.

How much therefore doth it concern every Commonwealth[56], in such a case, to see and beware, that *Warwick*'s Ghost be not conjur'd up again, to act a Part in some new Tragedie!*

---

* The earl's "tragedie" is related, and its vividness urged on the reader, in the sixteenth-century compilation, which retained its fame in the seventeenth, *The Mirror for Magistrates*. Lily B. Campbell, ed., *The Mirror for Magistrates* (Cambridge, U.K.: Cambridge University Press, 1938), pp. 204–5.

# The Right Constitution of a Commonwealth.

[MP 77, 20–27 Nov. 1651]

The Romans having justly and nobly freed themselves from the Tyranny of Kings, and being in time brought to understand that the interest of Freedom consists in a due and orderly Succession of the Supreme Assemblies; they then made it their care, by all good ways and means, to fortifie the Commonwealth, and establish it in a free enjoyment of that Interest, as the onely bar to the return of Kings, and their main security against the subtil mining of Kingly humours and usurpations. The publicke *Rostra*, or Pulpits, sounded out the commendations of Freedom; their [24] *Augurs*, or Prophets, found *Freedom* written in the entrails of Beasts, and collected it from the flight of the auspicious bird[57], the Sun-daring Eagle, spreading her wings aloft over the Capitol: the common people also, in their common[58] discourses, breathed nothing but Freedom; and used the frequent mention of it, as a Charm against the return of Tyranny.[59]

Nor was it without reason, that this brave and active people were so studiously devoted to the preservation of their Freedom, when they had once attained it, considering how easie and excellent it is above all other Forms of Government, if it be kept within due bounds and order. It is an undeniable Rule, *That the People* (that is, such as shall be successively chosen to represent the People) *are the best Keepers of their own Liberties;* and that for these following Reasons.

First, because they never think of usurping[60] over other mens Rights, but minde[61] which way to preserve their own. Whereas, the case is far otherwise among Kings and Grandees, as all Na-[25]tions in the world have felt to some purpose: for they naturally move within the circle of domination, as in their proper Centre; and count it no less Security than Wisdom and Policy, to brave it over the People. Thus *Suetonius* tells us, how *Caesar, Crassus,* and another, *Societatem iniere, nequid ageretur in Repub. quod displicuisset ulli e tribus: Made a bargain between themselves, that nothing should be done in the Commonwealth that displeased either of them three.** Such another Triumvirate of Grandees was that of *Augustus, Lepidus,* and *Antonie,* who agreed to share the world between themselves; and traced the same paths as the other did, to the top of worldly Tyranny, over the ruines of their Countries Liberties: they sav'd and destroy'd, depress'd and advanc'd whom they pleased, with a wet Finger.† But whilst the Government remained untouch'd in the peoples Hands, every particular man lived safe, (except the Ambitious) and no man could be undone, unless a true and satisfactory reason were rendered to the world for his destruction.

[26] Secondly, the People are best Keepers of their own Liberty, because it is ever the Peoples care to see, that Authority be so constituted, that it shall be rather a burthen than benefit to those that undertake it; and be qualified with such slender advantages of profit or pleasure, that men shall reap little by the enjoyment. The happy consequence whereof is this, that none but honest, generous, and publick Spirits, will then desire to be in Authority, and that onely for the Common good. Hence it was, that in the Infancy of the Romane Liberty, there was no canvasing of Voices; but single and plain-hearted men were called, intreated, and in a manner forced with importunity to the Helm

---

* Suetonius, *Life of Julius Caesar,* XIX.2. "Another" was Pompey.
† Easily or lightly; without hesitation (*Oxford English Dictionary,* s.v. "finger").

of Government, in regard of that great trouble and pains that followed the imployment. Thus *Cincinnatus* was fetch'd out of the Field from his Plow, and placed (much against his will) in the sublime Dignity of Dictator: so the noble *Camillus,* and *Fabius,* and *Curius,* were, with much adoe, drawn from the recreation of Gardening, to the trouble of Governing: and the Consul-yeer [27] being over, they returned with much gladness again to their private employment.[62]

## [MP 78, 27 Nov.–4 Dec. 1651]

A third Reason why the People in their Supreme Assemblies successively chosen, are the best Keepers of their Liberty, is,[63] because as motion in Bodies natural, so succession in civil, is the grand preventive of corruption. The Truth of this will appear very clearly, if we weigh the effects of every standing Authority from first to last in the Romane State: for whilst they were governed by a continued Power in one and the same Hands, the People were ever in danger of losing their Liberty: sometimes in danger of being swallowed up by Kingly aspirers, witness the design of *Maelius, Manlius,* and others; sometimes in danger of a surprise by a Grandee Cabinet or Junta[64], who by contracting a particular Interest, distinct from that which they had in common with the people, so ordered the matter in time, that partly by their own strength, and partly by advantage[65] of Power, to gratifie and curb whom they pleased, and to wind in other Councils[66] [28] and parties to their own, they still brought the lesser into such subjection, that in the end they were forced all either to yeild to the pleasure of the Grandees, or be broken by them. By these practices, they produced that upstart Tyranny of the *Decemviri,* when ten men made a shift to enslave the Senate, as well as the people. Lastly, by continuing power too long in the hands of particular persons, they were swallow'd up[67] by two Triumvirates of Emperors by turns, who never left pecking at one another, till *Julius* and *Augustus,* having beaten all Competitors out of the Field, subjected all to the will of a single Emperour. If this were so among the Romans, how happy then is any Nation, and how much ought they to joy in the Wisdom and Justice of their Trustees, where certain Limits

Succession in power is the grand preventive of Corruption.

and Bounds are fixed to the Powers in being, by a declared succession of the supreme Authority in the hands of the People![68]

[MP 79, 4–11 Dec. 1651]

[69]A fourth Reason is, because a succession of supreme Powers doth not onely keep them from corruption, but it kills that grand Cankerworm of a Com-[29]monwealth, to wit, Faction: for, as Faction is an adhering to, and a promoting of an Interest, that is distinct from the true and declared Interest of State: so it is a matter of necessity, that those that drive it on, must have time to improve their slights and projects, in disguising their designs, drawing in Instruments and Parties, and in worming out of their opposites. The effecting of all this, requires some length of time: therefore the only prevention[70] is a due succession and revolution of Authority in the Hands of the People.

A succession of Supreme Power kills that Canker-worm of a Common-wealth, to wit, Faction.

That this is most true, appears not onely by Reason, but by Example: if we observe the several turns of Faction in the Romane Government. What made their Kings so bold, as to incroach and tyrannize over the People, but the very same course[71] that heightned our Kings heretofore in *England,* to wit, a continuation of Power in their own Persons and Families? Then, after the Romans became a Commonwealth, was it not for the same Reason, that the Senate fell into such heats[72] and fits a-[30]mong themselves? Did not *Appius Claudius* and his Junta, by the same means, Lord it[73] over the Senate? Whence was it, that *Sylla* and *Marius* caused so many proscriptions, cruelties, and combustions in *Rome,* but by an extraordinary continuation of Power in themselves? How came it to pass likewise, that *Julius Caesar* aspired, and in the end attained the Empire? and, that the People of *Rome* quite lost their Liberty, was it not by the same means? For, had not the Senate and People so long protracted the Power[74] of *Pompey* and *Caesar;* had *Pompey* had less command in *Asia,* and *Caesar* less in *Gallia, Rome* might have stood much longer in the possession of her Liberty.

After the death of *Caesar,* it was probable enough, they might then have recovered their Liberty, but that they ran again into the same Error, as before: for by a continuation of Power in the hands of *Octavius, Lepidus,* and *Antonie,* the Commonwealth came to be rent and divided into three several Factions; two of which being worn out by each other, onely *Octavius* re-[31]mained; who considering, that the Title of perpetual Dictator was the ruine of his Father *Julius,* contin-ued the Government onely for a set-time, and procured it to be setled upon himself but for ten yeers. But what was the effect of this continu-ation of Power? Even this, That as the former protractings had been[75] the occasions of Faction, so this produced a Tyranny: for, at the end of every ten yeers, he wanted no pretence to renew a lease of the Govern-ment; and by this means so played his Cards, that at length[76] he easily and utterly extinguished the small remains of the Roman Freedom.

The Observation then arising from hence, is this, that the onely way for a people to preserve themselves in the enjoyment of their Freedom, and to avoid those fatal inconveniences of Faction and Tyranny, is, to maintain a due and orderly succession of Power and Persons. This was, and is, good Commonwealths[77] Language; and without this Rule, it is impossible any Nation should long subsist in a State of Freedom. So that the Wisdom, the Piety, [32] the Justice, and the self-denial of those Governours in Free-States, is worthy of all honour and admiration, who have, or shall at any time as willingly resign their Trusts, as ever they took them up; and have so far denied themselves, as to prefix Lim-its and Bounds to their own Authority. This was it that made *Brutus* so famous in the beginning of the Romane Commonwealth.[78] For this also it was, that History hath left so reverend a remembrance of *Scipio, Camillus,* and *Virginus*[79]*;* as did *Cato* likewise of *Pompey:* whilst the ten Grandee Usurpers, with *Sylla,* and *Caesar,* and the Names of others that practised the contrary, are left as odious upon the Roman Record, as the Name of *Richard* the third[80], will be in our modern Chronicle, to all Posterity.

[MP "79" (80), 11–18 Dec. 1651]

A fifth Reason to prove the Life of Liberty lies in succession of Powers and Persons, is, because it is the onely Remedy[81] against Self-seeking, with all the powerful Temptations and Charms of self-interest: for the attaining of particular ends, requires length of time, as well as the creat-ing and promoting [33] of a Faction: both these designs must lie long

A succession
of Powers &
Persons is the
onely remedy
against self-
seeking.

in fermentation, or else they can never gain the beloved opportunity to bring matters to perfection. The Truth of this appears likewise in the Story of the Romane State: for, as long as all Authority was confined within the Walls of a standing Senate, they being more studious of their own, than the common good, in a short time the Commonwealth was turned altogether into a private; insomuch, that the people became not onely incapable of any Honour and Authority; but well-nigh reduced to flat beggery. Hence it was, that so many Quarrels and Combustions arose one after another: for, the Great Ones having made use of their time, in drawing all to themselves, the People were forc'd to live upon borrowing; and when they could borrow no longer, they fell into a general Mutiny, and forsook the City: nor could they be pacified till all Accounts were quitted; and then, with much adoe, they were wrought upon with the Eloquence of *Menenius Agrippa,* with his excellent Fable of a Mutiny in a [34] natural Body, among the Members against the Belly.*

Thus, as the first Insurrection was occasioned by the Usury and Exactions of the Great Ones; who by their long continuance in Power, had drawn all unto themselves: so the second was occasioned by the Lordliness of those ten Persons, who being elected to do Justice, according to the Laws, made use of their time, onely to confirm their Power, and Greaten themselves, by replenishing their own Coffers, ingrossing of Offices, and preferring their own Kindred and Alliances: and at length, improved Self-Interest so high, that they domineered, like absolute Tyrants, advancing and depressing whom they pleased, without respect of Merit or Insufficiency, Vice or Vertue; so that having secured all in their own Hands, they over-ruled[82] their Fellow-Senators at pleasure, as well as the People.[83]

Many more instances of After-times might be given; but these are sufficient whereupon to ground this Observation[84], That as the first Founders of the Roman [35] Liberty did well in driving out their

---

* Livy, *Ab Urbe Condita,* II.32. The fable was well known in the Renaissance and was famously told in Sir Philip Sidney's *An Apology for Poetry* and in the opening scene of Shakespeare's *Coriolanus.*

Kings; so on the other side, they did very ill in setling a standing Authority within themselves: for, by this means, lying open to the Temptations of Honour and Profit, (which are Sails too big for any humane bulk) they were immediately swallowed up of Self[85]; and taking their rise from the opportunity of a continued Power, made use of the Publick only to advance their Private, whereby they put the Commonwealth[86] into frequent flames of discontent and sedition; which might all have been prevented, could they have denied themselves at first, and setled the State Free indeed, (as they ought to have done) by placing an orderly succession of supreme[87] Authority in the Hands of the People.[88]

### [MP 81, 18–25 Dec. 1651]

A sixth Reason, why a Free-State is much more excellent than a Government by Grandees or Kings; and, that the People are the best Keepers of their own Liberties, is,[89] because, as the end of all Government is (or ought to be) the good and ease of the People, in a secure enjoyment of their Rights, without [36] Pressure and Oppression: so questionless the People, who are most sensible of their own Burthens, being once put into a capacity and Freedom of Acting, are the most likely to provide Remedies for their own Relief; they onely know where the shooe wrings,* what Grievances are most heavy, and what future Fences they stand in need of, to shelter them from the injurious Assaults of those Powers that are above them: and therefore it is but Reason, they should see that none be interested in the supreme Authority, but Persons of their own election, and such as must in a short time return again into the same condition with themselves, to reap the same Benefit or Burthen, by the Laws enacted, that befalls the rest of the People. Then the issue of such a Constitution must needs be this, That no Load shall be laid upon any, but what is common to all, and that always by common consent; not to serve the Lusts of any, but onely to supply the Necessities of their Country.

The end of all Government, being the good & ease of the people, they best know where the shooe pinches.

* Proverbial.

But when it happens, that a supreme Power long continues in the Hands of [37] any Person or Persons; they, by greatness of place, being seated above the middle Region of the People, sit secure from all windes and weathers, and from those storms of violence that nip and terrifie the inferiour part of the World: whereas, if by a successive Revolution of Authority, they came to be degraded of their Earthly Godheads, and return into the same condition with other Mortals, they must needs be the more sensible and tender of what shall be laid upon them. The strongest Obligation that can be laid upon any Man in pub-lick Matters, is, To see that he ingage in nothing but what must either offensively or beneficially reflect upon himself: for as, if any be never so good a Patriot, yet if his power be prolonged, he will finde it hard to keep Self from creeping in upon him, and prompting him to some Ex-travagancies for his own private Benefit; so, on the other side, if he be shortly to return to a condition common with the rest of his Brethren, self-Interest[90] bindes him to do nothing but what is Just and Equal; he himself being to reap the [38] good or evil of what is done, as well as the meanest of the people.

This without controversie must needs be the most Noble, the most Just, and the most excellent way of Government in Free-States; with-out which, it is obvious to common sense, no Nation can long con-tinue in a state of Freedom: as appears likewise by Example out of the Romane Story. For what more noble Patriots were there ever in the World, than the Romane Senators were, whilst they were kept under by their Kings, and felt the same Burthens of their fury, as did the rest of the people? but afterwards being freed from the Kingly yoke, and having secured all power within the hands of themselves and their posterity, they at length fell into the same Absurdities that had been before committed by their Kings; so that this new yoke be-came more intolerable than the former. Nor could the people finde any Remedy, untill[91] they procured that necessary Office of the Tribunes; who being invested with a temporary Authority by the peoples Elec-tion, remained the more sensible [39] of their condition, and were as Moderators between the Power of the Great Ones, and the Rights of the People.

What more excellent Patriot could there be than *Manlius,* till he became corrupted by Time and Power? Who more Noble, and Courteous, and Well-affected to the common good, than was *Appius Claudius*[92] at first? but afterwards, having obtained a Continuation of the Government in his own hands, he soon lost his primitive Innocency and Integrity, and devoted himself to all the Practices of an Absolute Tyrant.[93] Many others might be reckon'd up. And therefore, hence it was, That when the Senate (for some Reasons) thought to continue *Lucius Quintius* in the Consulship longer than the usual time; that gallant Man utterly refused it,* and chose rather to deny himself, than that a Precedent so prejudicial to the Romane Freedom should be made for his sake, by a Prerogative[94] of Authority in his hands, beyond the ordinary Custome.[95]

[MP 82, 25 Dec. 1651–1 Jan. 1652]

A seventh Reason why a people qualified with a due and orderly succession of their Supreme Assemblies, are the [40] best keepers of their own Liberties, is, Because[96], as in other Forms, those persons onely have access to Government, who are apt to serve the lust and will of the Prince, or else are parties or[97] compliers with some powerful Faction: so in this Form of Government by the People, the door of Dignity stands open to all (without exception) that ascend thither by the steps of Worth and Vertue: the consideration whereof hath this noble effect in Free-States, That it edges mens spirits with an active emulation, and raiseth them to a lofty pitch of designe and action.

> In this Government the door of Dignity stands open to all that ascend thither by the steps of Worth and Vertue.

The truth of this is very observable in the Romane State[98]: for, during the Vassalage of that People under Kings, we read not of any notable Exploits, but finde them confined within a narrow compass, oppress'd at home, and ever and anon ready to be swallowed up by their enemies. After this Government of Kings was abolished, you know that of Grandees in a standing Senate was next erected; under which Form, they made shift to enlarge their bounds a little: but the most they could

* Livy, *Ab Urbe Condita,* III.21.

then do, [41] was only to secure themselves from the attempts of the banished *Tarquins*, and those petty neighbours that envied the small increase of their Dominion. But at length, when the State was made free indeed, and the People admitted into a share and interest in the Government, as well as the Great Ones; then it was, and never till then, that their thoughts and power began to exceed the bounds of *Italy*, and aspire towards that prodigious Empire. For, while the road of Preferment lay plain to every man, no publike work was done, nor any Conquest made; but every man thought he did and conquered all for himself, as long as he remained valiant and vertuous: it was not Alliance, nor Friendship, nor Faction, nor Riches, that could advance men; but Knowledge, Valour, and vertuous Poverty, was preferred above them all.

For the confirmation whereof, we finde in the same Story, how that many[99] of their brave Patriots and Conquerors were men of the meanest Fortune, and of so rare a temper of spirit, that they little cared to improve them, or enrich [42] themselves by their publike employment: so that when they died, they were fain to be buried at the publike charge. We finde *Cincinnatus*, a man of mean fortune, fetch'd from the Plough, to the dignity of a Dictator: for he had[100] no more than four acres of land, which he tilled with his own hands. Yet so it[101] happened, that when the Roman Consul with his whole Army was in great peril, being circumvented and straitned by the *Equuns*[102], and the City of *Rome* it self in a trembling condition[103]; then, with one consent, they pitch'd upon *Cincinnatus*, as the fittest man for their deliverance: and he behaved himself so well[104], with so much magnanimity, integrity, and wisdom, that he relieved the Consul, routed and utterly subdued the Enemy, and gave as it were a new life to his Countries Liberties: which work being over, he with all willingness quitted his Authority, and returned to the condition of a painful private life.

This Example might seem strange, but that we know it was ordinary in that State, till it grew corrupt again: for, we read also, how *Lucius Tarquin*, (not of [43] the Tyrants family) a man of mean fortune, yet of great worth, was chosen General of the Horse, and drawn to it out of the Country, in which place he surpassed all the Romane youth for gallant behaviour. Such another plain Country-fellow was *Attilius Regulus,* the scourge of *Carthage* in his time; of whom many eminent points of Bravery were[105] recorded: as were also most of those Heroick spirits that succeeded, down to the times of *Lucius Paulus*[106] *Emilius,* by whose Conquests, the first charms and inchantments of Luxury were brought out of *Asia* to *Rome,* and there they soon swallowed up the remainders of primitive integrity and simplicity. And yet it is very observable also, that so much of the ancient severity was remaining still even in the time of this *Paulus,* the famous General, that a Silver dish, that was part of the Spoil, being given to a son-in-law of his, who had fought stoutly in that war, it was thought a great reward; and observed by the Historian,* to be the first piece of plate that ever was seen in the Family.

[44] This Observation then arises from this Discourse,[107] That as *Rome* never thrived till it was setled in a Freedom of the People; so that Freedom was preserved,[108] and that[109] Interest best advanced, when all Places of Honour and Trust were exposed to men of Merit, without distinction; which happiness could never be obtained, until[110] the people were instated in a capacity of preferring whom they thought worthy, by a Freedom of electing men successively into their Supreme Offices and Assemblies. So long as this Custome continued, and Merit took place, the people made shift[111] to keep and encrease their Liberties: but when it lay neglected, and the stream of Preferment began to run along with the favour and pleasure of particular powerful men, then Vice and Compliance making way for Advancement, the people could keep their Liberties no longer; but both their Liberties and themselves were made the price of every man's Ambition and Luxury.

The People are the best Keepers of their Liberty, because they only are concerned in the point of Liberty.

[MP 83, 1–8 Jan. 1652]

The eighth Reason, why the People in their Assemblies are the best Keepers [45] of their Liberty, is,[112] because it is they onely that are concerned in the point of Liberty: for, whereas in other Forms the main

* Plutarch, *Life of Aemelius Paulus,* XXVIII.11–13.

Interest and Concernment both of Kings and Grandees, lies either in keeping the People in utter ignorance what Liberty is, or else in allowing and pleasing them onely with the name and shadow of Liberty in stead of the substance: so in Free-States the People being sensible of their past condition in former times[113], under the Power of Great Ones, and comparing it with the possibilities and enjoyments of the present, become immediately instructed, that their main Interest and Concernment consists in Liberty; and are taught by common sense, that the onely way to secure it from the reach of Great Ones, is, to place it in the Peoples Hands, adorned with all the Prerogatives and Rights of Supremacy. The Truth of it is, the Interest of Freedom is a Virgin that every one seeks to deflower; and like a Virgin, it must be kept from[114] any other Form, or else (so great is the Lust of mankinde after dominion) there follows a rape upon the [46] first opportunity. This being considered, it will easily be granted, That Liberty must needs lie more secure in the Peoples than in any others hands, because they are most concerned in it: and the careful eyeing of this Concernment, is that which makes them both jealous and zealous; so that nothing will satisfie, but the keeping of a constant Guard against the Attempts and Incroachments of any powerful or crafty Underminers.

Hence it is, that the[115] People having once tasted the Sweets of Freedom, are[116] so extreamly affected with it, that if they discover, or do but suspect the least Design to incroach[117] upon it, they count it a Crime never to be forgiven for any consideration whatsoever. Thus it was in the Romane State, where one gave up his Children, another his Brother to death, to revenge an Attempt against common Liberty: divers also sacrificed their Lives, to preserve it; and some their best Friends, to vindicate it, upon bare suspicion; as in the Cases of *Maelius,* and *Manlius,* and others, after manifest viola-[47]tion, as in the Case of *Caesar.*

Nor was it thus onely in *Rome;* but we finde also as notable instances of revenge in the Free-People of *Greece,* upon the same occasion. But the most notable of all, is that which happened in the Island of *Corcyra,* during the war of *Peloponnesus:* where the People having been rook'd of Liberty by the slights and power of the Grandees, and afterwards by the assistance of the Free-states[118] of *Athens* recovering it again, took occasion thereupon to clap up all the Grandees, & chop'd off ten of their Heads at one time, in part of satisfaction for the Injury: but yet this would not serve the turn; for, some delay being made in executing of the rest, the People grew so inraged, that they ran, and pull'd down the very Walls, and buried them in the ruines and rubbish of the Prison.

We see it also in the Free-State of *Florence,* where *Cosmus* the first Founder of the *Tuscan*-Tyranny, having made shipwrack of their Liberty, and seized all into his own Hands; though he enslaved their Bodies, yet he could not [48] subdue their Hearts, nor wear their past Liberty out of Memory; for upon the first opportunity, they sought revenge, and a recovery; forcing him to fly for the safety of his Life: and though afterwards he made way for his Return and Re-establishment by Treachery, yet now after so long a time, the old Freedom is fresh[119] in memory, and would shew it self again upon a favourable occasion.

But of all Modern Instances, the most strange is that of the Land of *Holstein;* which being deprived of Liberty, and about seventy yeers[120] since made a Dutchy, and an Appendix to the Crown of *Denmark;* though the Inhabitants be but a Boorish, poor, silly Generation, yet still they retain a sense of Indignation at the loss of their Liberty; and being given to drink, the usual Complement in the midst of their Cups, is this, *Here is*[121] *a health to the remembrance of our Liberty.*

Thus you see what an impression the love of Freedom makes in the minds of the people: so that[122] it will be easily concluded, They must be the best [49] Keepers of their own Liberties; being more tender and more concerned in their security, than any powerful pretenders whatsoever.

[MP 84, 8–15 Jan. 1652]

The ninth Reason to justifie a Free-State, is,[123] because in Free-States the People are less Luxurious, than Kings or Grandees use to be. Now, this is most certain, that where Luxury takes place, there is as natural a tendency to Tyranny, as there is from the Cause to the Effect: for, you know the Nature of Luxury lies altogether in Excess. It is a Universal

The Government of a Free State is less Luxurious, than Kings or Grandees

Depravation of Manners, without Reason, without Moderation; it is the Canine appetite of a corrupt Will and Phant'sie, which nothing can satisfie; but in every Action, in every Imagination, it flies beyond the Bounds of Honesty,[124] Just, and Good, into all Extremity: so that it will easily be granted, That Form of Government must needs be the most excellent, and the Peoples Liberty most secured,[125] where Governours are least exposed to the baits and snares of Luxury.

The evidence of this may be made out, not onely by Reason, but by Ex-[50]amples old[126] and new. And first, by Reason, it is evident, That the People must needs be less luxurious than Kings or the Great Ones, because they are bounded within a more lowly pitch of Desire and Imagination: give them but *panem & circenses;* Bread, Sport and Ease, and they are abundantly satisfied. Besides, the People have less means and opportunities for Luxury, than those pompous standing powers, whether in the hands of one or many: so that were they never so much inclined to Vice or Vanity, yet they are not able to run on to the same measure of Excess and Riot. Secondly, as it appears they are less Luxurious; so, for this Cause also, it is cleer, They (that is, their successive Representatives) must be the best Governours; not onely, because the current of succession keeps them the less corrupt and presumptious; but also, because, being the more free from luxurious Courses, they are likewise free from those oppressive[127] and injurious Practices, which Kings and Grandees are most commonly led and forced[128] unto, to hold up the port and splendor of their Ty-[51]ranny, and to satisfie those natural appetites of Covetousness, Pride, Ambition and Ostentation, which are the perpetual Attendants of Great Ones, and Luxury. Thus much for Reason.

Now, for Example, we might produce a Cloud of Instances, to shew, That Free-States, or the People duely qualified with the Supreme Authority, are less devoted to Luxury, than the Grandee or Kingly Powers: but we shall give you onely a few.

The first that comes in our way is the State of *Athens,* which, whilst it remained free in the Peoples Hands, was adorned with such Governours as gave themselves up to a serious, abstemious, severe course of Life; so that whilst Temperance and Liberty walked hand in hand, they improved the points of Valour and Prudence so high, that in a short time they became the onely Arbitrators of all Affairs in *Greece.* But being at the height, then (after the common fate of all worldly Powers) they began to decline; for, (contrary to the Rules of a Free-State) permitting some men to greaten themselves, by [52] continuing long in Power and Authority, they soon lost their pure Principles of Severity and Libertie: for, up-started[129] those thirty Grandees, (commonly called the Tyrants) who having usurped a standing Authority unto themselves, presently quitted the old Discipline and Freedom, gave up themselves first to Charms of Luxury, and afterwards to all the practices of an absolute Tyranny. Such also was the condition of that State, when at another time (as in the dayes of *Pistratus*[130]) it was usurp'd in the hands of a single Tyrant.

From *Athens* let us pass to *Rome,* where we finde it in the dayes of *Tarquin,* dissolved into Debauchery. Upon the change of Government, their manners were somewhat mended, as were the Governours in the Senate: but that being a standing Power, soon grew corrupt; and first let in Luxury, then Tyranny, till the people being interested in the Government, established a good Discipline and Freedom both together; which was upheld with all Severity, till the ten Grandees came in [53] play after; whose[131] Deposition, Liberty, and Sobriety began to breath again, till the dayes of *Sylla, Marius,* and other[132] Grandees that followed down to *Caesar,* in whose time Luxury and Tyranny grew to such a height, that unless it were in the Life and Conversation of *Cato,* there was not so much as one spark, that could be raked out of the ashes, of the old Roman Discipline and Freedom; so that of all the World, onely *Cato* remained as a Monument of that Temperance, Virtue and Freedom, which flourished under the Government of the People.[133]

Omitting many other Examples, our Conclusion upon[134] these Particulars shall be this, That since the Grandee or Kingly Powers, are ever more luxurious, than the popular are, or can be: and since Luxury ever brings on Tyranny, as the onely bane of Liberty; certainly the Rights and Priviledges of the People, placed and provided for, in a due and orderly succession of their Supreme Assemblies, must needs remain more secure in their own Hands, than in any others whatsoever.[135]

[MP 85, 15–22 Jan. 1652]

In a Free-State, the People are ever more magnanimous and valiant.

[54] A tenth Reason, to prove the excellency of a Free-State or Government by the People, above any other Form of Government, is,[136] because under this Government, the People are ever indued with a more magnanimous, active, and noble temper of Spirit, than under the Grandeur of any standing power whatsoever. And this arises from that apprehension which every particular Man hath of his own immediate share in the publick Interest, as well as of that security which he possesses[137] in the enjoyment of his private Fortune, free from the reach of any Arbitrary Power. Hence it is, that whensoever any good success or happiness betides the Publick, every one counts it his own: if the Commonwealth conquer, thrive in Dominion, Wealth or Honour, he reckons all done for himself; if he sees[138] Distributions of Honour, high Offices, or great Rewards, to Valiant, Vertuous, or[139] Learned Persons, he esteems them as his own, as long as he hath a door left open to succeed in the same Dignities and Enjoyments, if he can attain unto the same measure of Desert. [55] This it is[140] which makes men aspire unto great Actions, when the Reward depends not upon the Will and Pleasure of particular Persons, as it doth under all standing Powers; but is conferred upon Men (without any consideration of Birth or Fortune) according to merit, as it ever is, and ought to be in Free-States, that are rightly constituted.

The Truth of this will appear much more evident, if ye list a little to take a view of the condition of People, under various Forms of Government: for, the Romanes of old, while under Kings, (as you heard before) remained[141] a very inconsiderable People, either in Dominion or Reputation; and could never inlarge their Command very far beyond the Walls of their City. Afterwards, being reduced unto that standing power of the Senate, they began to thrive a little better, &, for a little time: yet all they[142] could do, was only to struggle that for a subsistence among bad Neighbours. But at length, when the People began to know, claim, and possess their Liberties in being govern'd [56] by a succession of their Supreme Officers and Assemblies; then it was, and never till then, that they laid the Foundation, and built the Structure of that wondrous Empire that overshadowed the whole World[143]. And truely the founding of it must needs be more[144] wonderful, and a great Argument of an extraordinary Courage and Magnanimity, wherewith the People was indued in[145] Recovery of Liberty; because their first Conquests were laid in the ruine of mighty Nations, and such as were every jot as free as themselves: which made the difficulties so much the more, by how much the more free (and consequently, the more couragious) they were, against whom they made opposition: for as in those dayes the World abounded with Free-States, more than any other Form, as all over *Italy, Gallia, Spain,* and *Africa,* &c. so specially[146] in *Italy,* where the *Tuscans,* the *Samnites,* and other Emulators and Competitors of the Romane Freedom,* approved themselves magnanimous Defenders of their Liberty against *Rome,* that they endured Wars so[147] ma-[57]ny yeers with utmost extremity, before ever they could [be] brought to bow under the Romane Yoke[148]. This magnanimous State of Freedom, was the cause also why *Charthage*[149] was enabled so long, not only to oppose, but often[150] to hazard the Romane Fortune, and usurp the Laurel. It brought *Hannibal* within view, and the *Gauls* within the Walls of the City, to a besieging of the Capitol; to shew, that their Freedom had given them the courage to rob her of her Maiden-head, who afterwards became Mistriss of the whole World. But what serves all this for, but[151] onely to shew, That as nothing but a State of Freedom could have enabled those Nations with a Courage sufficient so long to withstand the Romane Power: so *Rome* her self also was beholden to this State of Freedom, for those Sons of Courage which brought the Necks of her Sister-States and Nations under her Girdle? And it is observable also in after-times, when Tyranny took place against[152] Liberty, the Romans soon lost their ancient Courage and Magnanimity; first under usurping Dictators, then [58] under Emperors, and in the end, the Empire it self.[153]

Now, as on the one side, we feel[154] a loss of Courage and Magnanimity, follow[155] the loss of Freedom: so, on the other side, the People

---

* In *The Case of the Commonwealth,* where this passage also appears, Nedham cites "Mach. *lib.* 2 *cap.* 2," an accurate reference to Machiavelli's *Discourses* (Knachel, p. 116).

ever grow magnanimous and couragious[156] upon a Recovery; witness at present, the valiant *Swisses,* the *Hollanders,* and not long since, our own Nation, when declared a Free-State, and a Re-establishment of our Freedom in the hands of the People procured, (though not secured) what noble Designs were undertaken and prosecuted with success? The Consideration[157] whereof, must needs make highly for the Honour of all Governours in Free-States, who have been, or shall be instrumental in redeeming and setting[158] any People in a fulness of Freedom, that is, in a due and orderly succession of their supreme Assemblies.

[MP 86, 22–29 Jan. 1652]

No determi-
nations are
carried but
by consent of
the People.

The eleventh Reason is[159], because in this Form no Determinations being carried, but by consent of the People; therefore they must needs remain secure out of the reach of Tyranny, and [59] free from the Arbitrary Disposition of any commanding Power. In this Case, as the People know what Laws they are to obey, and what Penalties they are to undergo, in case of Transgression; so having their share and interest in the making of Laws, with the Penalties annexed, they become the more inexcusable if they offend, and the more willingly submit unto punishment when they suffer for any offence. Now the case is usually far otherwise, under all standing Powers: for, when Government is managed in the hands of a particular Person, or continued in the hands of a certain number of Great Men, the People then have no Laws but what Kings and Great Men please to give: Nor do they know how to walk by those Laws, or how to understand them, because the sense is oftentimes left at uncertainty; and it is reckoned a great Mystery of State in those Forms of Government, That no Laws shall be of any sense or force, but as the Great Ones please to expound them: so as[160] by this means, the People many times are left as it were with-[60]out Law[161], because they bear no other construction and meaning, but what sutes with particular mens Interests and Phant'sies; not with Right Reason, or the Publike Liberty.

For the proof of this under Kingly Government, we might run all the world over; but our own Nation affords[162] Instances enough in the

Practices of all our Kings: yet this Evil never came to such a height, as it did in the Raign of *Henry* the seventh; who by usurping a Prerogative of expounding the Laws after his own pleasure, made them rather Snares, than Instruments of Relief, (like a grand Catch-pole) to pill, poll, and geld the Purses of the People; as his Son *Harry* did after him, to deprive many Gallant Men both of their Lives and Fortunes. For, the Judges being reputed the Oracles of the Law, and the power of creating Judges being usurp'd by Kings, they had a care ever to create such, as would make the Laws speak in Favour of them, upon any occasion. The Truth whereof hath abundantly appeared in the dayes of the late King[163], and his Father *James*, whose [61] usual Language was this: *As long as I have power of making what Judges and Bishops I please, I am sure to have no Law nor Gospel but what shall please me.*[164]

This very providing[165] for this Inconvenience, was the great Commendation of *Lycurgus* his Institution in *Sparta;* who, though he cut out the *Lacedemonian* Commonwealth[166] after the Grandee fashion, confirming the Supremacy within the Walls of the Senate[167], (for their King was but a Cypher) yet he so ordered the matter, that he took away the Grandeur; that as their King was of little more value than any one of the Senators; so the Senate was restrained by Laws, walking in[168] the same even pace of subjection with the People; having very few Offices of Dignity or Profit allowed, which might make them swell with State and Ambition; but were prescribed also the same Rules of Frugality, Plainness, and Moderation, as were the Common People: by which means immoderate lusts and desires being prevented in the Great Ones, they were the less inclined to Pride and Oppression; and no great profit or pleasure [62] being to be gotten by Authority, very few desired it; and such as were in it, sate free from Envie, by which means they avoided that odium and emulation which[169] uses to rage betwixt the Great Ones and the People in that Form of Government.

But now the case is far otherwise in the Commonwealth of *Venice,* where the People being excluded from all interest in Government, the power of making and executing of Laws, and bearing of Offices, with all other Immunities, lies onely in the hands of a standing Senate, and their Kindred, which they call the *Patrocian,* or Noble Order. Their

Duke, or Prince, is indeed restrained, and made just such another Officer as were the *Lacedemonian* Kings; differing from the rest of the Senate, onely in a Corner of his Cap, besides a little outward Ceremony and Splendor: but the Senators themselves have Liberty at random, Arbitrarily to ramble, and do what they please with the people: who excepting the City it self, are so extreamly oppress'd in all their Territories, living by no [63] Law, but the Arbitrary Dictates of the Senate, that it seems rather a Junta, than a Commonwealth[170]; and the Subjects take so little content in it, that seeing more to be enjoyed under the Turk, they that are his Borderers take all opportunities to revolt[171], and submit rather to the mercy of a Pagan-Tyranny. Which disposition if you consider, together with the little Courage in their Subjects, by reason they press them so hard; and how that they are forced, for this cause, to relie upon Forrain Mercenaries in all warlike Expeditions, you might wonder how this State hath held up so long; but that we know the Interest of Christendom, being concerned in her Security, she hath been chiefly supported by the Supplies and Arms of others.

Therefore our Conclusion[172] shall be this, That since Kings, and all standing Powers, are so inclinable to act according to their own Wills and Interests, in making, expounding, and executing of Laws to the prejudice of the Peoples Liberty and Security: and seeing the onely way to prevent Arbitra-[64]riness, is, That no Laws or Dominations[173] whatsoever should be made, but by the Peoples Consent and Election: therefore it must of necessity be granted, that the People are the best Keepers of their own Liberties, being setled in a due and orderly succession of their supreme Assemblies.

[MP 87, 29 Jan.–5 Feb. 1652]

A Free-State is most sutable to the Nature and Reason of mankinde.

[174]A twelfth Reason is, because this Form is most sutable to the Nature and Reason of Mankinde: for, as *Cicero* saith[175], *Man is a noble Creature, born with Affections to rule, rather than obey; there being in every man a natural appetite or desire of Principality.** And therefore the Reason

* Perhaps a further reference to Cicero, *De Officiis*, I.19.

why[176] one man is content to submit to the Government of another, is, not because he conceives himself to have less right than another to govern; but either because he findes himself less able, or else because he judgeth it will be more convenient for himself, and that community whereof he is a Member, if he submits[177] unto another's Government. *Nemini*[178] *purere vult animus a naturâ bene informatus, nisi,* &c. saith the same *Cicero:* that is to say, in honest English, *A minde well in-*[65]*structed by the light of Nature, will pay obedience unto none, but such as command, direct, or govern, for its good and benefit.** From both which passages and expressions of that Oracle of Humane wisdom, these three Inferences do naturally arise: First, that by the light of Nature people are taught to be their own Carvers and Contrivers, in the framing of that Government under which they mean to live. Secondly, that none are to preside in Government, or sit at the Helm, but such as shall be judged fit, and chosen by the People. Thirdly, that the People are the onely proper Judges of the convenience or inconvenience of a Government when it is erected, and of the behaviour of Governours after they are chosen: which three Deductions[179] appear to be no more, but an Explanation of this most excellent Maxime, That the Original and Fountain of all just Power and Government is in the People.

This being so, that a Free-State-Government by the People, that is, by their successive Representatives, or supreme Assemblies, duely chosen, is most na-[66]tural, and onely sutable to the Reason of mankinde: then it follows, that the other forms, whether it be of a standing Power in the Hands of a particular person, as a King; or of a set number of Great Ones, as in a Senate, are besides the Dictates[180] of Nature, being meer artificial devices of Great Men, squared out onely to serve the Ends and Interests of Avarice, Pride and Ambition of a few, to a vassalizing of the Community. The Truth whereof appears so much the more, if we consider, That a[181] Consent and free Election of the People, which is the most natural Way and Form of governing, hath no real effect in the other Forms; but is either supplanted by Craft and Custome, or swallowed up by a pernicious pretence of Right (in one or many)

* Ibid., I.4.

to govern, onely by vertue of an Hereditary succession. Now certainly, were there no other Argument to prove the excellency of Government by the People, &c. beyond the other Forms; yet this one might suffice, That in the Peoples Form, men have Liberty to make use of that Reason and Understanding God hath given [67] them, in chusing of Governours, and providing for their own safety in[182] Government: but in the other Forms of a standing[183] Power, all Authority being entailed to certain Persons and Families, in a course of inheritance, men are always deprived of the use of their Reason about choice of Governours, and forced to receive them blindely, and at all adventure[184]: which course being so destructive to the Reason, common Interest, and Majesty of that Noble Creature, called Man, that he should not in a matter of so high consequence as Government, (wherein the good and safety of all is concerned) have a Freedom of Choice and Judgement, must needs be the most irrational and brutish Principle in the World, and fit onely to be hissed out of the World, together with all Forms of standing Power (whether in Kings, or others) which have served for no other end, but transform[185] Men into Beasts, and mortified mankinde with misery through all Generations.

The Truth of this is evident all the World over; first, by sad Examples of [68] Monarchy: for, the Kingly form having been retained in a course of Inheritance, men being forced to take what comes next for a Governour, whether it be Male or Female, a wise Man or a Fool, Good or Bad; so that the major part of Hereditary Princes, have been Tyrannous and Wicked by Nature, or made so by Education and Opportunity: the People have been for the most part banded[186] to and fro, with their Lives and Fortunes, at the Will and Pleasure of some one single unworthy Fellow, who usually assumes the greater confidence in his unrighteous dealing, because he knows the People are tied in that Form to him and his, though he practice all the Injustice in the World. This was it that brought on Tyranny in *Rome,* first under their Kings, afterwards under Emperors: for it is to be observed out of the[187] Story, that all those Emperors which ruled by right of Inheritance, proved most of them no better than savage Beasts, and all of them Wicked except *Titus.* 'Tis true indeed, That a Nation may have some respite

and recruit now and then, by the Ver-[69]tue and Valour of a single
Prince; yet this is very rare; and when it doth happen, it usually lasts[188]
no longer than for his Life, because his Son or Successor (for the most
part) proves more weak or vitious, than himself was Virtuous, as you
may see in the several Lists of Kings throughout *Great Britain,** *France,*
*Spain,* and all the World. But this is not all the Inconvenience, that
Hereditary Princes have been and are for the most part Wicked in
their own Persons: for, as great Inconveniences happen by their being
litigious[189] in their Titles; witness the bloody disputes between[190] the
Princes of the Blood in *France,* as also in *England,* between the two
Houses of *Yorke* and *Lancaster;* to which many more might be reckoned out of all other Kingdoms; which miseries, the people might have
avoided, had they not been tied to one particular Line of Succession.
Therefore, if any Kingly Form be tolerable, it must be that which is by
Election, chosen by the Peoples Representatives, and made an Officer
of Trust by them, to whom they are to be accountable. And [70] herein,
as Kings are onely tolerable upon this account, as Elective; so these
Elective Kings[191] are as intolerable upon another account, because their
present Greatness gives them opportunity ever to practise such slights,
that in a short time, the Government that[192] they received onely for
their own Lives, will become entailed upon their Families, whereby the
Peoples Election will be made of no effect further, than[193] for Fashion,
to mock the poor People, and adorn the Triumphs of an aspiring[194]
Tyranny; as it hath been seen in the Elective Kingdoms of *Bohemia,*
*Poland, Hungaria*[195], and *Sweden;* where the Forms of Election were,
and are still retained; but the Power swallowed up, and the Kingdoms
made Hereditary; not only in *Sweden,* by the Artifice of *Gustavus Eri-
cus;* but also in *Poland,* and the Empire, where the peoples right of
election was soon eaten out by the cunning of the two Families of
*Casimira*[196] and *Austria.*

---

* One list Nedham will have had in mind is that of Scottish kings in *The
Grounds and Reasons of Monarchy* (n.p., 1650) by his literary partner John Hall;
another, from the same year, that of English kings in Henry Parker, *The True
Portraiture of the Kings of England* (London, 1650; reprinted in Scott, *Somers
Tracts,* 6:77–103).

Let this serve to manifest,[197] that a Government by a free Election and Consent of the People, setled in a due and [71] orderly succession of their supreme Assemblies, is more consonant to the light of Nature and Reason, and consequently much more excellent than any Hereditary standing Power[198] whatsoever. To take off all mis-constructions; when we mention *the People,* observe all along, that we do not mean the confused promiscuous Body of the People, nor any part of the people who have forfeited their Rights by Delinquency, Neutrality, or Apostacy, *&c.* in relation[199] to the divided state of any Nation; for they are not to be reckon'd within the Lists of the People[200].

[MP 88, 5–12 Feb. 1652]

In this Government there are fewer opportunities of Oppression and Tyranny, then under any other Form. The thirteenth Reason, to prove the excellency of a Free-State above any other Form, is,[201] because in Free-States there are fewer opportunities of Oppression and Tyranny, than in the other Forms. And this appears, in that it is ever the care of Free-Commonwealths[202], for the most part, to preserve, not an Equality, (which were irrational and odious) but an Equability of Condition among all the Members; so that no particular Man or Men shall be permitted to grow over-great in Power; nor any Rank of Men be al-[72]lowed above the ordinary Standard, to assume unto themselves the State and Title of Nobility.

The Observation of the former, secures the Peoples Liberty from the reach of their own Officers, such as being entrusted with the Affairs of high Trust and Imployment, either in Campe and Council,[203] might perhaps take occasion thereby to aspire beyond Reason, if not restrained and prevented.

The Observation of the later[204], secures the People from the pressures and Ambition of such petty Tyrants, as would usurp and claim a Prerogative, Power, and Greatness above others, by Birth and Inheritance. These are a sort of Men not to be endured in any well-ordered Commonwealth; for they alwayes bear a Natural and Implacable Hate towards the People, making it their Interest to deprive them of their Liberty; so that if at any time it happen, that any great Man or Men whatsoever, arrive to so much Power and Confidence, as to think of usurping, or to be in a Condition [73] to be tempted thereunto; these are the first that will set them on, mingle Interests with them, and become the prime Instruments in heaving them up into the Seat of Tyranny.

For the clearing of these Truths; and first, to manifest the Inconvenience of permitting any persons to be[205] over-great in any State; and that Free-States that[206] have not avoided it, have soon lost their Liberty, we shall produce a File of Examples. In *Greece* we finde, that the Free-State of *Athens* lost its Liberty upon that account once, when they suffered certain of the Senators to over-top the rest in power; which occasioned that multiplied Tyranny, made famous by the name of the thirty Tyrants: at another time, when by the same Error they were constrained, through the power of *Pistratus*[207], to stoop unto his single Tyranny.

Upon this score also, the people of *Syracusa* had the same misfortune under the Tyrant *Hiero,* as had they of *Sicily* under *Dyonisius* and *Agathocles.*

[74] In *Rome* also the case is[208] the same too: for during the time that Liberty was included within the Senate, they gave both *Maelius* & *Manlius* an opportunity to aspire, by permitting them a growth of too much Greatness: but by good fortune escaping their clutches, they afterwards fell as foolishly into the hands of ten of their Fellow-Senators, called the *Decemviri,* in giving them so much power as tempted them unto Tyranny. Afterwards, when the people scuffled, and made a shift to recover their Liberty out of the hands of the Senate, they committed the same Error too, by permitting of[209] their Servants to grow over-great; such as *Sylla,* who by power tyrannized and made himself Dictator for five yeers, as *Caesar* afterwards setled the Dictatorship upon himself for ever: and after *Caesar*'s death, they might have recovered their Liberty again, if they had taken care (as they might easily have done) to prevent the growing Greatness of *Augustus,* who gaining power first, by the courtesie & good will of the Senate and People, made use of it to establish himself in a Tyranny, which [75] could never after be extinguished, but in the ruine of the Roman Empire it self.

Thus also the Free-State of *Florence* foolishly ruined it self by the greatning of *Cosmus;* first, permitting him to ingross the Power, which gave him opportunity to be a tyrant; & then as foolishly forcing him to declare himself a Tyrant, by an unseasonable demand of the power back out of his hands. Many more instances might be fetch'd out of *Milan, Switzerland,* and other places: but we have one neerer home, and of a later date, in *Holland;* whereby, permitting the Family of *Orange* to greaten a little more than beseemed a Member of a Free-State, they were insensibly reduced to the last cast, to run the hazzard of the loss of their Liberty.

Therefore one prime Principle of State, is,[210] To keep any man, though he have deserved never so well by good success or service, from being too great or popular: it is a notable means (and so esteemed by all Free-States) to keep and preserve a Commonwealth from[211] the Rapes of Usurpation.[212]

## [MP 91, 26 Feb.–4 Mar. 1652]

In this form all Powers are accountable for misdemeanours in Government.

A fourteenth Reason, (and though [76] the last, yet not the least) to prove a Free-State or Government by the People, setled in a due and orderly succession of their supreme Assemblies, is much more excellent than any other Form, is,[213] because in this Form, all Powers are accountable for misdemeanors in Government, in regard of the nimble Returns and Periods of the Peoples Election: by which means, he that ere-while was a Governour, being reduced to the condition of a Subject, lies open to the force of the Laws, and may with ease be brought to punishment for his offence; so that after the observation of such a course, others which succeed, will become the less daring to offend, or to abuse their Trust in Authority, to an oppression of the People. Such a course as this, cuts the very throat of all Tyranny; and doth not onely root it up when at full growth, but crusheth[214] the Cockatrice in the Egg, destroys it in the Seed, in the principal,[215] and in the very possibilities of its being for ever after. And as the safety of the People, is the Soveraign and Supreme Law; so an esta-[77]blishment of this Nature, is an impregnable Bulwark of the Peoples safety, because without it, no certain Benefit can be obtained by the ordinary Laws; which if they should be dispensed by uncontrolable, unaccountable Persons in Power, shall never be interpreted, but in their own sense; nor executed, but after their own Wills and Pleasure.

Now, this is most certain, That as in the Government of the People, the successive Revolution of Authority by their consent, hath ever been the onely Bank against Inundations of Arbitrary Power and Tyranny; so on the other side, it is as sure, That all standing Powers have and ever do assume unto themselves an Arbitrary Exercise of their own dictates at pleasure, and make it their onely Interest to settle themselves in an unaccountable state of Dominion[216]: so that, though they commit all the injustice in the World, their custome hath been still to perswade men, partly by strong pretence of Argument, and partly by force, that they may do what they list; and that [78] they are not bound to give an account of their Actions to any, but to God[217] himself. This Doctrine of Tyranny hath taken the deeper Root in mens mindes, because the greatest[218] part was ever inclined to adore the Golden Idol of Tyranny in every Form: by which[219] means the rabble of mankinde being prejudicated in this particular, and having plac'd their corrupt humour or interest in base fawning, and the favour of present Great Ones; Therefore if any resolute Spirit happen to broach and maintain true Principles of Freedom, or do at any time arise to so much courage, as to perform a noble Act of Justice, in calling Tyrants to an account, presently he draws all the enmity and fury of the World about him. But in Commonwealths it is and ought to be otherwise; for, in the Monuments of the Grecian and Romane Freedom, we finde, those Nations were wont to heap all the Honours they could invent, by publick Rewards, Consecration of Statues, and Crowns[220] of Laurel, upon such worthy Patriots: and as if on earth all were too little, they inroll'd them [79] in heaven among the[221] Deities. And all this they did out of a Noble sense of Commonweal-interest;[222] knowing that the life of Liberty consists in a strict hand, and zeal against Tyrants and Tyranny, and by keeping persons in power from all the occasions of it: which cannot be better done, than (according to the custom of all States that are really free) by leaving them liable to account: which happiness was never seen yet under the sun, by any Law or Custom established, save onely in those States, where all men are brought to taste of Subjection as well as Rule, and the Government setled by a due succession of Authority, by consent of the People.

In *Switzerland* the people are free indeed,[223] because all Officers and Governours in the Cantons, are questionable by the People in their successive Assemblies.

The Inference from the fore-going particulars, is easie, That since Freedom is to be preserved no other way in a Commonwealth, but by keeping Officers and Governours in an accountable state; and since it appears no standing [80] Powers can never be called to an account[224] without much difficulty, or involving a Nation in Blood or Misery. And since a revolution of Government in the Peoples hands, hath ever been the onely means to make Governours accountable, and prevent the inconveniences of Tyranny, Distraction, and Misery; therefore for this, and those other reasons fore-going[225], we may conclude, That a Free-State, or Government by the People, setled in a due and orderly succession of their supreme Assemblies, is far more excellent every way, than any other Form whatsoever.[226]

# All Objections Against
# the Government of the People,
# Answered.

[MP 92, 4–11 Mar. 1652]

Considering, That in times past, the People of this Nation were bred up and instructed in the brutish Principles of Monarchy, by which means they have been the more averse from entertaining Notions of a more noble Form: and remembring, that not long since we were put into a better course, upon the declared Interest of a Free-State, or Commonwealth; I conceived nothing could more highly tend to the propagation of that good Interest, and the Ho-[82]nour of its Founders, than to manifest the Inconveniences and ill Consequences of the other Forms; and so to root up their Principles, that the good People[227], who but the other day were invested[228] in the possession of a more excellent way, may (in order to their re-establishment) understand what Commonwealth-Principles are and[229] thereby become the more resolute to defend them against the common Enemy; learn to be true Commonwealths men, and zealous against Monarchick-Interest, in all its appearances and incroachments whatsoever. To this end we have set down our Position, That a Free-State, or Government by the People, setled in a due and orderly succession of their supreme Assemblies, is the most excellent Form of Government; which (I humbly conceive) hath been sufficiently proved, both by Reason and Example: but because many pretences of Objection are in being, and such as by many are taken for granted; therefore it falls in of course, that we may refute them: which being done with the same evidence of Reason and [83] Example, I doubt not but it will stop all the Mouths, not onely of Ignorance, but even of Malice and Flattery, which have presumed to prophane that pure way of a Free-State, or Government by the People.

That Objection of Royalists, and others, which we shall first take notice of, is this, *That the erecting of such a Government would be to set on Levelling and Confusion.*

For answer, If we take Levelling in the common usage and application of the term in these days, it is of an odious signification, as if it levell'd all men in point of Estates, made all things common to all, destroyed propriety, introduced a community of enjoyments among men; which is a Scandal fastned by the cunning of the common Enemy upon this kinde of Government, which they hate above all others; because, were the People once put in possession of their Liberty, and made sensible of the great Benefits they may reap by its injoyment, the hopes of all the Royal Sticklers would be utterly extinct, in regard it would be the likeliest means [84] to prevent a return of the Interest of Monarchy: for no Person or Parties seeking or setting up a private Interest of their own, distinct from the Publick, it will stop the Mouths of all Gain-sayers. But[230] the Truth is, This way of Free-State, or Government by the People in their successive Assemblies, is so far from introducing a community, that it is the onely preservative of Propriety in every particular: the Reasons whereof are plain: for, as on the one side, it is not in Reason to be imagined, that so choice a Body, as the Representative of a Nation, should agree to destroy one another in their several Rights and Interests: on the[231] other side, all Determinations being carried in this Form by common Consent, every Man's particular Interest must needs be fairly provided for, against the Arbitrary disposition of others; therefore, whatever is contrary to this, is levelling indeed; because it placeth every Man's Right under the Will of another, and is no less

*A Free state the only preservative against Levelling and confusion of propriety.*

than Tyranny; which seating it self in an unlimited uncontrollable Prerogative over others without their [85] Consent, becomes the very bane of propriety; and however disquieted, or in what Form soever it appears, is indeed the very Interest of Monarchy.

Now that a Free-State, or successive Government of the People, &c. is the onely preservative of Propriety, appears by Instances all the World over; yet we shall cite but a few.

Under Monarchs, we shall finde ever, That the Subjects had nothing that they could call their own; neither Lives, nor Fortunes, nor Wives, nor any thing else that the Monarch pleased to command, because the poor people knew no remedy against the levelling Will of an unbounded Soveraignity; as may be seen in the Records of all Nations that have stoop'd under that wretched Form: whereof we have also very sad Examples in *France,* and other Kingdoms, at this very day, where the People have nothing of Propriety; but all depends upon the Royal Pleasure, as it did of late here in *England.* Moreover, it is very observable, That in Kingdoms where the People have enjoyed any thing of Liberty and Propriety, they have been [86] such Kingdoms onely, where the frame of Government hath been so well tempered, as that the best share of it hath been retained in the Peoples Hands; and by how much the greater influence the People have had therein, so much the more sure and certain they have been, in the enjoyment of their Propriety.[232]

To pass by many other Instances, consider how firm the *Aragonians* were in their Liberties and Properties, so long as they held their hold over their Kings in their supreme Assemblies; and no sooner had *Philip* the second deprived them of their share in the Government, but themselves and their properties[233] became a prey (and have been ever since) to the Will and Pleasure of their Kings.

The like also may be said of *France*[234], where, as long as the Peoples Interest bore sway in their supreme Assemblies, they[235] could call their Lives and Fortunes their own, and no longer: for, all that have succeeded since *Lewis* the eleventh, followed his levelling pattern so far, that in short time they destroyed the Peoples Property, and became the [87] greatest Levellers in Christendom. We were almost at the same pass[236] here in *England:* for, as long as the Peoples Interest was preserved by frequent and successive Parliaments; so long we were in some measure secure of our Properties: but as Kings began to worm the People out of their share in Government, by discontinuing of Parliaments; So they carried on their levelling design, to the destroying of our Properties; and had by this means brought it so high, that the Oracles of the Law and Gospel spake it out with a good levelling Grace, *That all was the King's, and that we had nothing we might call our own.*

Thus you see how much Levelling, and little of Propriety[237], the people have had certain under Monarchs; and if any at all, by what means and upon what terms they have had it. Nor hath it been thus onely under Kings; but we finde, the People have ever had as little of Property[238] secure, under all other Forms of standing Powers[239]; which have produced as errant Levellers in this particular, as any of the Monarchies. In the [88] Free-State of *Athens,* as long as the People kept free indeed, in an enjoyment of their successive Assemblies, so long they were secure in their Properties[240], and no longer. For, to say nothing of their Kings, whose History is very obscure, we finde, after they were laid side, they erected another Form of standing Power, in a single Person, called, a Governour, for Life; who was also accountable for misdemeanours: but yet a Tryal being made of nine of them, the People saw so little security by them, that they pitch'd upon another standing Form of Decimal Government[241]; and being oppress'd by them too, they were cashier'd. The like miseries they tasted under the standing power of Thirty, which were a sort of Levellers more rank than all the rest; who put to death, banished, pill'd, and poll'd whom they pleased, without Cause or Exception; so that the poor people having been tormented under all the Forms of standing Power, were in the end forced (as their[242] last remedy) to take Sanctuary under the Form of a [89] Free-State, in their successive Assemblies.

And though it may be objected, That afterwards they fell into many divisions and miseries, even in that Form: yet whoever observes the Story, shall finde, it was not the fault of the Government, but of themselves, in swerving from the Rules of a Free-State, by permitting the continuance of Power in particular hands; who having an opportunity thereby to create Parties of their own among the People, did for their own ends, inveigle, ingage, and intangle them in popular Tumults and Divisions. This was the true Reason of their Miscarriages[243]. And if ever any Government of the People did miscarry, it was upon that account[244].

Thus also the *Lacedemonians,* after they had for some yeers tryed the Government of one King, then of two Kings at once of two distinct Families; afterwards came in the *Ephori,* as Supervisers of their Kings: after (I say) they had tryed[245] themselves through all the Forms of a standing Power, and found them all to be Levellers of the Peoples [90] Interest and Property[246], then necessity taught them to seek shelter in a Free-State, under which they lived happily, till by a forementioned[247] Error of the *Athenians,* they were drawn into Parties by powerful Persons, and so made the Instruments of Division among themselves, for the bringing of new Levellers into play; such as were *Manchanidas* and *Nabis,* who succeeded each other in a Tyranny.

In old *Rome,* after the standing Form of Kings was extinct, and a new one established, the people found as little of safety and property as ever: for, the standing Senate, and the *Decemviri,* proved as great Levellers, as Kings: so that they were forced to settle the Government of the People by a due and orderly[248] succession of their supreme Assemblies. Then they began again to recover their propertie[249], in having somewhat they might call their own; and they happily enjoyed it, till, as by the same Error of the *Lacedemonians* and *Athenians,* swerving from the Rules of a Free-State, lengthning of power in particular hands, they were drawn and di-[91]vided into Parties, to serve the lusts of such powerful men as by craft became their Leaders: so that by this means (through their own default) they were deprived of their Liberty long before the dayes of Imperial Tyranny. Thus *Cinna, Sylla, Marius,* and the rest of that succeeding Gang, down to *Caesar,* used the Peoples favour, to obtain a continuation of power in their own hands; and then having sadled the people with a new standing Form of their own, they immediately rooted up the Peoples Liberty and Property, by Arbitrary Sentences of death, Proscriptions, Fines, and Confiscations: which strain[250] of levelling, (more intolerable than the former) was maintained by the same Arts of Devillish Policy down to *Caesar;*

who striking in a Favourite[251] of the People, and making use of their Affections to lengthen power in his own hands: at length, by this Errour of the people, gained opportunity to introduce a new levelling Form of standing power in himself, to an utter and irrecoverable ruine of the Romane Liberty and property[252].

[92] In *Florence* they have been in the same case there, under every Form of standing power. It was so, when the Great Ones ruled: it was so under *Goderino*,* it was so under *Savanarola* the Monk. When they once began to lengthen power by the peoples Favour, they presently fell to levelling and domineering, as did *Cosmus* afterwards, that crafty Founder of the present Dukedom.

Upon the same terms, the Republick of *Pisa* lost themselves, and became the prey of several Usurpations.

*Mantua* was once a Free-City of the Empire; but neglecting their successive Assemblies, and permitting the Great Ones, and most Wealthy, to form a standing power in themselves: the people were so vexed with them, that one *Passerimo* getting power in his own hands, and then lengthening it by Artifice, turn'd Leveller too, subjecting all to his own will; so that the poor people, to rid their hands of him, were forced to pitch upon another, as bad, and translate their power into a petty Dukedom, in the hands of the Family of *Gonzaga*.

[93] We may from hence safely conclude[253] against all objecting Monarchs and Royalists, of what name and Title soever, that[254] a Free-State or Commonwealth by the people in their successive Assemblies is so far from levelling or destroying propertie[255], that in all ages it hath been the onely preservative of Liberty and property, and the onely remedy against the Levellings and Usurpations of standing powers: for, it is cleer, That Kings[256] and all standing powers are the Levellers.

## [MP 93, 11–18 Mar. 1652]

[257]A second Objection in the Mouths of many, is this, That *the erecting of such a Form in the Peoples hands, were the ready way to cause confusion*

---

* Presumably Soderino. Yet the spelling was reproduced from *Politicus* and was retained in the republication of 1767.

*in Government; when all persons (without distinction) are allowed a right
to chuse and be chosen members of the supreme Assemblies.*[258]

For answer to this, know, we must consider a Commonwealth[259] in
a twofold condition: either in its setled state, when fully stablished and
founded, and when all men were[260] supposed Friends to its establishment; or else when it is newly founding or founded, and that in the
close of a civil War, upon the ruine of [94] a former Government, and
those that stood for it; in which case it ever hath a great party within it
self, that are enemies to its establishment.

A Free state
gives no cause
of confusion.

As to the first, to wit, a Commonwealth in its setled and composed
state, when all men within it are presumed to be its Friends, questionless, a right to chuse and to be chosen[261], is then to be allowed the
people, (without distinction) in as great a latitude, as may stand with
right Reason and Convenience, for managing a matter of so high Consequence as their Supreme Assemblies; wherein somewhat must be left
to humane Prudence; and therefore that latitude being to be admitted
more or less, according to the Nature, Circumstances, and Necessities
of any Nation, is not here to be determined.

But as to a Commonwealth under the second consideration, when it is
founding, or newly founded, in the close of a Civil War, upon the ruine of
a former Government; In this case, (I say) to make no distinction betwixt
men; but to allow the conquered part of the people an equal right to
chuse and to [95] be chosen, &c. were not onely[262] to take away all proportion in policy, but the ready way to destroy the Commonwealth, and
by a promiscuous mixture of opposite Interests, to turn all into confusion.

Now, that the Enemies of Liberty, being subdued upon the close of
a Civil War, are not to be allowed sharers in the Rights of the people,
is evident, for divers Reasons: not onely because such an allowance
would be a means to give them opportunity to sow the seeds of new
Broyls and Divisions, and bring a new hazard upon the Liberties of
the People, (which are Reasons derived from Convenience): but there
is a more special Argument from the equity of the thing, according to
the Law and Custom of Nations, That such as have commenced War,
to serve the Lusts of Tyrants against the Peoples Interest, should not
be received[263] any longer a part of the people, but may be handled as
slaves when subdued, if their Subduers please so to use them; because

by their Treasons against the Majesty of the people, (which they ought to have [96] maintained) they have made forfeiture of all their Rights and Priviledges, as Members of the People; and therefore if it happens in this case at any time, That any Immunities, Properties or Enjoyments be indulged unto them, they must not take them as their own by Right, but as Boons bestowed upon them by the peoples courtesie.

The old Commonwealth of *Greece* was[264] very severe in this particular: for, as they were wont to heap up all Honours they could vent, upon such as did or suffered any thing for the maintenance of their Liberty; so, on the other side they punished the Underminers of it, or those that any wayes appeared against it, with utmost extremity; persecuting them with Forfeitures, both of Life and Fortune; and if they escaped with Life, they usually became slaves: and many times they persecuted them, being dead, branding[265] their Memories with an Eternal Mark of Infamy.

In old *Rome* they dealt more mildly with the greatest part of those that had sided with the *Tarquins* after their Expulsion: but yet they were not restored [97] to all their former Priviledges. In process of time, as oft as any conspired against the Peoples Interest, in their successive Assemblies; after they had once gotten them, themselves were banished, and their Estates confiscated, not excepting many of the Senators, as well as others; and made for ever incapable of any Trust in the Commonwealth[266].

Afterwards, they took the same course with as many of *Catiline's* Fellow-Traytors and Conspirators, as were worthy any thing; and had no doubt sufficiently paid *Caesar's* Abettors in the same Coin, but that he wore out all opposites with his prosperous Treason. Thus *Millain*[267], and the rest of those States, when they were free, as also the *Swisses* and *Hollanders,* in the Infancy of the *Helvetian* and *Belgick* Freedoms, who took the same course with all those unnatural Paricides and Apostates, that offered first to strangle their Liberty in the Birth, or afterwards in the Cradle, by secret Conspiracy, or open violence. Nor ought this to seem strange, since if a right of Conquest may be used over a Forain, who onely is to be accounted [98] a fair, enemy: much more against such, as against the light of Nature, shall engage themselves in so foul practices, as tend to ruine the Liberty of their Native Country.

Seeing therefore that the people in their Government, upon all occasions of Civil War against their Liberties, have been most zealous in vindicating those Attempts upon the heads of the Conspirators: seeing also, that upon the close of a Civil War, they have a Right; and not onely a Right, but usually a very great Resolution to keep out those Enemies of Liberty, whom they conquer, from a participation of any Right in Government: therefore in this case also, as well as the former, we may conclude, That they in their successive Assemblies, are so far from levelling the Interest of Government into all hands, without distinction, that their principal care is ever to preserve it in their own, to prevent the return of new Wars, old Interests, and Confusion.

### [MP 94, 18–25 Mar. 1652]

[268]But there is a third Objection against it, drawn from a pretending[269] inconvenience of such a succession; al[99]ledging, That *the management of State-Affairs requires Judgement and Experience; which is not to be expected from new Members comming into those Assemblies upon every election.*

Now, because the very Life of Liberty lies in a succession of Powers and Persons; therefore it is meet I should be somewhat precise & punctual by way of answer to this particular. Observe then, that in Government two things are to be considered: *Acta Imperii,* and *Arcana Imperii:* that is, *Acts of State,* and *Secrets of State.* By Acts of State, we mean the Laws and Ordinances of the Legislative Power: these are the things that have most influence upon a Commonwealth[270], to its ill or well-being; and are the onely Remedies for such bad Customes, Inconveniences, and Incroachments as afflict and grieve it. Wherefore, matters of grievance being matters of common sense, and such are obvious to the people, who best know where the shooe pinches[271] them; certainly, there is no need of any great skill or judgement in passing or applying a Law for Remedy[272], which is the [100] proper work of the people in their supreme Assemblies; and such, as every ordinary Understanding is instructed in by the Light of Nature: so that, as to this, there can be no danger by instituting an orderly succession of the people.

*Affairs of State as well managed under a Free-State as under any Form.*

But as for those things called *Arcana Imperii,* Secrets of State, or the executive part of Government, during the Intervals of their Supreme Assemblies; these things being of a Nature remote from ordinary apprehensions, and such as necessarily require prudence, time, and experience, to fit men for management: Much in Reason may be said, and must be granted, for the continuation of such Trusts in the same hands, as relate to matter of Counsel[273], or Administration of Justice, more or less, according to their good or ill-behaviour. A prudential continuation of these, may (without question) and ought to be allowed upon discretion; because, if they do amiss, they are easily accountable to the peoples Assemblies. But now the case is otherwise, as to these Supreme Assemblies, where a few, easie, [101] necessary things, such as common sense and reason instruct men in, are the fittest things for them to apply themselves unto: and there the Peoples Trustees are to continue, of right, no longer than meer Necessity requires, for their own redress and safety; which being provided for, they are to return into a condition of Subjection and Obedience, with the rest of the people, to such Laws and Government as themselves have erected: by which means alone, they will be able to know whether they have done well or ill, when they feel the effects of what they have done. Otherwise, if any thing happen to be done amiss, what way can there be for remedy? since no Appeal is to be had from the Supreme Body of the People, except a due course of Succession be preserved from hand to hand, by the Peoples choice; and other persons thereupon admitted (upon the same terms) into the same Authority.

This is the truth, as we have made manifest both by Reason and Example: therefore we shall adde a little to our former Discourse[274], by way of Illustration.

[102] In *Athens,* when govern'd by the People, we finde, it was their course to uphold constant returns and periods of Succession in their Supreme Assemblies, for remedy of Grievances; and they had a standing Council[275], called the *Areopagus,* to whom all their Secrets of State were committed, together with the administration of Government during the Intervals of those Assemblies, at whose return they were accountable; and warily continued, or excluded, as the People found cause.

In *Sparta* they had the like; as also in *Rome,* after the People had once got their successive Assemblies, wherein they passed Laws for Government: and not knowing how to be rid of their hereditary Senate, they permitted them and their families to continue a standing Council[276]; but yet controllable by, and accountable to their Assemblies, who secluded and banished many of them for their misdemeanours: so that by this means the people had an opportunity to make use of their Wisdom, and curb their Ambition.

In *Florence* (when free) the Govern-[103]ment was after the same Mode.[277]

In *Holland* also, and *Switzerland,* they have their Supreme Assemblies frequent by Election, with exceeding benefit, but no prejudice to Affairs: for the frequencie of those successive Meetings, preserves their Liberty, and provides Laws; the Execution whereof is committed to others, and affairs of State to a Council[278] of their own choice, accountable to themselves: where their State-concernments very seldom miscarry, because they place and displace their Counsellors[279] with extraordinary care and caution.

By these particulars, you may perceive the vanity of the aforesaid Objection, and how slender a pretence it is against that excellent course of Successive Assemblies; since affairs of State are as well disposed (or rather better) under this Form, than any other.

## [MP 95, 25 Mar.–1 Apr. 1652]

A fourth Objection commonly used against the Constitution of a Free-State, or Government by the People in their successive Assemblies, is this: *That such a Government brings great Damage to the* [104] *Publike, by their frequent Discontents, Divisions, and Tumults, that arise within it.*

Discontents &
Tumults, no
natural effects
of a Free-State.

For answer to this, it is requisite that we take notice of those Occasions which are the common causes of such humours in this Form: which being once known, it will easily appear whence those Inconveniences do arise, and not from any default in the nature of the Government: they are commonly these three.

First, when any of their fellow-Citizens, or Members of the Commonweal, shall arrogate any thing of Power and Priviledge unto themselves, or their Families, whereby to Grandize or greaten themselves, beyond the ordinary size and standard[280] of the People. We finde this to be most true, by the course of affairs in the Romane State, as they are recorded by *Livy;* who plainly shews, that upon the expulsion of the *Tarquins,* though the senate introduced a new Government, yet their retaining the power of the old within the hands of themselves and their Families, was the occasion of all those af-[105]ter-Discontents and Tumults that arose among the People. For, had *Brutus* made them free, when he declared them so; or had the Senate a little after, followed the advice and example of *Publicola,** and some others as honest as he; all occasion of Discontent had been taken away: but when the People saw the Senators seated in a lofty posture over[281] them; when they felt the weight of that State and Dignity pressing upon shoulders that were promised to be at ease, and free; when they found themselves exempted from the enjoyment of the same common Priviledges, excluded from all Offices, or Alliance with the Senators; their purses emptied of Money, their bellies of Meat, and their hearts of Hope: then it was, that they began to grumble and mutiny; and never until they got a power to bridle the Great ones, by an happie succession of their Supreme Assemblies.[282]

A second Occasion of the peoples being inclined to Discontent and Tumult, under their Free Form of Government, appears in Story to be this: When they [106] felt themselves not fairly dealt withal, by such as became their Leaders and Generals. Thus[283] in *Syracusa, Dionysius* cloathing himself with a pretence of the peoples Liberties[284]; and being by that means made their General[285], and then making use of that power to other ends than was pretended, became the Fire-Brand of that State, and put the people all into Flames, for the expulsion of him, who had made a Forfeiture of all his glorious pretences.†

* Livy, *Ab Urbe Condita,* II.8.
† Perhaps a reference to Plutarch, *Life of Dion,* XLIV.

Thus in *Sparta* the people were peaceable enough under their own Government, till they found themselves over-reached, and their credulity abused by such as they trusted, whose designs were laid in the dark, for the converting of Liberty into Tyranny, under *Manchanidas* and *Nabis.* In old *Rome,* under the peoples Government, it is true, it was a sad sight oftentimes to see the people swarming in tumults, their shops shut up, and all trading given over throughout the City, and somtimes the City forsaken and left empty.

But here, as also in *Athens,* the Occasion was[286] the same: for, as the people [107] naturally love Peace and Ease; so finding themselves often out-witted and abused by the slights and fears of the Senate, they presently (as it is their Nature upon such Occasions) grew out of all patience. The case was the same also, when any one of their Senators, or of themselves, arrived to any height[287] of power by insinuating into the peoples favour, upon specious and popular pretences, and then made a forfeiture of those pretences, by taking a contrary course. Thus *Sylla* of the Senatorian order, and *Marius* of the Plebeian, both got power into their hands, upon pretence of the peoples good, (as many others did before and after, not onely in *Rome,* but in other Free-States also) but[288] forfeiting their pretences by taking Arbitrary courses, they were the sole Causes of all those Tumults and Slaughters among the Romanes, the infamy whereof hath most injuriously been cast upon the peoples Government, by the profane pens of such as have been bold in Pension or Relation in the Courts of Princes.

Thus *Caesar* also himself, striking as a [108] Favorite of the people upon fair pretences, and forfeiting them, when in power, was the onely cause of all those succeeding Civil Broyles and Tragedies among the people.

A third Occasion of the Peoples being inclined to Discontent and Tumult in a Free-State, is this, when they are sensible of Oppression. For, I say again, The people are naturally of a peaceable temper, minding nothing, but a free Enjoyment: but if once they finde themselves circumvented, misled, or squeezed by such as they have intrusted, then they swell like the Sea, and over-run the Bounds of Just and Honest, ruining all before them.

In a word, there is not one precedent of Tumults or Sedition can be cited out of all Stories[289], by the Enemies of Freedom, against the peoples Government; but it will appear likewise thereby, that the people were not in fault, but either drawn in, or provoked thereto, by the Craft or Injustice of such fair Pretenders as have had by-ends of their own, and by-designs upon the publick Liberty.

[109] Nevertheless, admit that the people were tumultuous in their own Nature; yet those Tumults (when they happen) are more easily to be borne, than these Inconveniences that arise from the Tyranny of Monarchs and[290] Great Ones: for popular Tumults have these three Qualities:

First, The Injury of them never extends further than some few Persons; and those (for the most part) guilty enough; as were the thirty Grandees in *Athens,* the Ten in *Rome,* and those other State-Mountebanks, that suffered for their Practices by the Peoples Fury.

Secondly, Those Tumults are not lasting, but (like fits) quickly over: for, an Eloquent Oration, or Perswasion, (as we see in the Example of *Menenius Agrippa*) or the Reputation of some grave or honest Man, (as in the Example of *Virginus*[291], and afterwards of *Cato*) doth very easily reduce and pacifie them.

Thirdly, The ending of those Tumults, though they have ruined some particulars, yet it appears they have [110] usually turned to the good of the Publick: for we see, that both in *Athens* and *Rome,* the Great Ones were by this means kept in awe from Injustice; the Spirits of the people were kept warm with high thoughts of themselves and their Liberty (which turned much to the inlargement of their Empire.)

And lastly, By this means they came off alwayes with good Laws for their profit, (as in the case of the Law of twelve Tables, brought from *Athens* to *Rome*)* or else with an Augmentation of their Immunities, and Priviledges (as in the case of procuring the Tribunes, and their

---

* The Law of the Twelve Tables formed the basis of the Roman Republican constitution. According to Livy, *Ab Urbe Condita,* III.32–33, during the preparation of the laws ca. 450 B.C., the Decemvirate sent an embassy to Athens in order to study the Solonian Constitution.

Supreme Assemblies) and afterwards in the frequent confirmation of them against the Incroachments of the Nobles.

Now the case is far otherwise under the standing power of the Great Ones; they, in their Counsels, Projects, and Designs, are fast and tenacious; so that the Evils under those Forms are more remediless. Besides, they reach to the whole Body of a Commonweal: and so the Evils are more Universal. And lastly, those Tumults, Quarrels, and Inconveniences [111] that arise from among them, never tend nor end, but to the farther oppression and suppression of the people in their Interest and Propriety.

For conclusion then: by these particulars you may plainly see the vanity of this Objection about Tumults, how far they are from being natural effects of the Peoples Government; insomuch, as by the Records of History, it appears rather that they have been the necessary consequences[292] of such Tricks and Cheats of Great Men, as in the dayes of yore have been put upon the people.

## [MP 96, 1–8 Apr. 1652]

A fifth Objection against the Form of a Free-State[293], or Government by the people in their successive Assemblies, and which we finde most in the Mouths of Royalists and Parasites, is this, That *little security is to be had therein for the more wealthy and powerful sort of men, in regard of that Liberty which the people assume unto themselves, to accuse or calumniate whom they please upon any occasion.*

For answer to this, know, That calumniation (which signifies ambitious [112] slandering of men, by whisperings, reports, or false accusations) was never allowed or approved in this Form of Government. 'Tis true indeed, that such Extravagancies there have been (more or less) in all Forms whatsoever; but in this, less than any: it being most in use under standing Powers of Great ones, who make it their grand Engine to remove or ruine all persons that stand in the way of them and their designes: And for this purpose, it hath ever been their common custom to have Instruments ready at hand; as we see in all the Stories of Kings and Grandees from time to time; yea, and by *Aristotle*

Calumniation less used under the peoples Government, than under any other Form.

himself,* together with the whole train of Commentators, it is particularly mark'd out *inter flagitia Dominationis,* to be one of the peculiar enormities that attend[294] the Lordly interest of Dominion[295].

The Romane State, after it grew corrupt, is a sufficient Instance; where we finde, that not onely the ten Grandees, but all that succeeded them in that domineering humour over the People, ever kept a Retinue well stock'd with [113] Calumniators and Informers, (such as we call *Knights of the Post*) to snap those that in any wise appeared for the Peoples Liberties. This was their constant trade, as it was afterwards also of their Emperours. But all the while that the People kept their power entire in the Supreme Assemblies, we read not of its being brought into any constant practice. Sometimes indeed, those great Commanders that had done them many eminent Services, were, by reason of some after-actions, called to an account[296]; and having, by an ingrosment of Power, render'd themselves suspected, and burthensome to the Commonwealth, were commanded to retire, (as were both the *Scipio*'s.)

And in the Stories of the *Athenian* Commonwealth, we finde, that by their lofty and unwary carriage, they stirr'd up the Peoples fear and jealousie so far, as to question and send divers of them into Banishment, notwithstanding all their former merits; as we read of *Alcibiades, Themistocles,* and others: whereas, if the Rules of a Free-State had been punctually observed, by pre-[114]serving a discreet revolution of Powers, and an equability, or moderate state of particular persons, there had been no occasion of Incroachment on the one part, or of Fear on the other; nor could the prying Royalist have had the least pretence or shadow of Invective against the Peoples Government in this particular[297].

Thus much of Calumniation, which is less frequent under the Peoples Form, than any other.

Now as to the point of Accusing, or liberty of Accusation by the People, before their Supreme Assemblies; it is a thing so essentially necessary for the preservation of a Commonwealth, that there is no possibility of having persons kept accountable without it; and, by

* Aristotle, *Politics,* V.ii.

consequence, no security of Life and Estate, Liberty and Property. And of what excellent use this is, for the publike benefit of any State, appears in these two particulars.

First, it is[298] apparent, that the reason wherefore Kings, and all other standing Powers, have presumed to abuse the People, is, because their continuation [115] of Authority having been a means to state[299] them in a condition of Impunity, the People either durst not, or could not assume a liberty of Accusation; and so have linger'd without remedy, whilst Great Men have proceeded without control to an Augmentation of their misery: whereas if a just Liberty of Accusation be kept in ure, and Great Persons by this means lie[300] liable to questioning, the Commonwealth[301] must needs be the more secure; because none then will dare to intrench, or attempt ought, against their Liberty; and in case any do, they may with much ease be suppress'd. All which amounts, in effect, to a full confirmation of this most excellent Maxime, recorded in Policie: *Maximè interest Repub. Libertatis, ut liberè possis Civem aliquem accusare:* It most[302] highly concerns the Freedom of a Commonwealth, that the People have liberty of accusing any persons whatsoever.

Secondly, it appears, this Liberty is most necessary, because, as it hath been the onely Remedy against the Injustice of great and powerful persons; so it [116] hath been the onely means to extinguish those Emulations, Jealousies, and Suspicions, which usually abound with fury in mens mindes, when they see such persons seated so far above, that they are not able to reach them, or bring them (as it becomes all earthly Powers)[303] to an account of their actions: of which Liberty when the People have seen themselves deprived in time past, it is sad to consider how they have flown out into such absurd and extraordinary courses, in hope of Remedy, as have caused not onely Distraction, but many times utter Ruine to the Publike. Most of those Tumults[304] in old *Rome*, were occasioned for want of this liberty in ordinary; as those that happened under the *Decemviri:* so that the People, not having freedom to accuse and question their Justice, were enflamed to commit sudden Outrages, to be revenged upon them. But when they had once obtained power to accuse or question any man, by assistance of their Tribunes; then we meet with none of those heats and fits among them; but they referr'd themselves over[305], with much content, to [117] the ordinary course of proceeding. A pregnant Instance whereof, we have in the Case of *Coriolanus;* who having done some injury to the people, they finding him befriended and upheld by the Great ones, resolved to be revenged upon him with their own hands; and had torn him in pieces as he came out of the Senate, but that the Tribunes immediately step'd in, and not onely promised, but appointed them a day of Hearing against him; and so all was calm again, and quiet: whereas, if this ordinary course of Remedy, in calling him to account, had not been allow'd, and he been destroy'd in a Mutiny, a world of sad Consequences must have befallen the Commonwealth[306], by reason of those Enormities and Revenges that would have risen, upon the ruine of so considerable a person.

In the Stories of *Florence* also, we read of one *Valesius,* who greatning himself into little less than the posture of a Prince in that Republike, he so confirm'd himself, that the people not being able to regulate his extravagancies by any ordinary proceedings, they [118] betook themselves to that unhappie remedy of Arms; and it cost the best blood and lives in that State, before they could bring him down: involving them in a world of Miseries, which might have been avoided, had they taken care to preserve their old Liberty of Accusation and Question, and being able to take a course with him in an ordinary way of progress[307].

Thus also in the same State, *Soderino,* a man of the same size, interest, and humour; when the People saw that they had lost their Liberty, in being unable to question him, ran like madmen upon a Remedy as bad as the Disease, and called in the Spaniard to suppress him[308]: so that turned almost to the ruine of the State, which might have been prevented, could they have repress'd him by the ordinary way of Accusation and Question[309].*

From these[310] Premises, then, let us conclude, That seeing the crooked way of Calumniation is less used under the Peoples Form of Government, than any other: and since the retaining of a Regular

* Machiavelli, *Discourses,* I.7.

course, for admitting and deci-[119]ding of all Complaints and Controversies by way of Accusation, is of absolute necessity to the safety
and well-being of a Commonwealth[311]; Therefore this Objection is of
as little weight as the rest, so as in any wise to diminish the Dignity
and Reputation of a Free-State, or Government by the People in their
successive Assemblies.

[MP 97, 8–15 Apr. 1652]

A sixth Objection against the Form of a Free-State, or Government by
the People; is alleadged by many, to this effect: *That People by nature are
factious, inconstant, and ungrateful.*

For answer, first, as to the point of being Factious, we have already
shewn, that this Government, stated in a succession of its Supreme
Assemblies, is the onely preventive of Faction; because, in creating
a Faction, there is a necessity, that those which endeavour it, must
have oportunity to improve their slights and projects, in disguising
their Designes; drawing in Instruments and Parties, and in worming out Opposites: the effecting of all which, requires some length
of time; which [120] cannot be had, and consequently, no Faction
form'd, when Government is not fixed in particular persons, but managed by due succession and revolution of Authority in the hands of
the People.

*Faction, inconstancy, and ingrati- tude, no natural effects of the peoples Government.*

Besides, it is to be considered, that the People are never the first or
principal in Faction: they are never the authors and contrivers of it, but
ever the parties that are drawn into Sidings by the influence of standing
Powers, to serve their interests and designes.

Thus *Sylla* and *Marius, Pompey* and *Caesar,* continuing power in
their own hands[312], cleft the Romane Empire at several times into several Parties: as afterwards it was cleft into three by the Triumvirate;
wherein the people had no hand, being (as they are alwayes) purely
passive, and passionately divided, according as they were wrought upon
by the subtil Insinuations of the prime Engineers of each Faction.

Thus *Italy* was divided into *Guelph* and *Gibelline;* and *France* torn in
two by the two Families of *Orleance* and *Burgundi:* also, by the *Guisians*

and their [121] Confederates; wherein[313] the people had no further[314] hand, than as they were acted by the perswasions and pretences of two powerful parties.

The case also was the same in[315] *England*, in times past, when the Grandee-Game[316] was in action between[317] the two Families of *Yorke* and *Lancaster.* So that it is clear enough, The people in their own nature are not inclined to be Factious, nor are they ever ingaged that way, farther than as their Nature is abused, and drawn in by powerful persons.

The second particular of this Objection, is Inconstancy; which holds true indeed in them that are debauched, and in the corrupted State of a Commonwealth, when degenerated from its pure Principles; as we finde in that of *Athens, Rome, Florence,* and others: but yet in *Rome* you may see as pregnant instances of that peoples constancy, as of any other sort of men whatsoever: for, they continued constant irreconcilable Enemies to all Tyranny in general, and[318] Kingly power in particular.

In like manner, when they had once [122] gotten their successive Assemblies, they remained so firm & stiff to uphold them, that the succeeding Tyrants could not in a long time, nor without extraordinary cunning and caution deprive them of that onely Evidence of their Liberty.

Moreover, it is observable of this people, That in making their Elections they could never be perswaded to chuse a known Infamous, Vitious, or unworthy Fellow; so that they seldom or never erred in the choice of their Tribunes and other Officers. And as in the framing of Laws, their aim was ever at the general Good, it being their own Interest, *quatenus* the people; so their constancy in the conservation of those Laws was most remarkable: for, notwithstanding all the crafty Devices and Fetches of the Nobles, the people could never be woo'd to a consent of abrogating any one Law, till by the alteration of Time, Affairs, and other Circumstances, it did plainly appear inconvenient.

But the case hath ever been otherwise under Kings and all standing Powers, [123] who usually ran into all the extreams of Inconstancy, upon every new Project, petty Humour, and Occasion, that seemed[319] favourable for effecting of their by-designs. And in order hereunto,

Stories will inform you, That it hath been their Custome, to shift Principles every Moon, and cashier all Oaths, Protestations, Promises, and Engagements, and blot out the Memory of them with a wet Finger.

This was very remarkable in the late King[320], whose inconstancy in this kinde, was beyond compare; who no sooner had passed any Promises, made Vows and Protestations, fix'd[321] Appeals in the High Court of Heaven, in the behalf of Himself and his Family; but presently he forfeited all, and cancell'd them by his Actions.[322]

As to the third point, of Ingratitude, it is much charged upon this Form of Government; because we read both in *Athens* and *Rome*, of divers unhandsome Returns made to some worthy Persons that had done high services for those Commonwealths; as *Alcibiades, Themistocles, Phocion, Miltiades, Furius,* [124] *Camillus, Coriolanus,* and both the *Scipio's;* the cause[323] of whose misfortunes is described by *Plutarch* and *Livy*, to be their own lofty and unwary carriage; Having (say they) by an ingrossment of power, rendred themselves suspected, and burthensome to the Commonwealth, and thereby stirred up the peoples fear & jealousie: whereas if they had kept themselves within the Rules of a Free-State, by permitting[324] a disceet Revolution of power in particular hands; there had been no occasion of incroachment on the one part, nor of fear on the other. Of all[325], the *Scipio's* indeed were most to be pitied, because their only[326] fault seems to be too much power and greatness, (which indeed is the greatest fault that Members of a Commonwealth can be guilty of, if seriously considered;) insomuch, that being grown formidable to their Fellow-Senators, they were by them removed: and so it appears to have been the act of the Nobles, (upon their own score and Interest) and not of the people. But as for *Camillus* and *Coriolanus*, they sufficiently deserved whatsoever[327] befel [125] them, because they made use of the power and reputation[328] they had gotten by their former merits, onely to maligne and exercise an implacable hate towards the peoples Interest. Nevertheless, the people restored *Camillus* again to his Estate and Honour, after some little time of Banishment.

And though this accident in a Free-State hath been objected by many, as a great deffect; yet others again do highly commend the humour: For (say they) it is not onely a good sign of a Commonwealths being in pure and perfect health, when the people are thus active, zealous, and jealous in the behalf of their Liberties[329], that will permit no such growth of power as may endanger it; but it is also a convenient means to curb the Ambition of its Citizens, and make them contain within due bounds, when they see there is no presuming after Inlargements, and Accessions of Powers and Greatness[330], without incurring the danger and indignation of the people.

Thus much of the Reason why the [126] people many times cast off persons that have done them eminent services: yet on the other side, they were so far from Ingratitude, that they have alwayes[331] been excessive in their Rewards and Honours, to such men as deserved any way of the Publike, whilst they conformed themselves to Rules, and kept in a posture suiting to Liberty[332]. Witness their Consecration of Statues, Incense, Sacrifices, and Crowns of Laurel, inrolling such men in the number of their Deities.

Therefore the crime of Ingratitude cannot in any peculiar manner be fastned upon the People: but if we consult the Stories of all standing Powers, we may produce innumerable testimonies of their Ingratitude toward such as have done them the greatest service; ill recompence being a Mystery of State practised by all Kings and Grandees, who (as *Tacitus* tells us)* ever count themselves disobliged, by the bravest actions of their subjects.

Upon this account, *Alexander* hated *Antipater* and *Parmenio,* and put the latter to death. Thus the Emperour *Ve-*[127]*spasian* cashiered and ruined the meritorious *Antonies*[333]. Thus also was *Alphonsus Albuquerque* served by his Master the King of *Portugal;* and *Consalvus* the Great, by *Ferdinand* of *Aragon:* as was also that *Stanley* of the House of *Derby,* who set the Crown upon King *Henry* the seventh's head. Thus *Sylla* the Romane Grandee destroyed his choicest Instruments that help'd him into the Saddle; as *Augustus* served his friend *Cicero,* and exposed him to the malice and murther of *Anthonie.*

* Machiavelli, *Discourses,* I.29, in discussing the ingratitude of princes, quotes Tacitus, *History,* IV.3 to that effect.

Innumerable are the Examples of this kinde, which evidence, that such unworthy dealings are the effect[334] of all standing Powers; and therefore more properly to be objected against them, than against the Government of the People.

[335]Thus having answered all, or the main Objections, brought by the adversaries of a Free-State; before we proceed to the Errours of Government, and Rules of Policie, it will not be amiss, but very convenient, to say some-[128]thing of that which indeed is the very Foundation of all the rest; to wit, *That the Original of all Just Power and Government is in the PEOPLE.*

# [129]    The Original of All Just Power
## Is in the People.

[MP 98, 15–22 Apr. 1652]

[336]Those Men that deny this Position, are fain to run up as high as *Noah* and *Adam,* to gain a pretence for their Opinion: alledging, That the primitive or first Governments of the World were not instituted by the consent and election of those that were governed, but by an absolute Authority invested in the persons governing.\* Thus they say our first Parent ruled, by a plenary Power and Authority in himself onely, as did also the Patriarchs before and after the Flood too, for some time, becoming Princes by vertue of a paternal right over all the Families of their own Generation and Extraction: so that the Fathers, by reason of their extraordinary long Lives, and the multiplicity of Wives, happened to [130] be Lords of Kingdoms or Principalities of their own begetting.

---

\* Nedham's target is Sir Robert Filmer, the theorist of patriarchal monarchy, whose *The Anarchy of a Limited or Mixed Monarchy* had been published in 1648 in London.

And so some deriving the Pedigree or Government of this Paternal Right of Soveraignty, would by all means conclude, *That the Original of Government, neither was nor ought to be in the People.*

For answer to this, consider, That Magistracy or Government is to be considered, as Natural, or as Political: Naturally he was a true publick Magistrate or Father of his Country, who in those Patriarchal times ruled over his own Children and their Descendants. This Form of Government was only temporary, and took an end not long after the Flood, when *Nimrod* changed it, and by force combining numbers of distinct Families into one Body, and subjecting them to his own Regiment, did, by an Arbitrary Power, seated in his own Will and Sword, constrain them to submit unto what Laws and Conditions himself pleased to impose on[337] them.

Thus the Paternal Form became changed into a Tyrannical. Neither of these had (I confess) their Original [131] in or from the People, nor hath either of them any relation to that Government which we intend in our Position.

But secondly, There is a Government Political, not grounded in Nature, nor upon Paternal Right by Natural Generation; but founded upon the free Election, Consent or mutual Compact of men entring into a form of civil society. This is the Government we now speak of, it having been in request in most ages, and still is: whereas the other was long since out of date, being used onely in the first age of the World, as proper onely for that time.

So that to prevent all Objections of this nature, when we speak here of Government, we mean onely the Political, which is by Consent or Compact; whose original we shall prove to be in the people. As for the Government of the *Israelites,* first under *Moses,* then *Joshua* and the Judges; The Scripture plainly shews, that they were extraordinary Governours, being of God's immediate institution, who raised them up by his Spirit, and imposed them upon that people; whose peculiar happiness it was in [132] cases of this nature, to have so infallible and sure a direction; so that their Government was a Theocracie, (as some have called it) having God himself for its onely Original: and therefore no wonder we have in that time & Nation, so few visible foot-steps of the peoples Election, or of an institution by Compact. But yet we finde after the Judges, when this people rejected this more immediate way of Government by God, (as the Lord told *Samuel, They have not rejected thee, but me*)* and desired a Government after the manner of other Nations; then God seems to forbear the use of his Prerogative, and leave them to an exercise of their own natural Rights and Liberties, to make choice of a new Government and Governour by suffrage and compact.

The Government they aimed at, was Kingly: God himself was displeased at it, and so was *Samuel* too; who, in hope to continue the old Form, and to fright them from the new, tells them, what Monsters in Government Kings would prove, by assuming unto themselves an Arbitrary Power, (not that a King might [133] lawfully and by right do what *Samuel* describes, but[338] onely to shew how far Kings would presume to abuse their power; which no doubt *Samuel* foresaw, not onely by Reason, but by the Spirit of Prophecie.) Nevertheless the people would have a King; say they, *Nay, but there shall be a King over us:* whereupon, saith God to *Samuel, Hearken to their voice.*† Where we[339] plainly see; first, God gives them leave to use their own natural Rights[340], in making choice of their own Form[341] of Government; but then indeed, for the choice of their Governor, there was one thing extraordinary, in that God appointed them one, he vouchsafing still in an extraordinary and immediate manner to be their Director and Protector: but yet, though God was pleased to nominate the person, he left the confirmation and ratification of the Kingship unto the people; to shew, that naturally the right of all was in them, however the exercise of it were superseded at that time, by his Divine pleasure, as to the point of nomination: for, that the people might understand it was their Right, *Samuel* calls them [134] all to *Mizpeh,* as if the matter were all to be done anew on their part; and there by lot, they at length made choice of *Saul,* and so immediately by proclaiming him with shouts and acclamations: and

---

* I Samuel 8:7.
† I Samuel 8:6–7.

then having had proof of his valour against the *Amorites,* they meet at *Gilgal,* and proclaim him King once again, to shew that (naturally) the validity of the Kingship depended wholly upon the peoples consent and confirmation. And so you see the first and most eminent evidence of the institution of Political Government in Scripture doth notoriously demonstrate, that its original is in or from the people; and therefore I shall wave any further instances in cases of the like nature out of Scripture, which are not a few. Onely let it be remembred, that *Peter* in his first Epistle, calls all Government the Ordinance of man,* (in the Original, *the creation of man,* a Creature of a mans making) to shew, that in all its forms it depends onely upon the will & pleasure of the people.

We might insist farther to evince the Truth of this by strength of Reason; but let this serve to assert the right of the [135] thing; and as for the rest, every man will easily believe it very consonant to reason, if he reflect upon the matter of fact, and consider, that it hath been the unanimous practice of all the Nations of the World, to assert their own Rights of Election and Consent (as often as they had opportunity) in the various turns of institution and alteration of Government. In *Italy* of old they had most Free-States, and few Princes; now all Princes, and no Free-States. *Naples,* after many Revolutions, is under *Spain, Rome* under a Pope, and under him one Senator, in stead of those many that were wont to be; *Venice* and *Genoa* have Senators and Dukes, but the Dukes are of small power; *Florence, Ferrara, Mantua, Parma,* and *Savoy,* have no Senators, but Dukes only, and they absolute; *Burgundy, Lorain, Gascoin,* and *Britany,* had once Kings, then Dukes, but now are incorporated into *France:* so all the Principalities of *Germany* that now are, were once imbodied in one entire Regiment: *Castile, Aragon, Portugal,* & *Barcelona,* were once distinct Kingdoms, but now united all to *Spain,* save *Portugal,* which fell off the other [136] day; *France* was first one Kingdom under *Pharamond,* afterwards parted into four Kingdoms, and at last become one again: *England* consisted of Free-States till the *Romans* yoked it, afterwards it was divided into seven

---

* I Peter 2:13–15.

Kingdoms, and in the end it became one again. Thus you see how the world is subject to shiftings of Government: and though it be most true, that the power of the Sword hath been most prevalent in many of these changes, yet some of them have been chiefly managed, (as they ought) by the peoples Consent; and even in those where the Sword hath made way, the peoples consent hath ever been drawn and taken in afterwards, for corroboration of Title; it having been the custom of all Usurpers, to make their investitures appear as just as they could, by getting the Communities Consent *ex post facto*, and entring into some compact with them, for the better establishing themselves with a shew of legality: which act of all Tyrants and Usurpers, is a manifest (though tacite) confession of theirs, *That* de jure *the original of all Power and Government, is and ought to be in the people.*

# Errours of Government;
# And Rules of Policie.

[MP 99, 22–29 Apr. 1652]

Having proved[342] that the Originall of all just Power and Government is in the People; and that the Government of the People, in a due and orderly succession of their supream Assemblies, is much more excellent than any other Form, I suppose it falls in of course, in the next place, to note, and observe those common Errors in Policie, wherein most Countries of the World, (especially that part of it called Christendome) have been long intangled; that when the mystery of Tyrannie is undress't, and stript of all its gaudy Robes, and gay Appearan-[146] ces, it may be hiss't out of the Civill part of Mankind into the company of the more barbarous and brutish Nations.

The first Errour that we shall observe in antient Christian Policie, and which hath indeed been a main foundation of Tyranny, is that corrupt Division of a State, into Ecclesiastical and Civil; A fault whereof our latest Refiners of Political Discourse, are as guilty in their Writings, as any others: But that there is the least footstep, in the Scripture, for Christians to follow such a Division of State, or to allow of a National way of Churching, which is the Root of that Division, could never yet be proved by any; and the contrary is very clear from the drift

One Errour in Government, is a corrupt division of a State into Ecclesiastical and civil.

and scope of the Gospel. We read, indeed, of the Common-wealth of *Israel*[343] being thus divided, and that it was done according to Rules and Constitutions of Gods own appointment; it being Gods way then, when he was pleased, to make choice of that people onely, out of all the World, to be his own peculiar, and so fixed his Church there in a Nationall Form: Then, it was confined and restrained to [147] that particular Nation, excluding all others. But if any man will argue from hence, that it is lawfull for any Nation now under the Gospel to follow this pattern; then it behoves him, 1. to prove, that God intended the Jewish Government as a pattern for us to follow under the Gospel. And if any man will pretend to this, then in the second place, it will concern him to prove, that we are to follow it in every particular, or onely in some particulars. That we are to follow it in every one, no sober man did ever yet affirm: And if they will have us to follow it in some particulars, relinquishing the rest, then it concerns him to produce some Rule or Command out of Scripture, plainly pointing out what parts of it we are to imbrace, and what not; or else he will never be able to make it appear, that the Form of the Commonwealth of *Israel* was ever intended, either in the whole, or in part, as a Pattern for Christians to follow under the Gospel. But never was any such Rule alleadged yet out of Scripture by those that pretend to a Nationall Church.[344]

And therefore, if we seriously reflect [148] upon the Design of God, in sending[345] Christ into the World, we shall find it was to set an end to that Pompous Administration of the Jewish Form; that as his Church and People were formerly confined within the Narrow Pale of a particular Nation, so now the Pale should be broken down, and all Nations taken into the Church: Not all Nations in a lump; nor any whole Nations, or National Bodies to be formed into Churches; for his Church or People, now under the Gospel, are not to be a Body Political, but Spiritual and Mystical: Not a promiscuous confusion of persons, taken in at adventure; but an orderly collection, a picking and chusing of such as are called and sanctified; and not[346] a company of men forced in, by Commands and Constitutions, of Worldly Powers and Prudence; but of such as are brought in by the Power and Efficacy of *Christs* Word and Spirit: for he himself hath said, *My Kingdome is not of this World; it* *is not from hence,** &c.[347] And therefore, that hand which hitherto hath presumed, in most Nations, to erect a Power, called Ecclesiastick, in equipage with the Civil, to bear sway, and bind [149] mens Consciences to retain[348] Notions, ordained for Orthodox, upon civill penalties, under colour of prudence, good order, discipline, preventing of Heresie, advancing of Christs Kingdome; and to this end, hath twisted the Spiritual Power (as they call it) with the Worldly and secular interest of State: This (I say) hath been the very right hand of Antichrist, opposing Christ in his way: Whose Kingdom, Government, Governours, Officers, and Rulers; Laws, Ordinances, and Statutes, being not of this World, (I mean, *jure humano,*) depend[349] not upon the helps and devices of Worldly wisdom.

Upon this score and pretence, the Infant Mystery of Iniquity began to work in the very Cradle of Christianity.

Afterwards it grew up by the indulgence of *Constantine,* and other Christian Emperours, whom though God used in many good things for the suppression of gross Heathen Idolatry, yet (by Gods permission) they were carried away, and their eyes so far dazled, through the glorious pretences of the Prelates and Bishops, that they could [150] not see the old Serpent in a new Form wrapt up in a Mystery; for, Satan had a new Game now to play, which he managed thus: First, he led a great part of the World away with dangerous Errours, thereby to find an occasion for the Prelates, to carry on the mystery of their Profession; and so, under pretence of suppressing those dangerous errors they easily scrued themselves into the Civil Power: and for continuing of it the surer in their own hands, they made bold to baptize whole Nations with the name of Christian, that they might (under the same pretence) gain a share of Power and Authority with the Magistrate in every Nation; which they soon effected.

The Infant, being thus nurst, grew up in a short time to a perfect man, the man of sin (if the Pope be the man, which is yet controverted by some:) for, the Prelates having gotten the power in their hands, began then to quarrel, who should be the greatest among them. At

---

* John 18:36.

length he of *Rome* bore away the Bell; and so the next step was, that, from National Churches they proceed to have a Mother-[151]Church of all Nations. A fair progress and pitch, indeed, from a small beginning: and now being up, they defied all with Bell, Book, and Candle, excommunicating and deposing Kings and Emperours, and binding mens Consciences still, under the first specious pretence of suppressing Heresie, to believe onely in their Arbitrary Dictates, Traditions, and Errours, which are the greatest Blasphemies, Errours, and Heresies, that ever were in the World. Now they were up, see what a do there was to get any part of them down again. What a Quarter and Commotion there was in *Germany*, when *Luther* first brake the Ice? And the like here in *England*, when our first Reformers began their Work: These men, in part, did well, but having banished the Popes actual Tyranny, they left the Seed, and Principle of it, still behind, which was, a State Ecclesiastical united with the Civil; for, the Bishops twisted their own interest again with that of the Crown, upon a Protestant Accompt; and by vertue of that, persecuted those they called Puritans, for not being as Orthodox (they said) as themselves.

[152] To conclude, if it be considered[350], that most of the Civil Wars, and Broiles, throughout *Europe*, have been occasioned, by permitting the settlement of Clergy-Interest, with the Secular, in National Formes, and Churches, it will doubtless be understood, that the Division of a State into Ecclesiastical and Civil, must[351] needs be one of the main Errors in[352] Christian Policy.

[MP 100, 29 Apr.–6 May 1652]

A second Error which[353] we shall note, and which is very frequent under all Formes of Government, is this; that care hath not been taken at all times, and upon all occasions of Alteration, to prevent the passage of Tyranny out of one Form into another, in all the Nations of the World: for, it is most clear, by observing the Affairs and Actions of past-Ages, and Nations, that the interest of absolute Monarchy, and its Inconveniencies, have been visible and fatal under the other Forms (where they have not been prevented) and given us an undeniable proof

The not preventing the passage of Tyranny, out of one Form into another, is a main Error of Policie.

of this Maxime by Experience in all Times; That the Interest of Monarchy may reside in the hands of many, as well as of a single person.

The Interest of absolute Monarchy, [153] we conceive to be an unlimited, uncontrolable, unaccountable station of Power and Authority in the hands of a particular person, who governs onely according to the Dictates of his own Will and Pleasure. And though it hath often bin disguised by Sophisters in Policy, so as it hath lost its own name, by shifting Formes; yet really, and effectually, the thing in it self hath bin discovered under the artificial covers of every Form, in the various Revolutions of Government: So that nothing more concerns a People established in a state of Freedom, than to be instructed in things of this Nature, that the means of its preservation being understood, and the subtil sleight of old Projectors brought into open view, they may become the more zealous to promote the one, and prevent the other, if any old game should happen to be plaid over anew, by any succeeding Generation.

It is very observable in *Athens*, that when they had laid aside their King, the Kingly power was retained still in all the after-turns of Government: for their Decimal Governours, and their Thirty (commonly called the [154] Tyrants) were but a multiplied Monarchy, the Monarchal Interest being held up as high as ever, in keeping the exercise of the Supremacy out of the peoples hands, and seating themselves in an unaccountable state of Power and Authority, which was somewhat a worse condition, than the[354] people were in before; for their Kings had Supervisors, and there were also Senatick Assemblies, that did restrain and correct them: but the new Governors having none, ran into all the heats and fits, and wild extravagancies, of an unbounded Prerogative: by which means, Necessity and Extremity opening the peoples Eyes, they, at length, saw all the Inconveniencies of Kingship wrapt up in new Forms, and rather increased, than diminished; so that (as the onely Remedy), they dislodged the Power out of those hands, putting it into their own, and placing it in a constant orderly Revolution of persons Elective by the Community. And now being at this fair pass, one would have thought there was no shelter for a Monarchal[355] Interest, under a popular Form too. But alas, they found the contrary; for, the people not

[155] keeping a strict Watch over themselves, according to the Rules of a Free State; but being won by specious pretences, and deluded by created Necessities, to intrust the management of Affairs into some particular hands, such an occasion was given thereby to those men to frame parties of their own, that by this means, they in a short time became able to stand upon their own legs, and do what they list without the peoples consent: and in the end, not onely discontinued, but utterly extirpated their successive Assemblies.

In *Rome* also, the Case was the same under every Alteration; and all occasioned, by the crafty contrivances of Grandising Parties, and the peoples own facility and negligence, in suffering themselves to be deluded: for, with the *Tarquin's*, (as it is observed by *Livy*, and others) onely the name King was expelled, but not the thing; the Power & Interest of Kingship was still retained in the Senate, and ingrossed by the Consuls: For, besides the Rape of *Lucrece*, among the other faults objected against *Tarquin*, this was most considerable, That he had [156] acted all things, after his own head, and discontinued Consultations with the Senate, which was the very height of Arbitrary Power. But yet as soon as the Senate was in the saddle, they forgat what was charged by themselves upon *Tarquin*, and ran into the same Errour, by establishing an Arbitrary, Hereditary, unaccountable Power in themselves, and their Posterity, not admitting the people (whose interest and liberty they had pleaded,) into any share in Consultation, or Government, as they ought to have done, by a present erecting of their successive Assemblies: so that you see the same Kingly Interest, which was in one before, resided then in the hands of many. Nor is it my Observation onely, but pointed out by *Livy*, in his second Book, as in many other places; *Cum à Patribus, non Consules, sed Carnifices*, &c. When (saith he) the Senators strove to create, not Consuls, but Executioners, and Tormentors, to vex & tear the people, &c.* And in another place of the same Book, *Consules, immoderatâ, infinitaq; potestate, omnes metus legum*, &c. The Consuls, having an immoderate and unlimited Power, turn-[157]ed the

---

* Livy, *Ab Urbe Condita*, II.56.8.

terror of Laws and punishments onely upon the people, themselves (in the mean while) being accountable to none but to themselves, and their Confederates in the Senate.*

Then the Consular Government being cashiered, came on the *Decemviri. Cum Consulari Imperio ac Regio, sine provocatione,* (saith my Author) being invested with a Consular and Kingly Power, without appeal to any other.†

And in his third Book he saith, *Decem Regum species erat,* it was a Form of ten Kings,‡ the miseries of the people being increased ten times more then they were under Kings, and Consuls: For remedy therefore, the ten were cashiered also; and Consuls being restored, it was thought fit for the bridling of their Power, to revive also the Dictatorship (which was a Temporary Kingship, used onely now and then upon occasion of Necessity) and also those Deputies of the people called Tribunes, which one would have thought had bin sufficient Bars against Monarchick Interest, especially being assisted by the peoples successive [158] Assemblies. But yet for all this, the people were cheated through their own neglect, and bestowing too much confidence and trust upon such as they thought their friends: For when they swerved from the Rules of a *Free-State,* by lengthning the Dictatorship in any hand, then *Monarchick-Interest* stept in there, as it did under *Sylla, Caesar,* and others, long before it returned to a declared Monarchal Form; and when they lengthned Commands in their Armies, then it crept in there, as it did under the afore-named persons, as well as *Marius, Cinna,* and others also; and even *Pompey* himself, not forgetting also the pranks of the two *Triumvirales,* who all made a shift under every Form, being sometimes called Consuls, sometimes Dictators, and sometimes Tribunes of the people, to out-act all the Flagitious Enormities of an absolute Monarchy.[356] It is also evident[357] in the Story of *Florence,* that that Commonwealth, even when it seemed most free, could never quite shake off the

---

* Ibid., III.9.4.
† Ibid., III.33.9.
‡ Ibid., III.36.5.

Interest of Monarchy: for, it was ever the business of one Upstart, or other; either in the Senate, or among the People, to make [159] way to their own ambitious Ends, and hoist themselves into a Kingly posture through the Peoples favour, as we may see in the Actions of *Savanarola* the Monk, *Soderino,* and the *Medices,* whose Family did (as we see at this day) fix it self at length in the State of an absolute Monarchy, under the Title of a Dukedom. Nor can it be forgotten, how much of Monarchy (of late) crept into the United Provinces.

Now the Use that is to be made of this Discourse, is this,[358] that since it is clear, the Interest of Monarchy may reside in a Consul, as well as in a King; in a Dictator, as well as in a Consul; in the hands[359] of many, as well as of a single person; and that its Custom hath bin to lurk under every Form, in the various turnes of Government, therefore as it concerns every people in a State of Freedome, to keep close to the Rules of a *Free-State,* for the turning[360] out of Monarchy (whether simple, or compound, both name and thing, in one or many) by which means onely they will be inabled to avoid this second Error in Policy; so they ought ever to have a Reverent and Noble re-[160]spect of such Founders of *Free-States,* and *Common-wealths,* as shall block up the way against Monarchick Tyranny, by declaring for the Liberty of the People, as it consists in a due and orderly succession of Authority, in their supream Assemblies.

## [MP 101, 6–13 May 1652]

A keeping
the people in
ignorance of
the essential
wayes and
meanes that
are necessary
for the peoples
Liberty, is
an Error in a
Free-State.

A third Errour in Policy, which ought especially notice to be taken of[361], and prevented in a *Free-State,* hath bin a keeping of the people ignorant of those ways and means that are essentially necessary for the preservation of their Liberty; for, implicite Faith, and blind Obedience, hath hitherto passed currant, and been equally pressed and practised by Grandees, both Spirituall and Temporal, upon the People; so that they have in all Nations shared the Authority[362] between them. And though many quarrels have risen in times past between Kings, and their Clergy, touching their several Jurisdictions, yet the mysteries of Domination have been still kept under lock and key: so that their Prerogative remained entire ever above the reach and knowledge of the People: by which means, Monarchs and other standing Powers, have seen their own Interest[363] provided [161] for, as well as in the Popes in this mysterious Maxime, *Ignorance*[364] *is the Mother of Devotion.*

But these things ought not to be so, among a people that have declared themselves a *Free-State:*[365] For, they should not onely know what *Freedome* is, and have it represented in all its lively and lovely Features, that they may grow zealous and jealous over it; but, that it may be a Zeal according to knowledge and good purpose: it is without all question, most necessary, that they be made acquainted, and throughly instructed in the Meanes and Rules of its preservation, against the Adulterous Wiles and Rapes of any projecting Sophisters that may arise hereafter.

And doubtless, this endeavour of mine, in laying down the Rules of preserving a *Free-State,* will appear so much the more necessary, if we consider, that all the Inconveniencies that in Times have happened under this Form, to imbroyl, or ruine it, have proceeded (as we have formerly proved) either from the peoples neglect, or rather ignorance of those Meanes and Rules that should be committed [162] unto them, both for Practice, and Observation: having therefore made brief Collections out of the Monuments of this kind of Learning, I shall here insert them, that the People of every Common-wealth[366], which mean to preserve their Freedom, may be informed how to steer their course, according to such Rules as have bin put in practice heretofore by, divers Nations.

First, it hath bin a Custom, not only to breed up all the young Fry in Principles of Dislike and Enmity against Kingly Government; but also to cause all that were capable of swearing, to enter into an Oath of Abjuration, to abjure a toleration of Kings, and Kingly Power, in time to come.

Thus *Brutus* bound the *Romans* by an Oath against Kings, *That they should never suffer any man again to reign*[367] *at Rome.**

It hath bin one Rule in all Free States, to abjure a toleration of Kings, and Kingly Government.

* Livy, *Ab Urbe Condita,* II.1.9–10.

Thus the *Hollanders* preserved themselves also, entering into an Oath of Abjuration,* not onely against King *Philip,* and his Family, but all Kings for ever.

And *Brutus,* to make sure work, did not onely do this, but divided the [163] Royal Revenues among the People; which was a good way to make them resolute to Extremity, knowing, That if ever any King came in play again, He would take all away again by vertue of his Prerogative and Crown: He brake also all the Images and Statues of the *Tarquins,* and he levell'd[368] their houses with the ground, that they might not remain as Temptations to any ambitious Spirits. Suitable to this policy, was that of *Henry* the 8th, who when he disposed of the Revenues of Abbies, demolished also the Building; saying, *Destroy the Nests, and the Rookes will ne're return again.* Which, questionless, was a most sure way, both in him, and *Brutus,* to be imitated, or neglected, as there may be occasion. But they thought, in a case of this Nature, that the convenience in keeping them, could not countervail the danger.

Secondly, It hath bin usual not to suffer particular persons to Grandise, or greaten themselves more than ordinary; for that, by the *Romans,* was called, *affectatio Regni,* an aspiring to Kingship: Which being observed in *Maelius* and *Manlius,* two noble *Ro-*[164]*mans,* that had deserved highly of the State, yet their[369] past-merits & services, could not exempt them from the just anger of the People, who made them Examples to Posterity: Yea, the Name of the latter, (though *Livy* cals him an incomparable man, had he not lived in a *Free-State,*)† was ever after disowned by his whole Family, that famous Family of the *Manlii;* and both the Name and Memory of Him, and of his Consulship, was rased out of all publike Records, by Decree of the Senate.[370]

The not keeping close to this Rule, had of late like to have cost the Low-countries, the loss of their Liberty[371]; for the Wealth of the House of *Orange,* grown up to excess, and permitting the last man to match into a Kingly Family, put other thoughts and designs into his head, than beseemed a member of a *Free-State;* which, had he not been

*It hath bin a Rule in all Free-States, not to suffer particular persons to Grandise more then ordinary.*

* In the year 1581.
† Livy, *Ab Urbe Condita,* VI.20.14.

prevented, by the Providence of God, and a dark night, might[372] in all probability, have reduced them under the Yoak of Kingly Power.*

Thirdly, Especial care hath been taken, *non Diurnare Imperia*, not to permit a Continuation of Command [165] and Authority[373], in the hands of particular persons, or families. This point we have been very large in: The[374] Romans had a notable care herein, till they grew corrupt. *Livy*, in his fourth Book, saith, *Libertatis magna custodia est, si magna Imperia esse non sinas, & temporis modus imponatur:* It is a grand preservative of Liberty, if you do not permit great Powers and Commands to continue long; and if so be you limit, in point of time.† To this purpose, they had a Law, called the *Emilian*[375] *Law, to restrain them;* as we find in the Ninth Book, where he brings in a Noble Roman, saying thus: *Hoc quidem Regno simile est;* And this,[376] indeed, is like a Kingship. That I alone should bear this great Office of the Censorship, *Triennium & sex menses*, three years and six moneths, contrary to the *Emilian*[377] *Law.*‡ In his third Book also, he speaks of it, as of a monstrous business, That the *Ides*[378] of May were come (which was the time of their years choice) and yet no new Election appointed: *Id-veró Regnum haud dubiè videre, deploratur in perspetuum libertas.* It without doubt seems no other than a Kingdom, and Liberty is utter-[166]ly lost for ever.§ It was Treason for any man to hold that high Office of the Dictatorship in his own hand, beyond six moneths. He that would see notable stuff to this purpose, let him read *Ciceroes* Epistles[379] to *Atticus*, concerning *Caesar*.‖ The care of that people, in this particular, appeared also, that they would not permit any man to bear the same Office twice together.

A third Rule in policy, not to permit a continuation of Command and Power in the hands of particular person[s] and families.

---

* William II of Orange, brother-in-law and ally of the exiled Charles II of England. Nedham refers to the attempted military seizure of Amsterdam by William's supporters in July 1650. William died in October of the same year.

† Livy, *Ab Urbe Condita*, IV.24.4. Nedham loosely paraphrases. The words ascribed by Livy to Mamercus Aemilius were: *Se, quod intra muros agendum esset, libertati populi Romani consulturum; maximam autem eius custodiam esse si magna imperia diuturna non essent et temporis modus imponeretur quibus iuris imponi non posset.*

‡ Ibid., IX.34.16.

§ Ibid., III.38.1–2.

‖ Cicero, *Letters to Atticus*, X.1.3, 4.2, 8.6.

This was observed likewise (as *Aristotle* tells us) in all the *Free-States* of *Greece.*

And in *Rome* we find *Cincinnatus,* one of the brave Romane Generals, making a Speech unto the People, to perswade them, to let him lay down his Command. Now the time was come, though the Enemy was[380] almost at their Gates, and never more need, than at that time, of his valour and prudence, as the people told him: but no perswasion would serve the turn; resign he would, telling them, *There would be more danger to the State, in prolonging his Power, than from the Enemy, since it might prove a President most pernicious to the Romane Freedome.**
Such another Speech was made by *M. Ru-*[167]*tilius Censorinus,* to the People, when they forced him to undergo the Office of Censor twice together, contrary to the intent and practice of their Ancestors; yet he accepted it: but (as *Plutarch* tells us) upon this condition; *That a Law might pass against the Title in that, and other Officers, least it should be drawn into President in time to come.*† Thus the People dealt also with their own Tribunes, the Law being, *That none of them should be continued two years together.* So tender were the Romans, in this particular, as one principal Rule and Means, for the preservation of their Liberty.[381]

[MP 102, 13–20 May 1652]

Not to let two of one Family bear Offices of Trust at one time.

A fourth Rule,[382] not to let two of one Family to bear Offices of High Trust at one time, nor to permit a Continuation of great Powers in any one[383] Family. The former, usually brings on the latter: And if the latter be prevented, there is the less danger in the former: but however, both are to be avoided: The reason is evident,[384] because a permission of them, gives a particular Family an opportunity, to bring their own private Interest into competition, with that of the Publique: from whence presently ensues [168] this grand inconvenience in State, the Affairs of the Commonwealth[385] will be made subservient to the ends of a

* This is perhaps a conflation of two passages of bk. 10 of Dionysius of Halicarnassus, *Roman Antiquities:* X.25.2–3; X.27.2–3.
† Plutarch, *Life of Caius Marcus Coriolanus,* I.1–2.

few persons; no Corn shall be measured, but in their bushel; nor any Materials be allowed for the Publick Work, unless they square well with the building of a private Interest, or Family. This therefore, was a principal point of State among the[386] Romans, *Ne duo vel plures ex una familia magnos Magistratus gerant eodem tempore;* Let not two or more of one Family, bear great Offices at the same time. And a little after it follows, *Ne magna Imperia ab unâ familiâ praescribantur,* Let not great Commands be prescribed, or continued, by one Family.

That little liberty which was left to the Romans, after that fatal stab given to *Caesar* in the Senate-house, might have been preserved, had they prevented his Kinsman *Octavius* from succeeding him in the possession of an extraordinary Power. The effecting whereof was *Ciceroes* work, and, indeed, his principal errour: as he often afterwards acknowledged;* which may serve to shew, *That the wisest man may be sometimes mistaken*[387]: For he brought [169] the other into play; whereas[388] had he quitted his spleen, and consulted his brain, he must questionless have seen, that a siding with *Anthony* had been more convenient, then with the other; who being once admitted into Power, soon drew the Parties, and Interests of his Uncle *Julius,* to become his own; and with a wet finger, not onely cast off his friend *Cicero,* but contrived the ruine of the Republick, and Him, both together.

The *Florentine* Family of the *Medices,* who hold an absolute Command at this day, made themselves, by continuing Power in their hands, in a short time so considerable, that they durst openly bid defiance to Publick[389] Liberty, which might have continued much longer, had not *Casinus*[390] been so easily admitted to succeed his Cousin *Alexander.*

It is observable also, of the same Family, that one of them being Pope, they then hatched Designs upon several parts of *Italy,* not doubting but to[391] carry them by favour of the Pope their Kinsman: but he dying before their Ends were effected, they then made a Party in the Conclave, for the [170] creating of *Julian de Medicis,* who was Brother to the former Pope, and had like to have carried it, till *Pompeius Columba*[392] stood up, and shewed them how dangerous and prejudicial

* Plutarch, *Life of Cicero,* XLVI.1.

it must of necessity prove, to the Liberties of *Italy,* that the Popedom should be continued in one house, in the hands of two brothers one after another.

What Effects the continuation of Power, in the Family of *Orange,* hath had in the *United Provinces,* is every mans observation; and that Nation sufficiently felt, long before the Project came to maturity, in this last mans dayes; and had he left a son of sufficient years behind him, to have stept immediatly into his place,* perhaps the Design might have gone on: but certainly that People have wisely improved their opportunity, (the Cockatrice being not flech'd) in reducing[393] that Family into a temper more suitable to a State and Interest of Liberty.

What made the antient Roman Senate, in a short time, so intollerable to that People, but because they carried all by Families; as the Senate of [171] *Venice* doth now at this day: where, if the Constitution were otherwise, the people would then (perhaps) be much more sensible what it is to be in a *State of Freedom.*

The Majesty and Authority of the Suffrages, or votes of the Supream Assembly to be kept intire. Fifthly, It hath bin usual in *Free-States,* to hold up the Majesty and Authority of their Suffrages, or Votes intire, in their Senators, or supream Assemblies: for if this were not look'd to, and secured from controle, or influence of any other Power, then *Actum erat de libertate,* Liberty and Authority became lost for ever. So long as the Roman people kept up their credit and Authority, as sacred, in their Tribunes, and Supream Assemblies, so long they continued really free: but when by their own neglect, they gave *Sylla,* and his Party, in the Senate, an opportunity of power to curb them, then their Suffrages (once esteemed as sacred) were troden under foot; for immediately after, they came to debate and act but by courtesie, the Authority left being by *Sylla,* after the expiration of his Dictatorship, in the hands of the standing Senate, so that it could never after be regained by the People. Nor did the Senate themselves keep it [172] long in their own hands: for when *Caesar* marched to *Rome,* he deprived them also of the Authority of their Suffrages; only in a formal way made use of them, and so under a

---

*William II's son, William III, was born a few days after the father's death. The accession of an infant gravely weakened the Orange interest in the Netherlands.

shadow of legality, he assumed that power unto[394] himself, which they durst not deny him.[395]

Just in the same manner dealt *Cosmus* with the *Flerentine Senate:* he made use of their Suffrages, but he had so plaid his Cards beforehand, that they durst not but yield to his Ambition. So also *Tiberius,* when he endeavored to settle himself, first brought the Suffrages of the Senate at his own Devotion, that they durst not but consent to his Establishment; and then so ordered the matter, that he might seem to do nothing, not only without their consent; but to be forced to accept the Empire by their intreaty: so that you see, there was an Empire, in Effect, long before it was declared in Formality.

From hence, therefore, we may clearly deduce the necessity of this Rule in a *Free-State,* from the practice of times past, that no State can prefer[396] its Freedom, but by maintaining the free [173] Suffrage of the People in full vigour, untainted with the influence, or mixture, of any Commanding Power.[397]

## [MP 103, 20–27 May 1652]

[398]A sixth Rule in Practice hath been this; to see, that the people be continually trained up in the Exercise of Arms, and the *Militia* lodged onely in the Peoples hands; or that part of them, which are most firm to the Interest of Liberty, that so the Power may rest fully in the Disposition of their Supream Assemblies. The happy consequence whereof, was ever to this purpose:

That nothing could at any time be imposed upon the people, but by their consent[399]; that is, by the consent of themselves; or of such as were by them intrusted: this was a Rule most strictly practised in all the *Free-States* of *Greece:* For, as *Aristotle* tells us, in his fourth Book of *Politicks,* they ever had special care[400] to place the Use and Exercise of Arms in the people: because (say they) the Common-wealth is theirs who held[401] the Arms.*

The people are to be continually trained up in the exercise of Armes, and the Militia lodged in the hands of those that are firm to the Interest of the Nation.

* Aristotle, *Politics,* IV.13.1.

The Sword, and Soveraignty, ever walk hand in hand together. The Romans were very curious in this particular, after they had gained a plenary [174] possession of Liberty in their Tribunes, and successive Assemblies, *Rome* it self, and the Territories about it, was trained up perpetually in Arms, and the whole Common-weal, by this means became one formal *Militia*, a generall Exercise of the best part of the people in the use of Arms, was the onely Bulwark of their Liberty: This was reckoned the surest way to preserve it both at home, and abroad: the Majesty of the People being secured thereby, as well against Domestick Affronts from any of their own Citizens, as against the forraign Invasions of bad Neighbors.

Their Arms were never lodged in the hands of any, but such as had an Interest in the Publick; such as were acted by that Interest, not drawn only by Pay; such as thought themselves well paid, in repelling Invaders, that they might with *Freedome* return to their Affairs: For, the truth is, so long as *Rome* acted by the pure Principles of a *Free-State*, it used no Arms to defend it self, but, such as we call, sufficient men; such, as for the most part were men of Estate, Masters of Families, that took Arms (only upon occasion) *pro* [175] *Aris & Focis,* for their Wives, their Children, and their Countrey. In those days there was no difference, in order, between the Citizen, the Husbandman, and the Souldier: for, he that was a Citizen, or Villager yesterday, became a Souldier the next, if the *Publick Liberty* required it; and that being secured, by repelling of Invaders, both *Forreign* and *Domestick,* immediatly the Souldier became Citizen again: so that the first and best brave Roman Generals, and Souldiers, came from the Plough, and returned thither when the Work was over.

This was the usual course even before they had gained their Tribunes and Assemblies; that is, in the Infancy of the Senate, immediately after the Expulsion of their Kings: for, then even in the *Senatick Assembly,* there were some Sparks of Liberty in being, and they took this course to maintain it.

The *Tarquins* being driven out, but having a Party left still within, that attempted to make several[402] Invasions, with confidence to carry all before them: and yet in the Intervalls, we find not any form of souldiery;

only [176] the *Militia* was lodged and exercised in the hands of that Party, which was firm to the *Interest of Freedom,* who upon all occasions, drew forth at a Nod of the *Senate,* with little charge to the Publick, and so rescued themselves out of the Clawes of Kingly Tyranny.

Nor do we find in after-times, that they permitted a Deposition of the Arms of the Common-wealth[403] in any other way, till that their Empire increasing, necessity constrained them to erect a continued stipendary Souldiery (abroad in forreign parts) either for the holding, or winning of Provinces. Then Luxury increasing with Dominion, the strict Rule and Discipline of *Freedome* was soon quitted; Forces were kept up at home, (but what the consequences were, stories will tell you) as well as in the Provinces abroad.

The Ambition of *Cinna,* the horid Tyranny of *Sylla,* the insolence of *Marius,* and the self-ends of divers other Leaders, both before, and after them, filled all *Italy* with Tragedies, and the World with wonder: so that in the end, the People[404] seeing what misery [177] they had brought on themselves, by keeping their Armies within the bowels of *Italy,* passed a Law to prevent it, and to employ them abroad, or at a convenient distance: the Law was, *That if any General marched over the River of Rubicon*[405], *he should be declared a publike Enemy.*

And in the passage of that River, this following Inscription was erected, to put the men of Arms in mind of their duty: *Imperator, sive miles, sive Tyrannus armatus quisquis, sistito vexillum armaq; deponito, nec citra hunc Amnem trajicitio:*[406] General, or Souldier, or Tyrant in Arms, whosoever thou be, stand, quit thy Standard, and lay aside thy Arms, or else cross not this River.*

For this cause it was, that when *Caesar* had presumed once to march over this River, he conceived himself so far ingaged, that there was no Retreat; no Game next, but have at all, advanceth[407] to *Rome* it self, into a possession of the Empire.

By this means it was, the Common-wealth[408] having lost its Arms, lost it self too, the Power being reduced both effectually and formally

* This inscription, now kept in the archaeological museum at Cesena, is generally regarded as a medieval or Renaissance forgery.

into the [178] hands of a single Person, and his Dependants, who, ever after, kept the Armes out of the hands of the People.

Then followed the erecting of a *Praetorian Band,* instead of a *Publick Militia*[409], he being followed herein by *Augustus,* and the rest of his Successors, imitated of latter-times by the Grand Seignor; by *Cosmus* the first great Duke of *Tuscany;* by the *Muscovite,* the *Russian,* the *Tartar,* and the *French,* who by that means are all Absolute; and it was strongly endeavored here too in *England* by the late King[410], who first attempted it by a Design of introducing Forreigners, *viz.* the *German Horse,* and afterwards by corrupting of the Natives; as when he laboured the Army in the North, in their return to rifle the Parliament, neglected Train-Bands; and at length, flew out himself into open Arms against the Nation.

So that you see, the way of *Freedome* hath bin to lodge the Arms of a Common-Weal, in the hands of that part of the People, which are firm to its Establishment.[411]

## [MP 104, 27 May–3 June 1652]

Seventhly, that Children[412] should be [179] educated and instructed in the Principles of *Freedom. Aristotle* speaks plainly to this purpose, saying; *That the institution of Youth, should be accommodated to that Form of Government, under which they live; forasmuch, as it makes exceedingly for preservation of the present Government, whatsoever it be.** The Reason of it appears in this; because all the Tinctures and Impression that men receive in their Youth, they retain in the full Age, though never so bad, unless they happen (which is very rare) to quell the corrupt Principles of Education by an Excellency of Reason, and sound Judgment.

*Children educated and instructed in the Principles of Freedom.*

And for confirmation of this, we might cite the various Testimonies of *Plutarch, Isocrates,* with many more, both Philosophers, Orators, and others, that have treated of this particular, touching the Education of Children, as it relates either to Domestick, or Civil Government: But

* Aristotle, *Politics,* V.9. Nedham paraphrases loosely.

we shall take it for granted, without more ado, supposing none will deny, of what effect it is, in all the Concernments of Mankind, either in Conversation, or in Action.

The necessity of this Point, appears [180] from hence, as well as the Reason; That if care be not taken to temper the Youth of a Common-Wealth, with Principles and Humours suitable to that Form, no sure settlement, or peace, can ever be expected: for Schools, Academies, with all other Seed-plots, and Seminaries of Youth, will otherwise be but so many Nurseries of Rebellion, publike Enemies, and unnatural Monsters that will tear the bowels of their Mother-Countrey: And this Neglect, if it follow an alteration of Government, after a Civil War, is so much the more dangerous; because, as long as Youngsters are nuzled[413] up in the old Ways and Rudiments, by the old ill-affected Paedagogues, there will ever be a hankering after the Old Government, which must ever be in a fair probability of return, when new Generations shall be catechised into old Tenets and Affections, contrary to the Establishment of a *Free-State:* That being taken for the declared Interest of this Nation. Therefore, the consequence of such Neglect is clearly this, That the Enmity will be immortal, a Settlement impossible: there must be a perpetual Disposition to Civil-[181]War, in stead of Civil Society.[414]

Upon this account[415] it was, that in *Plutarch* and *Isocrates,* we find so many good Testimonies of the great care that was had amongst all the *Free-States* of *Greece* in this particular, which tyed up their Paedagogues and Teachers, to certain Rules; and selected certain Authors to be read onely, as Classical, for the Institution of their Youth: And, that it was so in the days of *Julius Caesar,* even in that barbarous Country of *Gallia,* appeares by *Caesars* own Commentaries, who tells, how that it was the main Office of those famous men amongst them called *Druides*[416], to breed up their Youth not onely in Religion, but also to instruct them in the Nature of a Common-wealth[417], and mould them with Principles, answerable to the Government[418].*

---

* Caesar, *Gallic Wars*, VI.14. Caesar does not say that the Druids instructed their pupils in matters of government.

If we reflect upon the two Grand Turns of State in *Rome,* the first, from a Monarchy to a *Free-State;* and then from a *Free-State,* to a Monarchy again; they minister matter of notable Observation in this particular.

In the first, we find how difficult it was for the Romans to preserve their [182] *Freedom* when they had gotten it, because most of the Youth had bin educated in Monarchical Principles, and such[419] Tutors were ever inclining that way upon the least opportunity: so that the sons even of *Brutus* himself, (who was the Founder of their Liberty) quitted that natural affection which they owed unto their Father, and Coun-trey; and being sway'd by the Monarchick Principles of corrupt Edu-cation, drew in a great part of the Roman Youth, (like themselves,) to joyn with them in a Design for the bringing back of the *Tarquins* to the Kingdom.

It is very observable also, what a do that Common-wealth[420] had to settle, so long as any of the old stock of Education were living, be-cause those corrupt points of Discipline and Government, wherewith they were seasoned when young, could not be worn out with Age; but hurried many of them along with the storm of every Insurrection and Invasion of the publike Enemy.

On the other side, in the Turn of a *Free-State,* to a *Monarchy* again, we see with what difficulty *Caesar* met, in setling his own Domination over a Peo-[183]ple that had been educated in a *Free-State,* and in Principles of *Freedom;* insomuch, that in the end it cost him his life, being stab'd for his Usurpation by a combination of some of the Senators, and the Fact applauded not onely by the People, but by *Cicero,** and all the Roman Writers, and others that had been bred up under the Form of *Freedom.*

And afterwards, when *Augustus* took upon him the Inheritance and Title, of his Uncle *Caesar,* he did it, *lento pede,* very slowly and warily, for fear of conjuring up the same spirit in the people, that had flown into revenge against his Uncle, for his Rape upon their Liberty.

And it is Noted by *Tacitus,* that among the other advantages that *Augustus* had for his Establishment, there was this: That he never

* For example, *De Officiis,* II.7.

declared himself, till, after many delayes and shifts, for the continuation of Power in his own hands, he got insensibly into the Throne, when the old men were most of them dead, and the young Generation grown up, having been pretty well educated and inured to his Lordly Domination. The words of [184] *Tacitus* are these: "All (saith he) was quiet in the City, the old names of the Magistrates remained unchanged; the young men were all born after *Augustus* his victory at *Actium:* and the greatest part of the old men, during the Civil Wars; when the *Free-State* was imbroiled and usurpt (in effect, though retained still in name by powerful and ambitious persons) so that when he assumed and owned the Empire, there was not one man Living, that had so much as seen the ancient Form of Government of a *Free-State*[421]; which indeed facilitated his Design very much, the Generation then Living, being by his Artifice and Power, bred up to his own Monarchy-Interest and Devotion."*

We might be larger, but this is enough, to shew of what consequence the careful Education of Youth, is, in the Constitution[422] of Government: and therefore, without doubt, it is one essential point to be observed in the Establishment of a *Free-State,* that all wayes and meanes be used for their seasoning and instruction in the principles of *Freedom.*

## [MP 105, 3–10 June 1652]

[423]The Eighth Rule, is, that which more [185] especially relates unto the People themselves in point of behaviour, *viz.* That being once possessed of Liberty, they ought to use it with moderation, lest it turn to licentiousness; which, as it is a Tyranny it self, so in the end it usually occasions the corruption and conversion of a Free State, into Monarchical[424] Tyranny: And therefore (by way of prevention) it is necessary to set down a few Cautions.

First, That in a Free State, it is above all things necessary to avoid Civil Dissention; and to remember this, That the uttermost Remedy is not

Cautions for the people to observe.

---

* Nedham paraphrases a passage from Tacitus, *Annals,* I.3–4.

The People are not to use the utmost remedy in all cases of male administration.

to be used upon every Distemper or Default of those that shall be intrusted with the Peoples Power and Authority: for, if one Inconvenience happen in Government, the correction, or curing of it by violence, introduceth a thousand: And for a man to think Civil War, or the Sword, is a way to be ordinarily used for the recovery of a sick-State, it were as great a madness, as to give strong Waters in a high Feaver: or as if he should let himself blood in the Heart, to cure the aking of his Head.

And therefore, seeing that Enormity of Tumult, Dissention, and Sediti-[186]on, is the main that hath been objected by Tyrants, & their Creatures, against the Peoples Government, the onely Expedient to confute it is, That those People, that are, or shall be setled, in a State of Freedom, do[425] (upon all occasions) give them the Lie, by a discreet and moderate behaviour in all their proceedings, and a due reverence of such as they have once elected, and made their Superiors.

And as this is most requisite on the one side; so on the other side, if there be just (but they must be sure it be just[426]) cause to use sharp and quick Remedies, for the Cure of a Common-wealth,[427] then (seeing all Majesty and Authority is really and fundamentally in the people, and but Ministerially in their Trustees, or Representatives) it concerns the people by all means to see to the Cure.

And that is, in a word, in such cases onely, as appear to be manifest intrenchments (either in design, or in being) by men of Power, upon the Fundamentals, or Essentials, of their Liberty, without which, Liberty cannot consist.

What those Essentials are, may be [187] collected out of the past-discourse; the sense[428] of all shall be illustrated by one instance.

It is that famous Contention which lasted for three hundred years in *Rome* betwixt the Senate and the People, about the dividing of such Lands as were conquered and taken from the Enemy.

The Senators, they sharing the lands amongst themselves, allowed little, or none, unto the people; which gave such Discontents, that the people made a Law to curb them; enacting, That no Senator should possess above 500 Acres of Land.

The Senators cryed, it was against their Liberty, thus to be abridged by the people: And the people cryed, it was inconsistent with Liberty, that the Senators should thus greaten themselvs by an ingrosment of wealth and power into their own hands. *Livy* saith,* The people in this, said right, and the Senators did wrong: but that they both did ill, in making it a ground of Civil Dissention; for, in process of time, when the *Gracchi*, who were supposed great Patrons of Liberty, took upon them to side with the people, [188] they did, instead of finding out some moderate wayes and Expedients to reduce the Senators to Reason, proceed with such heat and violence, that the Senate being jealous of their own safety, were forced to chuse *Sylla* for their General: which being observed by the people, they also raised an Army, and made *Marius* their General: so that here you see it came to a down-right Civil-War.

The occasion, indeed, was given by the Senators; (for, there was no reason they should Grandise themselves in so gross a manner as they did) but yet the occasion ought not to have bin so taken, and prosecuted with such violence as it was by the People: for seeing more temper-ate wayes had been practised by their Ancestors, and might have been found out again, to curb the Ambition of their Nobility in the Senate: Therefore, the People ought, first, to have tryed those wayes again, and have used all other means to have brought things about, rather than by a misguided heat and violence to rush into Arms; which as it is the most desperate Remedy, so it ought never to be used, but when all [189] other courses have been tried in vain, and when the Publick Liberty is really concerned by an imminent Danger, or invincible Necessity: For, this Quarrel, which questionless might have been composed, was, through indiscretion, made the ground of so bloudy a Civil-war, that what through Fines, Banishment, inhumane Cruelties, acted on both sides, Defeats in the open Field, and Massacres within the City, it cost

---

* Nelson, *Greek Tradition*, pp. 92–93, observes that "Livy said no such thing about the Licinian law" (the subject of the "famous Contention"). Nelson suggests that Nedham may have been misremembering another passage of Livy (*Ab Urbe Condita*, IV.51) or recalling Sallust, *Bellum Iugurthinum*, xxii [xlii?]. Alternatively, or additionally, Nedham's account may bear some debt to Florus, *Epitome of Roman History*, I. 47 and II. 1, a work that is itself based upon portions of Livy's work that are not extant.

the best Bloud and Estates of the Nobility and Commons; and in the end, it cost them also their Liberty.

For it is worthy observation, that out of the Root of this Civil war, sprang that Noble one[429], which was managed between *Pompey* and *Caesar*, and which will serve to illustrate the other part of our discourse, in shewing, When it is that the people may make use of the utmost, remedy; that is[430], in case of an intrenchment, manifestly designed, & acted upon the Publick Liberty. For *Caesar* having given manifest cause of Suspition to the *Senat* & people, by his acting amongst his Soldiers[431]; and then by a down-right march with them over *Rubicon* towards *Rome*, (which was [190] treason by the Law) this was a plain usurpation, and drew an invincible necessity, upon the people, and *Senate*[432], to arm form their Liberty, and commence a Civil war under the conduct of *Pompey*; so that this last war was necessary as the other was needlesse, if they could have kept within the bounds of prudence, and moderation.

We have a very notable[433] instance also in our own Nation, which may serve for a Just example to all the world in point of behaviour.[434] If we run over the Catalogue of the late Kings[435] defaults in government, we find extraordinary patience in the people, notwithstanding his extraordinary incroachments from time to time. It were needless to reckon up the several Monopolies, Impositions, and other oppressions of the People, both in soul and body, which are made publick and known to all the World; together with that highest of all Practices, not onely in dissolving Parliaments abruptly, but professedly designing the ruine of Parliaments, in depriving the People of their due Succession. Yet notwithstanding all this, that desperate Remedy of the Sword was for-[191]born, untill invincible Necessity did put it into their hands, for the preservation of themselves, with their Rights and Liberties.[436]

And so by these Examples, any people in a State of Freedom, may be sufficiently instructed how to demean themselves, for the avoiding of Licentiousness, Tumult, and Civil Dissention, which are the principal Inconveniences charged by Royalists, upon Free-States and Common-wealths:[437] from hence, also, may be observed all the necessary points of prudence, and forbearance, which ought to take place in

In What Case the Romans used the utmost remedy

respect of Superiors, till it shall evidently appear unto a people, *that there is a Design on foot to surprize and seize their Liberties.*[438]

## [MP 106, 10–17 June 1652]

[439]A second Caution, is, in relation to their Elective Power, that in all Elections of Magistrates, they have an especiall Eye upon the Publick, in making choice of such persons onely, as have appeared most eminent, and active, in the Establishment and[440] Love of Freedom.

In such hands the Guardianship of Liberty may be safely[441] placed, because such men have made the Publick Inte-[192]rest, and their own, all one; and therefore will neither betray, nor desert it, in prosperity or adversity; whereas men of another qualification and temper, if they get into Authority, care not to serve the Publick any further[442], than the publike serves them, and will draw off and on[443] as they find their Opportunity: Yea, and take this for a certain Rule, that if any person be admitted into Power, that loves not the Common-wealth[444], above all other considerations, such a man is (as we say) every mans money; any State-Marchant may have him for a Factor: and for good consideration, he will often make Returns upon the Publike Interest, have a stock going in every Party, and with men of every Opinion, and (if occasion serve) truck with the Common-Enemy, and Common-wealth[445], both together.

But that you may see, I do not speak without book, it is *Aristotles* opinion, as well as mine; who saith, in the first[446] of his *Politicks,* being thus translated, *Per negligentiam mutatur status Reipublicae, cum ad Potestates assumuntur illi qui praesentem statum non amant:* The Form of a Common-wealth[447] is then [193] altered by negligence, when those men are taken into Power, which do not love the present Establishment,* it is not onely a way to preserve a Common-wealth, to avoid those that hate it, but those also are as much to be avoided, that do not love it; that is, who are not earnestly wedded to it by an inward active principle of Affection: And the reason is very evident, because their Affections

---

* Aristotle, *Politics,* V.3.

being of an indifferent Nature, remain ready to run out into any Form, Interest, or Party, that offers it self upon the least alteration or temptation whatsoever. For this, we might give you instance[448] enough, and too much; but waving them, it may suffice, that most of the Broils, Tumults, and Civil Dissentions, that ever hapned in Free-States, have been occasioned by the Ambitious, Treacherous, and Indirect Practices of such persons admitted into Power, as have not been firm in their hearts to the Interest of Liberty.

The truth of this is (omitting many others) to be seen in the Romane State[449], after its Liberty was fully setled in a Succession of the Peoples supream Assemblies.

[194] For the Nobility in the Senate, being men of another Interest (however they pretended) and, sometimes by cunning, sometimes by corrupting, getting Trust from the People, did by combination and complyance with their Fellow-Senators, so garble, perplex, and turmoil the Peoples Affairs, Concernments, and Understandings, that at length, what they could never have done by force, as Opposites, they effected by fraud, as Friends, to deprive the People of a quiet and comfortable enjoyment of their Freedome.

*Faction, Alliance, & Affection is to be avoided in all Elections.* A third Caution is, That in all their Elections of any into the Supream Court, or Councels, they be not led by any bent[450] of Faction, Alliance, or Affection, and that none be taken in, but purely upon the account of merit.

The former course hath ever bin the occasion of discontents, sidings, and Parties.

The latter, stops the mouths of men, that perhaps are contrary minded, and draws the consent and approbation of all the World, when they see men put in Authority, that have a clear re-[195]putation of transcendent Honesty and Wisdom.

A fourth Caution, is, That as it is the secret of Liberty, that all Magistrates, and publike Officers, be kept in an accountable state, liable to render an account of their Behaviour and Actions; and also, that the *That people are to avoid all false charges against persons in Authority.* people have freedom to accuse whom they please: so on the other side, it concerns them, above all things, to avoid false Charges, Accusations, Calumniations[451] against Persons in Authority, which are the greatest abuses and blemishes of Liberty, and have been the most frequent Causes of Tumult and Dissention.

The Banishment, called *Ostracism,* among the *Athenians,* was instituted (at first) upon a just and noble ground: so[452] was that called *Petatism,* among the *Lacedemonians,** to turn such out of the Commonwealth[453], who had rendered themselves suspected against the common Liberty: but yet the abuse of it afterwards proved most pernicious, to the imbroyling of those States with Civil Dissention, when it was perverted by some petulant spirits, to an opposition of some few (and but few) of [196] their best deserving Citizens.

The Romans also, in their state of Liberty, retained this freedom also, of keeping all persons accountable and accusing whom they pleased, but then they were very cautious also, to retain that Decree of the Senate, called, *Turpilianum*[454], in full force and vertue, whereby a severe Fine was set on the Heads of all Calumniators, and false Accusers.†

The due Observation of this Rule preserved that State a long time from Usurpation by men in power on the one side, and from popular clamour and Tumults on the other side.

A fifth Caution is, That, as by all means they should beware of Ingratitude, and unhandsome Returns, to such as have done eminent services for the Common-wealth[455]; So it concerns them, for the publike peace and security, not to impose a Trust in the hands of any person or persons further, than as they may take it back again at pleasure.

*As the people are to avoid ingratitude, so likewise to have a care not to intrust any particular persons, with an unlimited Power.*

The Reason is, because, (as the Proverb saith) *Honores mutant mores,* Honours change mens manners;‡ Accessions, and Continuations of Power and [197] Greatness, expose the mind to temptations: They are Sailes too big for any Bulk of Mortality to steer an even course[456] by.

The Kingdoms of the World, and the Glories of them, are Baites that seldome failes[457] when the Tempter goes a fishing: and none but he, that was more than man, could have refused them. How many Free-States & Common-wealths have paid dear for their Experience in this

---

* Diodorus Siculus, XI.86–87.
† The law, passed in A.D. 61, is described by Tacitus, *Annals,* 14.41.
‡ Proverbial.

particular? who by trusting their own servants too far, have been forced, in the end to receive them for their Masters. Nor is it to be wondred at by any, considering that immoderate Power soon lets in high and ambitious thoughts; and where they are once admitted, no Design so absur'd, or contrary to a mans principles, but he rusheth into it, without the least remorse or consideration: for the Spirit of Ambition, is a Spirit of Giddiness, it foxes men that receive it, and makes them more drunk than the spirit of Wine.

So that were they never so wise, just, and honest before, they afterwards become the contrary, meer sots, *non compos mentis,* being hurried on with-[198]out fear or wit, in all their undertakings: And therefore, without question, it highly concerns a People that have redeemed and rescued their Liberties out of the hands of Tyranny, and are declared a Free-State, so to regulate[458] their Affairs, that all Temptations, and Opportunities of Ambition, may be removed out of the way: or else there follows a necessity of Tumult and Civil Dissention, the common consequence whereof hath ever been a Ruine of the publike Freedome.

This[459] *Caesar,* who first took Arms upon the Publick Score, and became the Peoples Leader, letting in Ambitious Thoughts to his unbounded Power, soon shook hands with his first Friends and Principles, and became another man: so that upon the first fair Opportunity, he turn'd his Armes on the Publick Liberty.

Thus did *Sylla* serve the Senate, and *Marius* also the People, being the same Tyrant, in effect, though not in name, nor in an open manner.

Thus did *Pisistratus* at *Athens, Agathocles* in *Sicily, Cosmos, Soderino,* and *Savaranola* in *Florence, Castrucio* in [199] *Luca,* and others, in many other places: Nor must it be forgotten what the Family of *Orange* would have done in *Holland;* for upon the very same account have Usurpations bin commenced in all *Free-States* throughout the World.[460]

Treason against the Peoples Liberties, not to be pardoned.

[MP 107, 17–24 June 1652]

The Ninth, and last Rule, for preservation of the *Publick Freedome,* is this[461], That it be made an unpardonable Crime, to incur the guilt of Treason against the Interest and Majesty of the People.

And for the clearing of this, it will be requisite to muster up those various Particulars that come within the compass of Treason, according to the Practice, and Opinion of other Nations. The 1. remarkable Treason in old *Rome,* after its *Establishment in a State of Freedome,* was that of *Brutus* his sons, who entered into a formal Conspiracy for the bringing back of the *Tarquins* to the Kingdom by force of Arms.[462]

This *Brutus* was the Founder of the Roman Liberty; and therefore one would have thought the young men might have obtained an easie pardon: But such was the zeal of the Romans, [200] for the preservation of their *Freedom,* that they were all put to death without mercy; and, that all others in time to come, might be deprived of the least hope of being spared upon the like occasion, their own Father was the man most forward to bring them to Execution.

This was Treason in gross: but in after-time, there started up more refined pieces of Treason; as may be collected out of the Actions of *Maelius* and *Manlius,* two persons that had deserved highly of the Common wealth[463]; but especially the latter, who saved it from ruine, when the *Gauls* had besieged the Capitol.

Nevertheless, presuming afterwards upon the People, because of his extraordinary Merits, He, by greating himself beyond the size of a good Citizen; and entertaining Thoughts and Counsels of surprising the Peoples Liberties, was condemned to death; but yet not without the Peoples pitty (as indeed it was an unhappy Necessity, that they should be forced to destroy him that had saved them from destru-[201]ction). To the same end came *Maelius* also, upon the like occasion.

Another sort of Treason there was contrived likewise against that People;

And that was by those Magistrates, called the *Decemviri,* touching whose Actions, and the Ground of their Condemnation, I onely let you know,

That you may be sufficiently informed by other Pens then mine; such as the Historian *Livy, Pomponius, Dionysius,* and others, that have written of the Roman Affaires and Antiquities.

A fourth sort of Treason against that People, was manifest Usurpation, acted over and over, long before the time of *Caesar.*

Some other Particulars also, there were, of less consideration, that came within the compass of Treason; And in all, they were very strict to vindicate the Interest of the Common-Wealth, without respect of Persons.

[202] To those passages out of the old Common-wealth[464] of *Rome*, let us add the rest we have to say about this point, out of the practices of the present State of *Venice*, the most exact for Punctillo's of that[465] Nature that ever was in the World; and therefore, questionless, it is the most principal cause of her so long continuance: It is, there, Death without mercy, for any man to have the least attempt, or thought, of conspiring against the Common-weal, and in several other Cases, as followeth.[466]

Secondly, it is Treason[467] in case any Senator betray Counsels: there it is an unpardonable Crime, and such a mortal sin, that draws on Death without mercy.

This severity also, was retained in the Roman State, where such as became guilty of this Crime, were either[468] burnt alive, or hanged upon a Gibbet: Hereupon, (saith *Valerius Max. lib.* 2.) when any matter was delivered, or debated, it was, as if no man had heard a syllable of what had been said among so many:* From whence it came to pass, that the Decrees of their Senate were called *Tacita*, that is to say; [203] things concealed; because never discovered, untill they came to Execution.[469]

Thirdly, it is Treason, without[470] mercy, for any Senators, or other Officers of *Venice*, to receive Gifts, or Pensions, from any forreign Prince, or State, upon any pretence whatsoever. It was an old Proverb among the Heathens[471], *That the gods themselves might be taken with gifts:* and therefore the consequences must needs be dangerous, in the inferiour Courts of States and Princes; since nothing can be carryed in this Case, according to *Native Interest,* and *Sound Reason;* but onely by Pluralities of Forreign Dictates, and Compliances: But in[472] *Venice* they are so free from this treacherous Impiety, that all States which transact with them, must do it above-board, consult before-hand with their brains, and not

---

* Apparently a reference to Valerius Maximus, *Factorum et Dictorum Memorabilium Libri Novem,* II.1a.

their purses: so that (as *Thuanus** saith) the King of *France* needs not use much labour to purchase an *Interest* with any Prince, or State in *Italy,* unless it be the *Venetian Republick,* where all Forreign Compliances, and Pensioners, are punished with utmost severity; but escape well enough, in other places.

[204] Fourthly, it is Treason for any of her Senators to have any private Conference with Forreign Ambassadors and Agents.[473] It is very observable also, among our Neighbours of the Low-Countries, that one Article of the Charge, whereby they took off *Barnevelts* head, was, for that he held familiarity and converse with the Spanish Ambassador, at the same time when *Spain* was an[474] Enemy.

Thus you have[475] a brief Description of Treason, in the most notable kinds of it, according to the Customes and Opinions of two of the most eminent *Free-States,* (which may serve instead of all the rest) that hath been in the World; who, as a principal Rule and Means for the preservation of *Freedom,* made it a Crime unpardonable, to incur the guilt of Treason, in any of these kinds, against the Interest and Majesty of the People in a *Free-State.*[476]

[MP 108, 24 June–1 July 1652]

We now return to the former[477] main Point of this[478] Discourse, in tracing out the Remainders of those Errours that have been received in the Practice of Policy.

[205] A fourth error in Policy, & which is indeed Epidemical, hath been the Regulation of affaires by Reason of State, not by the[479] strict Rule of Honest.[480] But for fear be[481] mistaken, you are to understand, that by Reason of State here, we do not condemn the equitable Results of prudence and right Reason: for upon determinations of this nature depends the safety of all states, and princes; but that reason of state that flowes from a corrupt principle to an indirect end; that reason of state, which is the states mans reason, or rather his will and lust, when he admits Ambition to be a reason, Perferment, Power, Profit, Revenge, and Opportunity, to be reason, sufficient to put him upon any designe

*Reason of State preferred before Rules of Honesty, is an Error in policy.*

---

* Jacques-Auguste de Thou (1553–1617).

of Action that may tend to the present advantage; though contrary to the Law of God, or the law of common honesty & of Nations.

A more lively description of this strange *Pocus* called Reason of State, take as followeth.[482] It is the most soveraign Commander, & the most important Counsellor. Reason of State is the Care and compass of the ship, the life of a State. That which answers all objections, and quarrels, about Mall [206] government. That's it, which makes[483] War, imposes Taxes, cuts off Offenders, pardons Offenders, sends and treats Ambassadors.

It can say and unsay, do and undo, baulk the Common Road, make High-wayes to become By-wayes, and the furthest about, to become the nearest Cut. If a difficult Knot come to be untied, which neither the Divine by Scripture, nor Lawyer by Case or precedent can untie, then Reason of State, or a hundred wayes more, which Idiots knows not, dissolves it. This is that great Empress which the *Italians* call *Raggione distato*. It can rant as a Souldier, complement as a Monsieur, trick it as a Juggler, strut it as a States man, and is as changable as the Moon, in the variety of her appearances.

But we may take notice of a more excellent way in oppsition to this sandy Foundation of Policy, called *Reason of State*,[484] *viz.* a simple reliance upon God in the vigorous and present actings of all Righteousness, exprest by honest men, in plain language, to this effect; *Fiat justitia, & fractus illabatur Orbis;* Deal uprightly, walke close [207] and real to your promises, and principles, though the Fabrick of Heaven and earth should fall, yet God is able to support, he expects but so much faith as will counterpoise a grain of mustard-seed. Besides, in following singly, a just and righteous principle, a man gains this advantage, that we[485] may go on boldly, with a mind free from that torturing sollicitude of success, (*he is subject to none of those heats and colds,

---

*The text preceding the parenthesis (which is merely a printer's mark) is taken from Charles Hotham, *Corporations Vindicated* (London, 1651), p. 25. Hotham's previous paragraphs (pp. 23–24) themselves reproduce reflections on "reason of state," which Nedham included in *Mercurius Politicus* in July 1651 and which in July 1652 reappeared in the editorial on the same subject that is reproduced here (*LP,* p. 210).

those fits and frights, wherewith men are perpetually vexed, for fear of discovery or miscarriage, when they have once intangled themselves in any by-acting of Engagements[486]) he either prospers, to the great good of his Nation, or else dies with honour and triumph.

But those that follow the other principle of *Humane Invention*, and serve that *Italian* Goddess, *Raggione di Stato*, they may live awhile as gods, but shall die like men, and perish like one of the Princes.

But because words will not serve the turn, take a few Examples of those many, that might be fetcht from all Ages, and Nations. It was *Reason of State*, made *Pharoah* hold the *Israe-*[208]*lites* in bondage, and afterwards, when they were freed, to endeavour to bring them back again to their old slavery: but you know what he came to; It was *Reason of State*, that made *Saul* to spare *Agag*, and plot the ruine of *David*.

It was *Reason of State*, that made *Jeroboam* to set up Calves in *Dan* and *Bethel*.

It was *Reason of State*, (and a shrew'd one too) when *Achitophel* caused *Absalom*, to defile his Fathers Concubines in the sight of all *Israel*. You know what end they both came to. It was the same, that caused *Abner*, first, to take part with the house of *Saul*; and that caused *Joab* to kil him after he came to be his Rival in Fame, and the Favour of *David*: their Ends were both bloudy.

Hence it was, that *Solomon* having pardoned *Adonijah*, thought fit afterwards to put him to death, upon a very slender occasion.

And *Jehu*, though he had Warrant from God to destroy all the house of *Ahab* his Master; yet, because in the Execution of it, he mingled *Reason of State*, in relation to his own *Interest*, [209] and minded the Establishment of himself thereby, more than the Command and Honour of God, in the Execution of Justice: therefore God cursed him for his pains, threatning by the mouth of the Prophet *Hosea*, to avenge the bloud of *Ahabs* family upon the house of *Jehu*.

It was *Reason of State*, that moved *Herod* to endeavour the destruction of Christ, as soon as he was born.

It was *Reason of State* in the Jewes, (lest the Romans should come and take away their Place and Nation) and in *Pilate*, (lest he should be thought no friend to *Caesar*) that made them both joyn in crucifying the Lord of Glory, and incur that heavy Curse, which at length fell upon the Jewish Place and Nation.

It is *Reason* of *State*, that makes the Pope and the Cardinals stick so close one to another, and binds them and the Monarchs of Christendom in one common Interest, for the greatning of themselves, and the inslaving of the People; for which, a sad destruction doth attend them.

[487]It was *Reason of State*, that destroyed so many millions of men (forsooth) in [210] the *Holy War;* that so Princes might not have time to take notice of the Popes Usurpation, nor the People leisure and opportunity to call their Princes to an account for their unbounded Tyranny.

It was *Reason of State,* that was pleaded in behalf[488] of *Borgia,* to justifie all his Villanies, in wading through so much bloud and mischief to a Principality in *Italy;* but he escaped not, to enjoy the fruit of all his labour.

It was the same Devil, that made *Henry* the 4. of *France,* to renounce his Religion, and turn Papist, to secure himself from Popish Reveng; but God punisht him, and sent a Popish Dagger through his heart.

It made *Richard* the Third in *England,* to butcher his own Nephew; for which, vengeance pursued him, being at last tied a thwart a horse back[489], naked and bloudy, like a Calf of the Shambles.

It made *Henry* the 7.[490] to extinguish the Line of *Plantagenet,* and his Son after him, not onely to dabble his hands in the bloud of many, but to persecute[491] the Protestants, notwithstanding that he fell heavy also upon the Papists.

[211] It made his Daughter *Mary* to fill up the measure of her Fathers iniquities, as they could not be expiated by the vertues of her sister, and Successor, whose only fault was, in following Reason of State so far, as to serve the Interest of Monarchy, above that of Religion, by upholding an Order of Prelacy; so that in her the direct Line of that Family ended.

After this, it was wicked Reason of State, that continued Monarchy, and brought in a Scotch-man upon us. This was *James,* who was so great an Admirer of Reason of State, that he adopted it for its own Darling, by the name of *King-craft:* and his Motto, *No Bishop, no King,* shewed, that he prefer'd Reason of State, before the Interest of Religion; as in other things, before honesty: witness, among many other, his quitting the Cause of God, and the *Palatinate*, to keep fair with the house of *Austria*: for which, and for the same Reason of State, put in practice by his Son *Charles*, for the ruine of Religion and Liberty, by a bloudy war, the whole Family hath been brought to a sad destruction.

These[492] Examples are sufficient to [212] shew that Reason of State, prefer'd before the Rule of Honesty, is an Errour in Policy with a vengeance; as they that will not believe, shall be sure to feel it, since it brings unavoidable Ruine, not onely to particular persons, but upon whole Families, and Nations.

## [MP 109, 1–8 July 1652]

A fifth Errour in Policy hath been this, *viz.* a permitting of the Legislative and Executive Powers of a State, to rest in one and the same hands and persons. By the Legislative Power, we understand the Power of making, altering, or repealing Laws, which in all well-ordered Governments, hath ever been lodged in a succession of the supream Councels of Assemblies of a Nation.

*A uniting of the Legislative and Executive Powers in one and the same hands, an Errour in Policy.*

By the Exccutive Power, we mean that Power which is derived from the other, and by their Authority transfer'd into the hand or hands of one Person, (called a Prince) or into the hands of many (called States) for the administration of Government, in the Execution of those Laws. In the keeping of these two Powers distinct, flowing in distinct Channels, so that they may never meet in one, save upon [213] some short extraordinary occasion consists the safety of a State.[493]

The Reason is evident; because if the Law-makers, (who ever have the Supream Power) should be also the constant Administrators and Dispencers of Law and Justice, then (by consequence) the People would be left without Remedy, in case of Injustice, since no Appeal can lie under Heaven against such as have the Supremacy; which, if once admitted, were inconsistent with the very intent and natural import of true Policy: which ever supposeth, that men in Power may be unrighteous; and therefore (presuming the worst) points alwayes, in all determinations, at the Enormities and Remedies of Government, on the behalf of the People.

For the clearing of this, it is worthy your observation; that in all Kingdomes and States whatsoever, where they have had any thing of Freedom among them, the Legislative and Executive Powers have been managed in distinct hands: That is to say, the Law-makers have set down Laws, as Rules of Government; and then put Power into the hands of others (not their own) to govern by those Rules; by [214] which means the people were happy, having no Governours, but such as were liable to give an account of Government to the supream Councel of Law-makers. And on the other side, it is no less worthy of a very serious observation; That Kings and standing States never became absolute over the People, till they brought both the making and execution of Lawes into their own hands: and as this Usurpation of theirs took place by degrees, so unlimited Arbitrary Power crept up into the Throne, there to domineer o're the World, and defie the Liberties of the People.

*Cicero,* in his second Book *de Offic.* and his third, *de Legibus,* speaking of the first institution of Kings, tells us, how they were at first left to govern at their own discretion without Laws.* Then their Wills[494], and their Words, were Law, the making and execution of Lawes was in one and the same hands.

But what was the consequence? Nothing but Injustice, and Injustice without Remedy, till the People were taught by Necessity to ordain Lawes, as Rules whereby they ought to go-[215]vern. Then began the meeting of the People successively in their supream Assemblies, to make Laws; whereby Kings (in such places as continued under the Kingly Form) were limited and restrained, so that they could do nothing in Government, but what was agreeable to Law; for which they were accountable, as well as other Officers were in other Forms of Government, to those supream Councels and Assemblies: Witness all the old stories of *Athens, Sparta,* and other Countries of *Greece,* where you shall find, that the Law-making, and the Law-executing Powers,

* Cicero, *De Officiis,* II.12; *De Legibus,* III.4–5.

were placed in distinct hands under every Form of Government: For, so much of Freedom they retained still under every Form, till they were both swallowed up (as they were several times) by an absolute Domination.

In old *Rome*, we find *Romulus* their first King cut in[495] pieces by the Senate, for taking upon him to make and execute Laws at his own pleasure. And *Livy* tells us, that the reason why they expel'd *Tarquin* their last King, was, because he took the Executive and Legislative Powers both into his own [216] hands, making himself both Legislator and Officer, *inconsulto Senatu*, without advice, and in defiance of the Senate.*

Kings[496] being cashiered, then their Standing-Senates[497] came in play, who making and executing Laws, by Decrees of their own, soon grew intolerable, and put the people upon divers desperate Adventures, to get the Legislative Power out of their hands, and place it in their own; that is, in a succession of their Supream Assemblies: But the Executive Power they left, part in the hands of Officers of their own, and part in the Senate; in which State it continued some hundreds of years, to the great happiness and content of all, till the Senate by sleights and subtilties got both Powers into their own possession again, and turned all into confusion.

Afterwards, their Emperors (though Usurpers) durst not at first turn both these Powers into the Channel of their own unbounded Will; but did it by degrees, that they might the more insensibly deprive the people of their Liberty, till at length they openly made and executed Laws at their own [217] pleasures, being both Legislators and Officers, without giving an account to any: and so there was an end of the Roman Liberty.

To come nearer home, let us look into the old Constitution of the Common-wealths[498], and Kingdomes of Europe: We find in the *Italian States; Venice*, which having the Legislative and Executive Power, confined within the narrow Pale of its Nobility in the Senate, is not so free as once *Florence* was with *Siena, Millan*, and the rest; before their

---

* Livy, *Ab Urbe Condita*, I.49.7.

Dukes, by arrogating both those Powers to themselves, worm'd them out of their Liberty.

Of all those States there, onely *Genoa* remains in a free posture, by keeping the *Power* of Legislation onely in their supream Assemblies, and leaving the Execution of Law in a titular Duke, and a Councel, the keeping of these Powers asunder within their proper Sphere, is one principal Reason why they have been able to exclude Tyranny out of their own State, while it hath run the Round in *Italy*.

What made the Grand Seignior absolute of old, but his ingrossing both these[499] Powers? and of late [218] the Kings of *Spain* and *France?* In ancient time the case stood far otherwise; for in *Ambrosio Morales* his Chronicle* you will finde, that in *Spain* the Legislative power was lodged onely in their supreme Councel[500], and their King was no more but an elective Officer, to execute such Laws as they made, and in case of failing[501], to give them an accompt, and submit to their judgements, which was the common practice; as you may see also in *Mariana:*† It was so also in *Aragon,* till it was united to *Castile,* by the Mariage of *Ferdinand,* and *Isabel;* and then both States soon lost their liberty, by the projects of *Ferdinand* and his successors, who drew the powers of Legislation and Execution of Law, within the verge and influence of the Prerogative Royall: whilest these two powers were kept distinct, then these States were free; but the ingrossing of them in one and the same hands, was the losse of their Freedom.[502]

*France* likewise was once as free as any Nation under Heaven: though the King of late hath done all, and been all in all, till the time of *Lewis* [219] the eleventh: he was no more but an Officer of State, regulated by Law, to see the Laws put in execution; and the Legislative Power

* Professor of Rhetoric at Alcalá de Henares, Morales (1513–91) was appointed *Cronista Real* in 1556. His *La Crónica General de España* was published in 1574. Morales may have been a source of Nedham's remarks on the constitution of Aragon in the same paragraph.

† Juan de Mariana (1536–1624), Spanish Jesuit priest and historian. Nedham may have had particularly in mind his *De Rege* (Toledo, 1599); or his *Historiae de rebus Hispaniae* (Toledo, 1592–1605), perhaps especially bk. 25. On him see Harald E. Braun, *Juan de Mariana and Early Modern Spanish Political Thought* (Aldershot, U.K.: Ashgate, 2007).

(that) rested in the Assembly of the 3. Estates; but *Lewis,* by snatching both these Powers into the single hands of himselfe, and his successors, rookt them of their Liberty; which they may now recover again, if they have but so much manhood, as to reduce the two Powers into their ancient, or into better Channels.

This pattern of *Lewis* was followed close by the late King of *England*[503], who by our ancient Laws, was the same here, that *Lewis* ought to have been in *France,* an Officer in trust, to see to the execution of the Lawes: but by aiming at the same ends which *Lewis* attained, and straining, by the ruine of Parliaments, to reduce the Legislative Power, as well as the Executive into his own hands, he instead of an absolute Tyranny, which might have followed his project, brought a swift destruction upon himself and[504] Family.

Thus you see it appears, that the keeping of these two Powers distinct, [220] hath[505] been a ground preservative of the peoples Interest, whereas their uniting hath been its ruine all along in so many Ages and Nations.

## [MP 110, 8–15 July 1652]

A sixth errour in *Policy,* observable in the practices of other times and Nations, hath been a reducing transactions, and in Interest[506] of the Publick, into the disposition and power of a few particuler persons. The ill consequences whereof have ever bin these; that matters were not wont to be carried by fair, friendly, and legal[507] debates, but by Design and Surprisal; not by freedom, and consent of the people, in their open Assemblies; but according to the premeditated Resolutions, and forestalments of Crafty projectors in private Cabinets, and Junto's; not according to the true Interest of State, but in order to the serving of mens ends; not for the benefit, and improvement of the people, but to keep them under as ignorant of true Liberty, as the Horse and Mule; that they might be Bridled and Sadled, & Ridden, under the wise pretences of being Governed and kept in Order. But the Grand and worse consequences of all, hath been this; [221] that such Colleagues, Partners, and Ingrossers of Power having once brought about their ends by lying

*Affairs of State transacted by a few, is an Errour in Policy.*

practies upon the people; have ever faln into fits of Emulation against themselves, and the next design hath ever bin to rook their fellows, and rid themselves of competitors; so that at length they have been their own executioners, and ruined one another. And had it been only the destruction of themselves, the matter were not considerable; but the people having by this means been torn with Civill dissentions, and the miseries of War, by being drawn into Parties, according to their severall humors and affections; the usuall event ever was, that in the end they have been seized as the prey of some single Tyrant.

An example of this there was in the State of *Athens,* under the Government of those thirty men, who usurped the power into their own hands, and were afterwards called the thirty Tyrants, for their odious behaviour; for *Xenophon* tells us, that they drew the determinations of all things into their own Closets, but seemed to manage them, *calculis & suffragiis Plebis,* [222] by the Votes of the people, which they had brought to their own devotion in the Assembly, to countenance their proceedings.* And their custom was, if any sort of men complained, and murmured at their doings, or appeared for the Publique, immediately to snap them off by the losse of life or fortune, under a pretence of being seditious, and turbulent fellows against the peace of their Tyranny. These Juncto-men had not been many moneths in possession, but they began to quarrel with one another; and the reason why the game went not on, against one another, was because the people took it out of their hands, and diverted the course of their spleen against each other, into a care of mutuall defence, they being assaulted on every side, by popular arms and clamors, for the recovery of liberty. So you see the event of these thirty mens combination, was no lesse then a civill War; and it ended in their banishment. But as great a mischief followed, for a new Junto of ten men got into their places, whose Government proving little lesse odious than the former, gave an occasion to new [223] changes, which never left shifting, till at last they fell into a single Tyranny. And the wilder sort of people, having by a sad experience, felt the fruits of their own error, in following the lusts and parties of particular

* Xenophon, *Hellenica,* II.iii.

powerful persons, grew wise; and combining with the honester sort, they all as one man, set their shoulders to the work, and restored the primitive Majesty, and Authority of their supreme Assemblies.

*Herodotus* in his second Book, tells us, that Monarchy being abolished in *Egypt*, after the death of King *Setho*, and a Declaration published for the freedom of the people, immediately the Administration of all Affaires was ingross't in the hands of twelve Grandees, who having made themselves secure against the people, in a few years fell to quarrelling with one another, (as the manner is) about their share[508] in the Government. This drew the people into severall parties, and so a civill Warre ensued; wherein *Psammeticus* (one of the twelve) having slain all his Partners, left the people in the lurch, and instead of a free State, seated himself in the pos-[224]session of a single Tyranny.*

But of all old instances, the most famous are the two Triumvirates that were in *Rome*. The first was that of *Pompey, Caesar,* and *Crassus,* who having drawn the affairs of the Empire, and the whole World into their own particular hands, acting and determining all in a private Junto of their own, without the advice or consent of the Senate and people, unless it were now and then to make stalking horses of them, for the more clearly[509] conveyance of some unpleasing design: These men, having made an agreement among themselves, that nothing should be done in the Commonwealth[510], but what pleased their own humor, it was not long ere the spirit of Ambition set them flying at the faces of one another, and drew the whole World upon the Stage, to act that bloody Tragedy, whose Catastrophe was the death of *Pompey,* and the Dominion[511] of *Caesar.* The second Triumvirate was erected after the fatall stab given to *Caesar* in the Senate, between *Octavius* (afterwards Emperor by the name of *Augustus,*) *Lepidus,* and *Antony:* these having drawn all [225] Affairs into their own hands, and shared the World between them, presently fell abandying against one another. *Augustus* picking a quarrell with *Lepidus,* gave him a lift out of his Authority, and confined him to a close imprisonment in the City. This being done first, he had the more hope and opportunity next for the outing

* Herodotus, *Histories,* II.141–53.

of *Anthony:* he picks a quarrel with him too, begins a new civill Warre, wherein *Rome* and a great part of the World was engaged to serve his ambition; and things being brought to the decision of a Battell, and the ruine of *Anthony,* he afterwards seated, and secured himself in the injoyment of a single Tyranny.

Omitting many other instances, here in *England,* it is worthy observation, that in the great contest between *Henry* the third, and the Barons, about the liberties of themselves and the people, the King being forced at length to yield, the Lords, instead of freeing the Nation indeed, ingrossed all power into their own hands, under the name of the Twenty-foure Conservators of the Kingdom, and behaved themselves like *totidem.* [226] *Tyranny,* so many Tyrants, acting all in their own Names, and in Junto's of their own, wholly neglecting, or else overruling Parliaments. But then not agreeing among themselves, there were three or four of them defeated the other twenty, and drew the intire management of Affairs into their own hands, *viz.* the Earles of *Leicester, Gloucester, Hereford,* and *Spencer;* yet it continued so not long; for, *Leicester* getting all into his own power, fell at enmity with *Gloucester,* and was defeated[512] by him.

At length, *Leicester* putting his Fortune to a Battel, was slain; and the King thereupon, getting all power back again took advantage of that opportunity for the greatning of himself, and Prerogative.

And so you see, All that the people got by the effusion of their bloud, and loss of their peace, was, That instead of one Tyrant, they had Twenty Four, and then Four; and after them, a single Usurper, (which was *Montfort,* Earl of *Leicester*) and he being gone, they were forced to serve their old Tyrant *Henry* the Third again, who by this means, became the more secure and [227] firm in his Tyranny: whereas if they had dealt like men of honour, and made the Nation as free as they pretended, not ingrossing all into[513] their own private hands, but instating the liberty of *England,* Paramount above the regall prerogative, in a due and constant course of successive Parliaments, (without which, liberty is but a meere name and shadow) then all the succeeding inconveniences had been surely prevented: the bloody bickering afterwards might have been avoided, their own persons and honors preserved, Kings either cashiered or regulated, as they ought to have been, and the whole Nation freed from those after-gripes and pangs, inflicted by that *Henry* and his corrupt Line of successors.[514]

The World affords many instances of this kinde, but these are sufficient to manifest the fatall consequences that have happened, in permitting publick transactions and interests to be ingrossed, and rest in the power of a few particuler persons, and that it deserves to be markt (as one saith) with a black Cole, as a most pernitious error in Policy.[515]

[MP III, 15–22 July 1652]

[228] A seventh error in Policy, is the driving[516] of Factions and Parties. Now that you may know what Faction is, and which is the factious Party in any State or Kingdom, afflicted with that infirmity: the onely way is first to finde out the true and declared Interest of State; and then if you observe any Designes, Counsels, Actings, or Persons, moving in opposition to that which is the true publick Interest, it may be infallibly concluded, that there lies the Faction, and the factious Party, which is so much the more dangerous, in regard it not only afflicts and tears Common-wealths[517] with divisions and discords at home, but in the end exposes them to the mercy (or rather) the malice[518] of some publick enemy, either at home, or from abroad, and brings a sad desolation, and ruine upon the Estates, lives, and liberties of the people.

There is a notable faction we read of in this *Roman* story, which was that of the *Decemviri,* who being intrusted with the Government, and the time of their trust expired, they instead of making a Resignation, combined together for the Perpetuation of [229] the power in their own hands, contrary to the intent of their first Election, and in defiance of that which twelve moneths before had been declared the interest of the Commonwealth.[519] The grand Engineer among them was *Appius Claudius,* who managed his designe by promising the Nobility, that if they would stick to the *Decemviri,* then the *Decemviri* would stick to them, and joyn with them, in keeping under the people and their Tribunes, and to defeat them of their successive Assemblies. By this means he sowed the seeds of an immortall enmity between the Senate and the people; though himself and his Collegues were notwithstanding deceived of their own establishment, and soon cashiered from their imperious Domination.[520]

Driving of Faction and Parties, a main Errour in Policy.

If we consider also what befell *Carthage*[521], and how it came to ruine: the story tells us, it was occasioned by their Factions, the whole Senate being divided betwixt two potent Families of *Hannibal* and *Hanno;* by which means they were disinabled, from carrying on their Warre with Unanimity[522] and alacrity, as was requi-[230]site against such wary Gamesters, as the *Romans,* who made such use of their Civil Dissentions, that they soon laid the glory of that famous Republick in the dust.

It was Faction and Civil Dissention that destroyed *Rome* itself; that is to say, her Liberty, and made her stoop under the Yoak of *Caesar.*

And it must not be omitted, that when her Liberty was first established, and *Tarquin* expelled, he had like to have made his way back again, by reason of their Divisions. And though he mist his aym there, yet *Pisistratus,* another Tyrant, being driven out of *Athens,* made a shift to get in again, by reason of their mutual Divisions.[523]

It was the same Devil of Faction, and Civil Dissention, (as *Philip de Comines* tells us) that made way for the Turk into *Hungaria,** as it let him in before into *Constantinople,* that admitted the *Goths* and *Vandals* into *Spain* and *Italy;* the *Romans* into *Jerusalem,* first under *Pompey;* and afterwards under *Vespasian* and *Titus.*

It was the cause why *Genoa,* for a time, was content to submit to the Family of *Sforza,* Dukes of *Millan.* It [231] brought the *Spaniard* into *Sicily* and *Naples;* and the *French* once into *Millain,* where they outed the aforenamed Family of *Sforza.*[524]

From hence, therefore, let us conclude, that no Errour is more dangerous, no Treason more pernicious to a Common-wealth[525], than the driving of Faction.

### [MP 112, 22–29 July 1652]

Breach of Vows and Promises, a main Error in Policy.

An Eighth and last Errour, observable in practice[526] of Times, and Nations, hath been a violation of Faith, Principles, Promises, and Engagements, upon every Turn of Time, and advantage. An Impiety that ought to be exploded out of all Nations, that bear the Name of

* Philippe de Commynes, *Memoires,* bk. 12, chap. 6.

Christians[527]: And yet we find it often pass, among the less discerning sort of men, for admirable Policy: and those Impostors that used it, have had the luck to be esteemed the onely Politicians. But yet, lest so many wise men of the World, as have been given up to this monstrous vanity, should be thought to have no reason for it, I remember, I find it usually exprest in *Machiavel,* to be this,[528] becaus the greatest part of the world being wicked, unjust, deceitful, full of treachery and circumvention, there is a Necessity [232] that those which are down-right, and confine themselves to the strict Rule of Honesty, must ever look to be over-reached by the Knavery of others. And take this for certain, (saith he) *Qui se virum bonum omnibus partibus profiteri studet, eum certè inter tot non bonos periclitari necesse est.** He which endeavours to approve himself an honest man to all parties, must of necessity miscarry among so many that are not honest: Because some men are wicked and perfidious, I must be so too. This is a sad inference, and fit onely for the practice of *Italy,* where he wrote it.

The ancient Heathen would have loathed this; and the *Romans* (who were the noblest of them all) did in all their actions detest it, reckoning plain honesty to have been the onely Policy, and the foundation of their Greatness, (*Favendo pietati fideique, populus Romanus ad tantum fastigii pervenerit*). The people of *Rome* attained to so great a height, by observing Faith and Piety: whereof you shall see[529] an Instance or two.

In the War between them, and *Porsena* King of the *Tuscans,* it so happ-[233]ened, that their City was besieged by *Porsena:* but peace being made, upon some advantagious Conditions for the *Tuscans,* the *Romanes,* for the performance of their[530] Conditions, were forced to yield up divers Noble Virgins.

These Virgins, after some time, made an escape from the *Tuscans,* and came back to *Rome,* but were demanded again.

Hereupon the Senate, though they were then recovered, and in a posture, able to have defied the *Tuscans,* and denied the performance of those harsh Conditions, chose rather to preserve their Faith

---

* Machiavelli, *Nicholas Machiavel's Prince,* trans. Dacres (London, 1640), chap. 18.

inviolable, then to take the present advantage; and so delivered up the Virgins.

The behaviour also of *Attilius Regulus,* is very memorable, who being prisoner at *Carthage,* and condemned to a cruel Death, was, notwithstanding, permitted to go to *Rome,* upon his bare Paroll, to propound certain Terms to the Senate; which if they yielded, then he was to have his liberty: if not, he was to return again to *Carthage,* and to suffer.[531]

The Senate not yielding, He, rather [234] then violate his Faith, did return and suffer, being put into a Barrel spiked with Nails, and tumbled down a Hill by the *Carthagenians.* Nor was it the temper onely of a few persons; but general throughout the whole Nation, as might be shown by innumerable Examples; especially in their Leagues and Treaties with other Nations.[532]

### [MP 113, 29 July–5 Aug. 1652]

[533]But that you may the better know, and avoid the impious Impostors, I shall[534] represent them in *Machiavels* own language; who in that unworthy book of his, entituled, *The Prince,* hath made a most unhappy Description of the Wiles that have been used by those Jugglers; and thereby left a Lesson upon Record, which hath been practised ever since by all the State-Rooks in *Christendom.* And therefore, since they have made so ill use of it, I suppose the best way to prevent the further operation of the poyson, is, to set it down here before you, (as I shall do *verbatim*[535], without adding, or diminishing a syllable) and then make two or three Inferences thereupon, for the practice of the people.*

*In what manner Princes ought to keep their Words.* How commenda-[235]ble[536] in a Prince it is to keep his Word, and live with Integrity, not making use of Cunning and Subtilty, every one knows well: Yet we see by Experience, in these our dayes, that those Princes have effected great matters, who have made small reckoning of keeping their

---

* Nedham makes very minor adjustments to the translation of chap. 18 by Edward Dacres in *Nicholas Machiavel's Prince.*

words, and have known by their Craft, how to turn and wind men about, and in the end overcome those who have grounded upon the Truth.

You must then know, there are two kinds of Combating or Fighting: the one, by Right of the Laws: the other, meerly by Force. That first way is proper to Men: The other is also common to Beasts. But because the first many times suffices not, there is a necessity to make recourse to the second: wherefore, it behoves a Prince to know how to make good use of that part which belongs to a Beast, as well as that which is proper to a Man.

This part hath been covertly shew'd to Princes by antient Writers; who say, that *Achilles,* and many others of those antient Princes, were intrusted to *Chiron* the *Centaure,* to be brought up under his Discipline: The morall [236] of this, having for their Teacher, one that was half a Beast, and half a Man, was nothing else, but that it was needful for a Prince to understand how to make his advantage of the one, and other Nature, because neither could subsist without the other.

A Prince then being necessitated to know how to make use of that part belonging to a Beast, ought to serve himself of the Conditions of the Fox, and the Lyon; for the Lyon cannot keep himself from Snares, nor the Fox defend himself against the Wolves. He had need then be a Fox, that he may beware of the Snares; and a Lyon, that he may scare the Wolves. Those that stand wholly upon the Lyon, understand not themselves.

And therefore a wise Prince cannot, nor ought not to keep his Faith given, when the observance thereof turnes to disadvantage, and the occasions that made him promise, are past: for if men were all good, this Rule would not be allowable; but being they are full of mischief, and will not make it good to thee, neither art thou tied to keep it with them: nor shall a Prince ever want lawfull occasions to [237] give colour to this breach. Very many modern Examples hereof might be alleadged, wherein might be shewed, how many Peaces concluded, and how many Promises made, have been violated and broken by Infidelity of Princes; and ordinarily things have best succeeded with him that hath bin nearest the Fox in condition.

But it is necessary to understand, how to set a good colour upon this Disposition, and be able to feign and dissemble throughly; and men are so simple, and yield so much to the present Necessities, that he who hath a mind to deceive, shall alwayes find another that will be deceived. I will not conceal any of the Examples that have been of late; *Alexander* the sixth never did any thing else, than deceive men, and never meant otherwise, and always found whom to work upon; yet never was there man that would protest more effectually, nor aver any thing with more solemn Oaths, and observe them less then he: nevertheless, his Couzenage thrived well with him, for he knew how to play his part cunningly.

[238] Therefore is there no necessitie for a Prince to be endued with all those above written qualities, but it behoves well that he seeme to be so: or rather I will boldly say this, that having those qualities, and alwaies regulating himself by them, they are hurtfull; but seeming to have them, they are advantageous, as to seeme pittyfull, faithfull, milde, religious, and indeed to be so (provided with all thou beest of such a composition, that if need require thee to use the contrary, thou canst, and know'st how to apply thy selfe thereto). And it suffices to conceive this, that a Prince, and especially a new Prince, cannot observe all these things, for which men are held good, he being often forced, for the maintenance of his State, to do contrary to his faith, charity, humanity, and religion. And therefore it behoves him to have a mind so disposed as to turn and take the advantage of all winds and fortunes; and as formerly I said, not forsake the good while he can; but to know to make use of the evil upon necessity. A Prince then ought to have a speciall care, that he never let fall any words, but what [239] are all seasoned with the five above written qualities: and let him seem to him that sees and knows him, all pitty, all faith, all integrity, all humanity, all religion; nor is there any thing more necessarie for him to seem to have, than the last quality: for all men in generall judge thereof, rather by the sight than by the touch; for every man, may come to the sight of him, few come to the touch and feeling of him; every man may come to see what thou seemest; few come to understand and perceive what thou art: and those few dare not oppose the opinion of many, who have the

Majesty of state to protect them. And in all mens actions, especially those of Princes, wherein there is no judgment to appeal unto, men forbear to give their censures till the events, and ends of thing. Let a Prince therefore take the surest courses he can to maintaine his life and state, the meanes shall alwaies be thought honorable, and commended by every one: for the vulgar is ever taken with the appearance and event of a thing, and for the most part of the people, they are but the vulgar, the others that are [240] but few, take place where the vulgar have no subssistence. A Prince there is in these daies, whom I shall not do well to name, that preaches nothing but peace and faith, but had he kept the one and the other, severall times had they taken from him his State and reputation.*

This is the old Court Gospel, which hath gained many thousand of Proselytes, among the great ones, from time to time, and the inferences arising thence in behalfe of the people, in briefe are these: That since the great ones of the world, have been very few that have avoyded this doctrine, therefore it concerns the people to keep a strict hand and eie upon them all, and impose not overmuch or long confidence in any.

If the Right of laws be the way of men, and force of beasts and great ones, not onely advised, but inclined to the latter, then it concernes any Nation or people to secure themselves, and keep Great men from degenerating into beasts, by holding up of law, liberty, priviledge, birthright, elective power, against the [241] ignoble beastly way of powerfull domination.

If of all beasts, a Prince should some times resemble the Lyon, and somtimes the Fox, then people ought to observe great ones in both the disguises, and be sure to cage the Lyon, and unkennel the Fox, and never leave till they have stript the one, and unrais'd the other.

If a Prince cannot, and ought not to keep his faith given, when the observance thereof turnes to disadvantage, and the occasions that made him promise, are past; then it is the Interest of the people, never to trust any Princes, nor ingagements and promises of men in power,

---

* The passage from Machiavelli ends here.

but ever to preserve a power within themselves, either to reject them, or to hold them to the performance whether they will or no. And if Princes shall never want occasions to give colour to this breach, then also it concernes the people, ever to make sure of the Instance, and not suffer themselves to be deluded with colours, shadows, and meere pretences.

Lastly, if it be necessarie for great ones to fain and dissemble throughly; [242] because men are so simple and yield so much to the present necessity (as *Machiavel* saith;)* and in regard he that hath a mind to deceive, shall alwayes finde another that will be deceived: then it concerns any people or Nation, to make a narrow search ever into the men, and their pretences and necessities, whether they be fained or not; and if they discover any deceipt hath been used, then they deserve to be slaves, that will be deceived any longer.[537] Thus I have noted the prime Errors of Government, and Rules of Policy. I shall now conclude with a word of Advice, in order to the chusing of the Supreme Assemblies.

### [MP 74, 30 Oct.–6 Nov. 1651]

Since[538] it appears, that the right, liberty, welfare, and safety of a people, consists in a due succession of their supreme Assemblies: surely then, the right constitution and orderly motion of them, is of the greatest consequence that can be, there being so much imbarqued in this Vessel, that if it should miscarry, all is irreparably lost, unless it can be recovered again out of the Sea of confusion. Therefore, as at all times there ought to be an [243] especiall care had to the Composure and Complexion of those great Assemblies, so much more after the confusion of a Civil Warre, where it is ever to be supposed, there will be many discontented humours a working, and labouring to insinuate themselves into the body of the people, to undermine the settlement and security of the Common-wealth, that by gaining an interest and share with the better sort, in the supreme Authority, they may attain those corrupt ends of Policy, which were lost by Power.

* Machiavelli, *Prince,* chap. 18.

In this case without question, there are severall men that ought to be taken into a strict consideration: There is the old Malignant and the new; against whom, not only the doores are to be shut, but every hole and cranny ought to be stopt, for fear they creep into Authority. There is likewise a tame Beast, more dangerous than the other two, which is that Amphibious animal, the neutrall of *Laodicea*,* that can live in either Element, sail with any winde on every point of the compasse, and strike in with Malignants of every sort, upon any occasion.

[244] This[539] is he that will undoe all, if he be not avoided; for in the form of an Angel of Light, he most slightly carries on the works of darkness. Let not him then, as to our present case, be so much as named upon an Election. Thus much for the Constitution of the supreme Assembly, or the manner of setling Authority upon the close of a Civil Warre, for the recovery of Liberty. What remains then, but that upon due caution for excluding the wilde Geese and the tame, the Malignant and the Neutrall, such a people may reasonably be put into possession of their right and interest in the Legislative power, and of all injoyment of it, in a succession of their supreme Assemblies.[540]

The onely way[541] to preserve liberty in the hands of a people, that have gained it by the Sword, is to put it in the peoples hands, that is, into the hands of such, as by a contribution of their purses, strength, and counsells, have all along asserted it, without the least stain of corruption, staggering, or apostasie; for in this case, these only are to be reckoned the people: the rest having either by a trayterous En-[245]gagement, Compliance, Neutrality, or Apostasie, as much as in them lies, destroyed the people, and by consequence made a forfeiture of all their Rights and immunities, as Members of a people. In this case therefore men ought to have a courage; and to have a care of the course of Election, and trust God with the success of a righteous Action; for nothing can be more righteous and necessary, than that a people should be put into possession of their native right and freedom: However, they may abuse it, it is their right to have it, and the want of it is a greater inconvenience, and drawes greater inconveniencies after it,

* Revelation 3:14–17.

than any can be pretended to arise from the injoyment, though they were presented in a multiplying glasse, to the eyes of discerning men. But now, as this holds true at all times, in all Nations, upon the like occasions of Liberty newly purchased, so much more in any Nation, where freedom, in a successive course of the peoples Assemblies, hath once been solemnly acknowledged and declared to be the interest of the Commonwealth; for, then a depriving [246] the people of their due, is a foundation for broils and divisions; and as *Cicero* defines faction to be a deviation from the declared interest of State: so in this case, if it happen that any shall desert a Common-wealth in its declared Interest, they immediately lose the name and honour of Patriots, and become Parties in a Faction.

# APPENDIX A

## The Edition of 1656

### TEXTUAL EMENDATIONS

I have made the following emendations to the text of 1656 (see p. cvi).

*Page and line*

| | | | |
|---|---|---|---|
| 9/5 | gate | *to* | gait |
| 14/15 | *an Oath | | an Oath |
| 14/margin | *Oaths | | Oaths |
| 21/23 | yeild | | yield |
| 32/12 | *tircenses* | | *circenses* |
| 33/21 | play after; | | play; after |
| 37/35 | Patrocian | | Patrician |
| 38/22 | and in Interests | | and Interests |
| 53/30 | Convenience: | | Convenience): |
| 85/15 | Emiliam | | Emilian |
| 85/19 | with doubt | | without doubt |
| 86/20 | own family | | one family |
| 87/15 | whertas | | whereas |
| 91/15 | Tragdeies | | Tragedies |
| 91/24 | trajicito | | trajicitio |
| 105/18 | *Free-State,* | | *Free-State.* |
| 106/4 | Commudaer | | Commander |
| 113/22 | freindly | | friendly |

| | | |
|---|---|---|
| 113/25 | prijectors | projectors |
| 115/8 | people in a few years, | people, in a few years |

## ADVERTISEMENT

At the back of the 1656 edition of *The Excellencie,* the publisher, Thomas Brewster, supplies an advertisement, or "Catalogue of Bookes." It lists three volumes (of which the third was an anonymous publication):

Sir Henry Vane, *The Retired Mans Meditations*

Thomas May, *A Breviary of the History of the Parliament of England*

*Lazarus and His Sisters Discourse of Paradice*

All three books were published in "1655," that is, by the modern calendar, between March 1655 and March 1656. Vane's book can be confidently dated to early July. Thomas May's book was a second edition.

# The Edition of 1767

## TITLE PAGE

---

## The Excellencie of a Free State

LONDON PRINTED FOR
A. MILLAR AND T. CADELL IN THE STRAND,
G. KEARSLY IN LUDGATE STREET, AND
H. PARKER IN CORNHILL.
MDCCLXVII

## THE PREFACE

---

### PREFACE TO THIS EDIT.

On the subject of government, no country hath produced writings so numerous and valuable as our own. It hath been cultivated and adorned by men of greatest genius, and most comprehensive understanding, MILTON, HARRINGTON, SYDNEY, LOCKE, names famous to all ages.

But, beside their incomparable writings, many lesser treatises on the same argument, which are little known, and extremely scarce, deserve to be read and preserved: in which number may be reckoned the small volume I now give the public, written by MARCH-AMONT NEDHAM, a man, in the judgment of some, inferior only to MILTON.

It was first inserted in the *Mercurius Politicus,* that celebrated state-paper, published "in defence of the Commonwealth, and for the information of the people"; and soon after re-printed in 12 mo,* under the following title, "The Excellencie of a Free-State. Or, The right constitution of a Commonwealth. Wherein all objections are answered, and the best way to secure the people's liberties discovered. With some errors of government, and rules of policie. Published by a well-wisher to posteritie. London, printed for Thomas Brewster, at the west end of Paul's, 1656."

An account of the author may be seen in *A. Wood's Athenae Oxonienses,* tho' drawn in bitterness of wrath and anger. If this volume shall be favorably received, the editor will go on to give other rare treatises on government in his possession, to the entertainment and benefit, as he hopes, of the public.

Reader, farewel,

Richard Baron

Below Blackheath, Jan. 1, 1767

TEXTUAL ADJUSTMENTS

Below is a list of the alterations made in 1767 to the text of 1656. Apart from the alterations, the edition of 1767 is faithful to the original, except that it overhauls the spelling and the use of capital letters, changes that I have not recorded. Some obvious misprints corrected in 1767 are also corrected in the present edition: see Appendix A, pp. 127–28.

Changes made in 1767 that revert to the text of *Mercurius Politicus* (whether or not with the knowledge of Richard Baron or Thomas Hollis) are asterisked (*).

* Today we would say a small octavo.

*Page and line [of this volume]*

| | *1656* | *1767* |
|---|---|---|
| 23/24 | Virginus | Virginius* |
| 33/21 | play after; | play; after* |
| 37/35 | Patrocian | Patrician* |
| 38/22 | and in Interests | and interests* |
| 40/18 | transform | to transform* |
| 40/26 | banded | bandied* |
| 41/25 | Hungaria | Hungary* |
| 41/30 | Casimira | Casimir*† |
| 44/29 | principal | principle* |
| 56/32 | their secrets | the secrets |
| 60/26 | (which . . . Empire.) | which . . . empire. |
| 68/26 | Antonies | Antonius* |
| 82/21 | notice to be taken of | to be taken notice of* |
| 85/13 | Emiliam | Emilian |
| 86/20 | own family | one family* |
| 87/15 | whertas | whereas |
| 91/24 | trajicito | trajicitio |
| 93/13 | nuzled | nursled |
| 101/29 | failes | fail* |
| 102/18 | This Caesar | Thus Caesar* |
| 101/5 | Petalism | Petatism |
| 113/19 | and Interest | and the interests‡ |
| 113/22 | freindly | friendly* |
| 115/8 | people in a few years, fell | people, in a few years fell |

On four occasions an asterisk was used in the text of 1767 to identify, in a corresponding footnote, "the late king" as Charles I. The text of 1656 has a new paragraph 56 at "In Athens"; that of 1767 does not. The text of 1767 normally gives more formality to the names and titles of kings (Henry IV and Lewis XI of France, Henry V and Henry VIII of England).

† *Mercurius Politicus has:* Casimire
‡ *MP has:* and interests.

# Corresponding Passages of
## *Mercurius Politicus*

### THE ENDNOTES

The endnotes that follow are signaled in the text of this edition (see p. cvii). They reproduce the words and passages of *Mercurius Politicus* (*MP*) that were altered in the 1656 edition of *The Excellencie* (*E*). (*Politicus* does not have the headings of the sections into which *The Excellencie* is divided.)

In the cause of intelligibility, all the English-language material from *Politicus* is given in roman type, even though much of the original is in italic. The print of *Politicus* is not always clear, and occasionally the transcription of the text has to be conjectural.

### [MP 71, 9–16 Oct. 1651]

1. *E omits:* We hear not of many Nations in this latter Age, wherein the People have been solemnly acknowledged and declared to be the Original and Fountain of Supremacy, or that they have been made thus to understand it; But whereever it hath been so presented to vulgar Apprehensions, it takes such deep Impression, that all the Arts under heaven can never wear it out of memory; nor will they ever rest, till they have sipt and tasted all of the sweets of Soveraignty.

2. the

3. Characters

4. this

5. The Observation then which naturally ariseth hence, is, That

6. *E substitutes this paragraph for:* Liberty declared or possest, is like the Golden fleece, or the Hesperian fruit, watcht by Argus his hundred eyes, or by ever-waking Dragons.

### [MP 73, 23–30 Oct. 1651]

7. *In MP the paragraph begins:* Liberty is the most precious Jewel under the Sun; And therefore when

8. old Roman

9. Bounds

10. lost it: they

11. a

12. they indeed

13. bonds

14. Vassals

15. Influence

16. Councell

### [MP 72, 16–23 Oct. 1651]

17. It is observed, that when

18. in regard that

19. Country that moved him to take Arms

20. secure

21. practises

22. Canuleius

23. perswasions

24. of Government

### [MP 70, 2–9 Oct. 1651]

25. When Rome was once declared

26. especiall

27. hatefull

28. Emperor, &c.

29. that

30. bound

31. Importunity

32. the

33. so that it seemes the People

34. the Senate. The People without the Senatick Councell were like Sulphur and Mercury, ever in motion or combustion, (as appears by the Story:) but the Senate were as Salt to season, fix and fasten the body of the people.

Nevertheless it is very observable, that this Commonwealth ever

35. irregular and unruly

[MP 68, 18–25 Sep. 1651]

36. is

37. Epaminondas

38. were

39. it having been

40. *E omits this passage, which MP takes from* The Case of the Commonwealth *(Knachel, pp. 117–18):*

In our own Countrey here, before that Caesars Tyranny took place, there was no such thing as Monarchy: For, the same Caesar tels us how the Britains were divided into so many severall States; relates how Cassevellanus was by the Common Councell of the Nation, elected in that their publique danger to have the principall Administration of State, with the business of War; And afterward how the severall Cities sent their Hostages unto him; whereby we perceive, it was of no old Monarchy, but like to the Gauls (with whom it was then one also in Religion) divided into Provinciall Regiments, without any entire Rule or Combination; onely in case of common peril by Invasion, &c. they were wont to chuse a Commander in Chief, much like the Dictator chosen by the Romans upon the like occasion. And now we see all the Western world (lately discovered) to be, as generally all Other Countries are *in puris naturalibus,* in their first and most innocent condition, setled in the same Form, before they came to be inslaved, either by some predominant Power from abroad, or some one among themselves, more potent and ambitious then his neighbours. Such also was the State heretofore, not onely of our Nation, but of France, Spain, Germany, and all the West parts of Europe, before the Romans did by strength and cunning unlock their Liberties: And such as were then termed Kings, were but as Generalls in War, without any other great Jurisdiction.

If we reflect likewise upon the antient State of Italy, we finde no other forms of Government but those of Free States and Commonweals, as the Tuscans, Romans, Samnits, and many others; nor is there any mention made of Kings in Italy, besides those of the Romans, and of Tuscany, which continued but a short time; for Tuscany soon became a free State, and as absolute enemies of Monarchy as the Romans; in the continuation of which enmity, they placed a kinde of an Heroick bravery.

41. inlargement of a People

42. Guicciardin

43. Pisistratus

44. their kings. Nor

45. reason, for as much as it is usuall

46. usually weighs

47. Title

[MP 37, 13–20 Feb. 1651]

48. at pleasure

49. dispossessed

50. that being

51. which

52. re-advancee

53. we may very well reinforce the conclusion made in our last two *[editorials]*, and learn,

54. with a share of Government, or in place of Trust, except he have, by some notable Series of Action, rendred himself utterly irreconcileable to the former power: for, otherwise, such

55. the new titular Tyrant

56. every new Commonwealth

[MP 77, 20–27 Nov. 1651]

57. birds

58. ordinary

59. *E omits:* No doubt but the famous Cobler's Crow was wont then to prattle in the same strain too, though afterwards, he were taught to crie χαῖρε Καῖσαρ. [*The story of the "cobler's crow" taught by its owner to say "ave caesar" to Augustus upon his return from Egypt was originally told by Macrobius,* Saturnalia, *II. 4.29–30. Nedham may have known it from the reference in Erasmus's* Apothegmata, *IV.42–43, or the plays of Robert Greene and Thomas Nashe.*]

60. *MP reads:*

following Reasons.

[*E changes the order of this paragraph, and that which follows, from that in MP. The first "reason" given in E for believing that the people are "the best Keepers of their own Liberties" is that printed as the second in MP. E reprints the following as its second reason.*] First, because it is ever the Peoples care to see, that Authority be so constituted, that it shall be rather a Burthen than a Benefit to those that undertake it, and be qualified with such slender Advantages of profit or pleasure, that men shal reap little by the enjoyment: The happie consequence whereof is this, that none but Honest, Generous, and Publick Spirits will then desire to be in Authority; and that only for the common good. Hence it was, that in the Infancy of the Roman Liberty, there was no canvasing for [*E has:* of] Voices, but simple and plain-hearted men were called, and intreated, and in manner forced with importunity to the Helm of Government, in regard of the great trouble and pains that followed the imployment: Thus Cincinnatus was fetch't out of the field from his Plough, and placed (much against his will) in the sublime dignity of Dictator; So the noble Camillus, and Fabius, and Curius were with much adoe drawn from the recreation of Gardening to the trouble of Governing; and the Consuler year [*E has:* Consul-yeer] being over, they returned with much gladness again to their privat employments [*E has:* employment].

Secondly, the people are the best Keepers of Liberty because they are not ambitious; They never think of usurping

61. minde onely

62. *E substitutes this paragraph for:*

A Third, and a Fourth Reason we adjourn til hereafter; In the mean time, this may serve partly to shew how great a happiness we may enjoy under a state of Liberty, being freed thereby so nobly from the late Inconveniencies of Kingly Power.

[MP 78, 27 Nov.–4 Dec. 1651]

63. *MP begins:* In the last, you had a Touch of some Reasons, justifying the form of a Free-State (or a Government by the People) to be much more excellent than the Grandee, or the Kingly Power: By the People, we mean such as shal be duely chosen to represent the People successively in their Supream Assemblies; And that the People thus qualified or constituted, are the best Keepers of their own Liberties, shal be farther made evident by Reasons[.]
A third Reason is,
64. Juncta
65. by their advantage
66. Counsels
67. up also
68. *E omits:* More of this hereafter.

[MP 79, 4–11 Dec. 1651]

69. *E omits:* To justifie the Excellency of a Free-State above a Kingly government, and to prove that the People, in a due and orderly succession of their Supream Assemblies, are the best Keepers of their own Liberties; we have already given you some Reasons, and shall here presume to set down one more.
70. Preventive
71. cause
72. such frequent heats
73. means, at length Lord it
74. Powers
75. had ever bin
76. last
77. This is good Common-wealth
78. Common-weal
79. Virginius
80. the name of Stuart

[MP "79" (80), 11–18 Dec. 1651]

81. *MP begins:* It hath in some measure been already proved, that the People, interested in a due and orderly succession of the supreme

Authority, are the best Keepers of their own Liberties; And that this qualification of a Free State (without which it cannot be free indeed) renders it so much more excellent then the Kingly, or any other form of Governmen[t] whatsoever[.] The life of Liberty lies in the Succession of Powers and Persons, as we shall farther demonstrate by Reason.

A Fift reason is, because as an orderly Succession and revolution of Authority in elected persons, is the grand preventive of Corruption and Faction, so it is the onely Remedy

82. they (much like our eleven impeached Members in the year 1647.) over-ruled

83. *E omits:* By this you see the first and second insurrection was caused by Necessity, the third and fourth hapned through Emulation: For, the great ones of the Senate taking advantage by their standing Authority, took care likewise to establish a [S]elf-interest, by confining of Marriages and Magistracie; They proceeded so far as to bear the people from marrying into their Families; and by this means (as they do now in Venice, for the most part) keeping a kind of State and Grandeur above the people, they the more easily made a shift to keep them out of all places of high trust and Au[t]hority.

84. ground an Observation, which shall be this:

85. SELF

86. Common-wealth

87. the supreme

88. *E omits:*

This (I say) still makes for the honor of all Governors in Free States, who have, or shall at any time deny themselves in settling limits and bounds to their own authority.


[MP 81, 18–25 Dec. 1651]

89. *MP begins:* In pursuance of our Position, That a Free State is much more excellent than a Government by Grandees, or Kings; and that the People are the best Keepers of their own Liberties; give leave to proceed yet farther upon the Accompt of Reason.

A sixth Reason is, because

90. Self interest

91. till

92. App. Claudius

93. Tyranny

94. prorogation

95. *E omits:* But after-times growing more corrupt, you shall find in story, that when the lengthning of Powers and Trusts in the same hands grew customary, it utterly spoiled all the brave Roman Patriots, insomuch, that most of the great Favourers and Defenders of the peoples interest, by the same means were tempted from the pure principles of Liberty, and in the end degenerated into Tyranny.

This may serve as a farther demonstration of the Equity and Noble-nesse of such Resolutions, as are taken up by Governours in Free-States, for setting Limits and bounds to the duration of Authority.

## [MP 82, 25 Dec. 1651–1 Jan. 1652]

96. *MP begins:* That a Free State is much more excellent then any other form of Government, & that the People, qualified with a due and orderly succession of their supreme assemblies are the best Keepers of their own Liberties, appears more evident still by Reason.

A Seventh Reason is, because

97. and

98. Story

99. how many

100. for, (to the admiration of more gay fellows and gawdy daies, be it spoken) he had

101. Yet it so

102. Equans

103. trembling condition despaired of safety

104. deliverance. But in what pickle did they finde him? Even following his plough in a poor rustick habit, a plain simple man and very unwilling, because he feared himself unfit, for so high an employment: But they who neglected all the Grandees and Gallants of Rome, to make choice of this poor man, constrained him to undertake it; and he behaved himself therein so well

105. are

106. L. Paulus

107. The Observation then, that ariseth from this discourse is this:

108. best preserved

109. their
110. till
111. made a shift

## [MP 83, 1–8 Jan. 1652]

112. *MP begins:* Our Design is still to prove, That a Free-State Government is much more excellent then any other form, Or that the People, instated in a due and orderly succession of their Supreme Assemblies, are the best Keepers of their own Liberties.

The eighth Reason is,

113. former Tyrannies
114. kept, free from mixture with
115. a
116. become
117. entrench
118. Free-Sta[t]e
119. still fresh
120. 60 years
121. Here's

122. mindes of the people, with how great a Spirit of Zeal and Revenge they are acted in its behalf, upon any occasion; and how jealous they are to preserve it, it being their onely delight, their Interest, their Life, and all; so that

## [MP 84, 8–15 Jan. 1652]

123. *MP begins:* To proceed in the justification of a Free State, or a Government by the people in a due and orderly succession of their supreme Assemblies; and to prove, that a Form thus qualified, is much more excellent than that of Kings, or Grandees, we are still upon the account of Reason.

A Ninth Reason is

124. honest
125. secure
126. both old
127. those many oppressive

128. led, and often forced

129. up started

130. Pisistratus

131. play; after whose (*E has:* play after; which).

132. the other

133. *E omits the passage below. In it, Nedham takes the verse from the translation of Lucan's* Pharsalia *(II. 280–91) by the poet and historian Thomas May, who died in 1650 (and whose relations with Nedham are discussed in LP, pp. 73–78). In the third line Nedham changes "sowre Cato" to "wise Cato"; in the last two lines he abbreviates May's text. The passage about William the Silent is taken, with two slight alterations of wording, from Fulke Greville's life of Sir Philip Sidney, which was first published in 1652 in London.* The Prose Works of Fulke Greville, Lord Brooke, *ed. John Gouws (Oxford, U.K.: Clarendon Press, 1986), pp. 13–14:* But that you may know what it was, take here the copy of old Catos countenance, as it was drawn by Lucan.

> These were his manners, this wise Cato's Sect,
> To keep a mean, hold fast the end, and make
> Nature his guide, die for his Count[r]ies sake.
> For all the World, not him, his Life was lent
> He thinks; his Feasts but hungers banishment,
> His choicest Buildings were but fence for cold,
> His best attire rough Gowns, such as of old
> Was Roman wear; and nothing but desire
> Of Progeny in him warm'd Venus fire:
> Father and Husband both to Rome was he,
> Servant to Justice, and strict Honestie.
> In none of Cato's acts creeps self-born pleasure,
> But in the publick good lay all his Treasure.

Thus you see what Cato was, and in him what the Governors of Rome were once, during the peoples Government: which being at an end, and the power put in other hands, their manners degenerated into luxury, and their liberty into Tyranny.

If we come down to later times, we find that the Free-States of Milan, Florence, Siena, and Luca, during their Liberty, were a severe and sober people, free from all those vanities and tyrannies wherewith they a[r]e now intangled, since they have been trampled on by ambitious, luxurious

Grandees and Princes; for, even in those States the lengthning of Powers in particular hands, brought on ambition and luxury to the losse of their Liberty; witness the actions of the two Families of Medices and Sforza.

If we look neerer home to such Free-States as are now in being, we find the United Provinces, while under a Tyranny, to abound in luxurious Governors and people, but much alter'd upon the very first appearance of Liberty, insomuch that Luxury and Tyranny flying both away together, they have lived ever since in a sober parcimonious condition (yet wealthy) under a grave and serious Government by the people. And the Family of Orange it selfe (before it grew corrupt) was in every respect suited unto this popular Form, as appears by that description of Prince William the Founder of their liberty, as it is set forth by Sir Fulk Grevil in the life of Sir Philip Sidney. For, when Sir Fulk came to visit him in the Town of Delph, he saith he found him thus accuoltred.

["]His uppermost garment was a Gown, yet such as (I dare confidently affirm) a mean student in our Inns of court, would not have been well-pleased to walk the streets in. Unbutton'd his Doublet was, and of like precious Matter and form to the other. His Wast-coat (which shewed it self under it) not unlike the best sort of those woollen knit ones, which our ordinary water-men row us in. His company about him were the Burgo-masters of that bear-brewing Town; and he so fellow-like encompassed with them, as I had not known his Face, no outw[ar]d signe of degree or merit, could have discovered the inequality of his worth or estate from that multitude. Notwithstanding, I no sooner came into his presence, but it pleased him to take knowledg of me; And even upon that (as if it had been a signall to make a change) his Respect to a stranger instantly begat Respect to himself in all about him: An outward passage of inward Greatnesse, which in a popular state is worth the observing.["] Thus farr Sr Fulk Grevil; which may serve to upbraid the Cours and conversation of the later Branches of that stock, who having by degrees forsaken their first Principles, and wedded themselves to the Bloud and Interrest of Rogalty, no sooner became infected with pride and Luxury, but they began to hatch Projects and designs, for the ruin of the Low-Country Liberty.

We might also cite another Instance from the free Cantons of Switzerland, by comparing their present State of Freedom, Industry, and

Sobriety, with the Luxury and Tyranny of former times in that Country, but we have been too large already. And as for Venice, though it bear the name of a Freestate, yet it have little of the Substance; for, the chief Power being deposited in the hands of a standing Senate of Grandees, the People must needs be to seek of their Freedom. And this is observable, that by how much the lesse they have of that Freedom which the united Provinces & the Cantons now enjoy, so much the more both they and their Governers are now inclined to Luxury, being (to speak mildly) of a more soft and delicate demeanour than is usuall in a state that is really free.

And thus much let us have further to say, it is no good signe of that Grandee Venetian Government's being pleasing to the People, since we finde by all our Intelligence that way, that the Islands in the Archipelago, and other of their Territories, are ready still, upon any opportunity (as they have been ever) to revolt unto the Turkish Government.

134. Our Conclusion therefore upon

135. *E omits:* More I might inlarge, but less I could not.


### [MP 85, 15–22 Jan. 1652]

136. *MP begins:* To go on upon our old Subject of a free-State or Government by the People, as it is constituted in a due and orderly succession of their supreme Assemblies; and to prove its excellency above all other Forms, wee shall make matters yet more evident by Reason.

A Tenth Reason is,

137. possesseth

138. see

139. and

140. This is it

141. while under Kings, remained

142. a little more, and for a little time; yet all that they

143. the World

144. the more

145. wherewith that people was endued upon the

146. especially

147. for

148. the yoak of the Romans

149. Carthage

150. many times

151. save

152. again of

153. *E omits:*

To avoid tediousness, let us come nearer home. In France, as long as the French retained their old Liberty, in the successive Assemblies of the People (wherein their King was but a Cypher) so long they produced Sparks of that ancient Courage, which was seen in the old Galls and Franks their predecessors, and no Nation did greater things abroad in Palestine and Egipt, besides all parts of Europe, till by a continuation of the supreme power in Charles the 7th, and a keeping it by craft in Lewis the 11th, they quite lost their Liberty; since which time they have been able to doe little, save the making of a few sallies into Italy, and some other places; but have suffered more at home, then they gained abroad; which want of success must of necessity be attributed chiefly to a defect of courage, since the loss of Liberty in the Generality of that people: For, the Country-men (whom they call Peasants) are only Spunges to the King, the Nobility, and their Landlords, having nothing of their own, but onely for the use of them, and are scarce allowed (as Beasts) enough to keep them able to do service; for, besides their Rent, they pay now more than two thirds to the King by which means that State is extremely weakned, having the worst Infantry under Heaven; for the greatest part of the people being miserably opprest, are becom heartless, weak and feeble, & consequently unfit for Military uses; so that (as one observs) they are first forced to borrow aide of the Swissers at a great charge; and secondly to compose their Armies for the most part of Gentlemen, which makes the loss of a Battel almost irrecoverable.

154. see

155. follows

156. gallant

157. Hollanders, and also our own Nation; whose high atchievments may match any of the Ancients, since the extirpation of Tyranny, and a re-establishment of our Freedom in the hands of the People: The consideration

158. settling

[MP 86, 22–29 Jan. 1652]

159. *MP begins:* That a Free State, or Government by the People, setled in a due and orderly succession of their supreme Assemblies, is much more excellent than any other Form, we shall farther illustrate by Reason.

The eleventh Reason is

160. that

161. Laws

162. will afford

163. Tyrant

164. *E omits:* Nor is it thus only in the government of Kings, but the same Inconvenience hath been seen also in that of the great ones, where they held a standing power in their own hands over the people: For, as in Rome, where Kings were expel'd, and the supremacy usurpt by the Senate, they made Laws at the pleasure of great men, without the suffrage or consent of the people in their successive Assemblies; so the execution of those Laws was committed onely to such as were of the Senatorian Order or Alliance, who never construed them in favour of the people, but onely so far still as would suit with the Lordly interest of the Senate, as is manifest by the several Decisions made in the Matrimoniall, Tribunitian, and Agrarian controversies in old Rome, betwixt the great ones, of the Senate and the people: yea, they proceeded so far, as to swear against the people, binding each other by oath and confederacy (saith Livy) to bridle, suppresse, and keep them under, not permitting them the enjoyment of any Office or Dignity in the Commonwealth; which practices are by him taxed of high imprudence; for, by this means the People grew desperate, & never gave over mutiny, till they gain'd a Right, not onely to the execution of Law, in being admitted to Offices, but also to the making of Laws, that nothing should passe for Law, but what was first ratified by consent in their solemne Assemblies.

165. The wary providing

166. Commonweal

167. of a standing Senate

168. Senate was strictly tyed up by Lawes, that they walked in

169. that

170. rather a Juncta then a Common-weal

171. opportunities (as I once mentioned before) to revolt

172. Therefore (to bee brief) our Conclusion

173. Determinations

## [MP 87, 29 Jan.–5 Feb. 1652]

174. *E omits:* Hitherto, We have pretty well cleared our way, to prove that a Free State, or a Government by a free election and consent of the People, setled in a due and orderly succession of their Supream Assemblies, is much more excellent than any other Form; But let us go on.

175. saith in the first of his Offices

176. wherefore

177. submit

178. *Nimini*

179. three Deductions of mine

180. Dictate

181. the

182. by

183. of Standing

184. at all adventure, from the hand of Chance, or Fortune

185. to transform

186. bandied

187. that

188. it lasts usually

189. being often litigious

190. betwixt

191. *MP reads:* Line of Succession. Therefore, if any Kingly Form be tollerable, it must be that which is by Election; and herein as Kings are tolerable only upon this Account of being Elective, so these Elective Kings

192. which

193. effect, farther than

194. of aspiring

195. Hungary

196. Casimire

197. *MP reads:* Casimire and Austria.

Neither are such grand Inconveniences to be found onely under the standing power of Kings, because they are Hereditary, but the same abound in like maner in the government of standing Senates, there being the same reason to prove inconveniences, because in this form they ever continue the same Hereditary course of Succession in their particular Families, usurping the same power (as Kings do) by birth, not receiving it from the consent of the people. The truth of this appeares by a survey of the constitution of the Roman Senate, which confined all right to government within their own Walls, Wills, and Families, to whom they affixed one common name of Honour, calling themselves the Patrician or Noble Order, just as they doe now in Venice, where none but the sons of the Senate are admitted to any dignity or power, but they all of them (without distinction) are admitted to the Helm, after they are once 25 years old; so that as in both those Commonweals the reasons and occasions of inconvenience are the same, as in the Kingly hereditary Form; so had I room I would have made Reasons and Examples walk hand in hand together, to make full proof of our position; and this I might have done, not onely in Rome and Venice, but also in Florence, Genoa, and even in Switzerland in time past, when the Cantons were prest under the weight of an Hereditary standing Nobility. But I have been too large already; let this serve to manifest

198. Form

199. Delinquency, or Neutrality, &c. in relation

200. the People, as shall be proved hereafter.

## [MP 88, 5–12 Feb. 1652]

201. *MP begins:* To proceed still in the maintenance of our Position, that a Free State, or Government by the People, constituted in a due and orderly Succession of their Supream Assemblies, is the most excellent Form, we shall add a few Reasons more.

The thirteenth reason is,

202. Free Commonweals

203. Camp or Councel

204. latter

205. grow

206. which

207. Pisistratus

208. In Rome the case was

209. permitting many of

210. *MP reads:* loss of their Liberty.

Now, on the other side, if you please to consider, you shall finde, that all States which have, from time to time, secured their Liberty, have done it meerely by reserving all Power only in the hands of the People, and never intrusting more than a moderate restrained Power in the hands of particular Persons; as wee see now it is their care in Switzerland, and the speciall care also of the Venetian Senat, to preserve themselves free from the usurpation of any of their Fellow Senators, as well as of their Duke: And it is attributed by a Countreyman of ours *[James Howell, whose* A Survay of the Signorie of Venice *(London, 1651), p. 6, Nedham loosely quotes]* to be one main cause of the long life of that Republick, that it was never yet usurpt by the Power or Policie of any of its Members. For (saith he) She puts sundry Restraints to the Power of the Duke, which are such, that it is impossible for him to attempt any thing against the Senate, or become a Tyrant.

Hereunto may be added the Limitations She puts also to the wealth of the Senators, that none of them grow over rich, but to such a Proportion, in regard it is a quality ever inherent, and Hereditary in the nature of man, that riches in excess puff up the minde, inciting it to ambition and high Attempts; nor is there a more catching Bait for one to take vulgar affections, and draw them after him than wealth: Therefore one of her prime Principles of state is,

211. great or popular, esteeming it a notable means (as indeed it hath been) in securing herself from

212. *E omits:*

Secondly, as to the permitting of any Sort, Rank, or Order of men, to assume unto themselves the state and Title of Nobility, I should proceed to prove it every jot as inconvenient as the other, and occasioning as dangerous oportunities of introducing tyranny into a Free-State; so, that it hath, not without good reason, been avoided in all States that ever were really Free: But it being a materiall discourse, I am forced to put it off till the next. In the mean time, this may serve in part to shew, That in a Free State, or Government by the people, so long as the Rules of it are cautiously observed, in preventing the over-growth of Grandeur in particular Persons, there will be fewer opportunities of oppression and tyranny, than in the governments of Kings, or the great Ones; and therefore by consequence it must needs be much more excellent and commodious than any other Form whatsoever.

## [MP 91, 26 Feb.–4 Mar. 1652]

213. *E omits the editorials of MP 89 and 90 (12–19 Feb., 19–26 Feb. 1652), which are reproduced in Appendix B. The first of them gives further reasons to support the thirteenth "reason"; the second advances a fourteenth; the editorial that follows consequently gives the fifteenth. It begins:* We have onely one Reason more to insist upon, for the proof of our Position, that a Free-state, or government by the People, setled in a due and orderly succession of their supreme Assemblies, is much more excellent than any other Form.

The Fifteenth, and last Reason, is,

214. crushes

215. the Principle

216. Domination

217. any but God

218. greater

219. every form, by reason of its outward splendor, and present power; by which

220. crown

221. their

222. Commonweal Interest

223. *MP reads:* consent of the People.

But yet we find this principle of Liberty in calling supreme Officers to account, was never totally extinct in other Forms; For, though the difficulty in questioning them is usually very great, because of the advantages which they draw to them-selves, and the opportunities that they have to frame practises of their own, through long continuance in authority, yet we can collect Precedents out of all Nations, whereby it appears, that the people have many times conquer'd all difficulties, and run the hazard of all extremities, rather then they would be accessary to the losse of their own Freedom, and leave mankind without noble examples of justice upon the proudest of all standing Powers, whether Kings or others.

First for Kings, give me leave to shew (what I once published upon another occasion *[in an anonymous pamphlet,* Anglia Liberata *(London,*

*1651): see the preface to the second impression of LP]* that tis no new thing for Kings to be deprived, or punish't with death for their crimes in government; We read of Amon, King of Judah, that was slain by a part of the people, Because he walked not in the way of the Lord. And though another part of the people were angry at it, and avenged his death upon those that did it, yet questionlesse the execution was just, according to the law of God, which was (without respect of persons) that Idolaters should die the death. And no doubt the punishment had been inflicted by a judiciall Processe, had not so great a party of the people been addicted to him and his wayes, and opposed it; which opposition of men of corrupt principles being creatures and vassals of Lordly Interest, is usually the cause in all cases of this nature, why Kings and continued Powers are not to be attached, as well as other malefactors, by an easie and ordinary course of justice.

In like maner we read, that the whole People tooke Amaziah King of Judah, and put him to death for his Idolatry; which seems by the words to have been don by judiciall process, in a full Assembly of the People, and speaks much to the honor of those who have had the courage to imitate so Heroick an Act of Justice, by a solemn and serious Proceeding. The like had been executed upon Joas the father of Amaziah by a part of the People, for his murther and Apostacie.

Profane stories (both old and new) are full likewise to the purpose. Romulus the first King of Rome, was for his Tyranny cut in pieces by the Senate; and Tarquin (their last King) with his whole Family was cashiered, the Government changed, by the same power, and upon the same occasion. Many years after Nero the Roman Emperor, was sentenced to death by the Senate; but being afterward cowed down by H[e?]liogabalus, so that they could not take the ordinary course, they were fain to deal with the Soldiery (upon whose strength he depended) to put him to death.

In France it is very observable, That the two famous changes made there in the Line Royal, depend upon Two such noble Pieces of Justice executed upon their Kings; the first upon Childerick the third King of France, who being judicially condemned in the Assembly of the People, the succession was then cut off from the Family of Pharamond, & confirmd to the race of Pepin; till Charls of Lorrain also, the last of Pepins race, was in like maner punisht by Parl. and the Crown was translated to the successors of Hugh Capet, who hold the same to this day; though

2. of this last Race also. viz. Lewis 3. and Charls the Gross, have bin judicially proceeded against in Parliament. And though the People, (for Reasons best known to Themselvs) forbear to put them to death; yet they were buried alive, being mued up within the melancholy wals of a Monastery, or closely confined within the Castle of Orleans.

In Spain too, we read of Suintilla, also of Don Alonso II. and Don Pedro, judicially proceeded against; The first by the fourth National Councel of Toledo; The second by publick Act of the Estates of the Realm in the Town of Valladolid, and the third by the Estates of Castile; but all for their Tyranny.

In Portugal, the like proceeding was had against Don Sancho the second. The like we finde passed against Henry of Poland that was K. of France, Henry of Swethlan; Christiern of Denmark; and Wenceslaus of Bohemia; as also against Edward 2. and Richard 2. here in England; and lately against the late Tyrant Charls, who was publickly beheaded; And though many of the rest were not, yet it is sufficient they were judged worthy of a Scaffold: And therefore it must needs be more honourable (after the late example of England) that the Judgments of God should be executed in publick before all the world, than that they should be stifled in a Dungeon, or the Majesty of them be lessned by paltry private Assassinations, or poysonings, acted upon Royall Tyrants and Offenders.

Thus you see, how notwithstanding the power and splendour of those gawdy things cald Monarchs, the People under them have made a shift (though not without much adoe) to keep them in an accountable condition, as the only means to abate the confidence and occasions of Tyranny. Where is to be noted, that the oftener they called them to Account, the better and easier they kept their Liberty.

Now for the other form of Power in standing Senates, the people have found every jot as great difficulties in keeping them in an Accountable condition, as well as Kings.

In Athens, when the Power of the People was usurp'd by the Thirty, in the form of a standing Senate; they presently flew out into all Extravagancies, and bore up so high, creating Parties by Favor, that the Comonwealth was brought neare to ruine, before they could bee made accountable and punisht. In Sparta, their Kings indeed were accountable to their Ephori, or standing Senate, but Senators to none, which was the cause of all afterenormities that befell the People, too large here to reckon.

In Rome as long as the Senate was accountable to none but themselvs, the People were swallowed up with their Liberties, which could never be regained, nor the Senate be fetched down from their unaccountable State, till the People, after long strugling, obtained their successive Assemblies. In Florence, observe all the scuffles between the Senators and the People, and afterwards between the Senate and their Dukes; As long as the People kept them to Account, so long they kept themselves and the People from the usurpation of Dukes. In Genoa, their liberty is preserved only by this means: that their Assemblies are successive, and their Duke accountable, &c. In Venice the People have nothing but the name and shadow of Liberty, becaus their Duke is to account only to the standing Senate (who have punisht about 6 or 7 of their Dukes for misgovernment) but the Senators accountable to none but themselvs, so that the People as to them are remediless. In Switzerland the People fare better, and are free indeed

224. Powers could ever be called to accompt

225. Reasons formerly published

226. *E omits:* Our next Cours shall be to refute all Objections to the contrary.

## [MP 92, 4–11 Mar. 1652]

227. the People

228. who being now invested

229. may (in order to the preservation of this Common-wealth) understand what Common-weal Principles are, and

230. interest of monarchy. But

231. so on the

232. Property

233. Proprieties

234. like may be said also of France

235. their Successive Assemblies, so long they

236. same pass too

237. how much of Levelling, and how little of Property

238. propriety

239. Power

240. Proprieties

241. Decennall Governors

242. the

243. those miscariages, as (if ever there be occasion) shall be made appear at large by the current of the Story:

244. that very account

245. tired

246. propriety

247. by the aforementioned

248. property as ever; for, as Livy tels us, They soon lost their Propriety under that erroneous constitution of a standing Senate; The great Ones not only deprived them of all interest in the Government, but even in ordinary enjoyments, eating them out with debt, usury, extortion, and circumvention; so that they were fain to beg, and many times make Mutinies and Uproars for Bread; and at last to leave the City, with a Resolution never to return, till they were perswaded back once by the eloquence of Menenius Agrippa; at another time wonn by the fair promises of Q. Hortensius. The same miseries rather increased than diminished under the other form of standing Power, called the Decemviri; during whose government the People were (besides the many other extremities) reduced to so much want, having no Propriety nor possession, that upon an uproar for Bread in the comon Forum, they set upon Appius Claudius, the chief of the Decemviri, with Curses and imprecations; so that he not with much adoe escaped at a Back-doore, he had bin torn in pieces. Thus you see how the Romans also shifted out of one standing Form to another, to no purpose till necessity taught them a remedy against those merciless Levellers, by setling the Government in the Peoples hands, by an orderly

249. recover a propriety

250. which new strain

251. in as a Favorite

252. *MP reads:* liberty and Property, as appears more at large in the Story.

In Venice, where the Government is in a standing Form, no man hath any Propriety in what he possesseth, in their Territories, save what the Senate please to allow him; for they may command what they please, upon any pretence, without the will and consent of the Owners, by vertue of their own Senatick Decrees, where the People have no interest, nor influence at all in the determinations of that supreme Assembly.

253. We might enlarge, but being too large already, we may (I suppose) safely conclude

254. Royallists that

255. destroying of Proprieties

256. Usurpations of all Standing powers. Add to the former Instances, the consideration of the former sad condition of Switzerland, and Holland, under standing Powers; with the flourishing state they have bin in ever since the expulsion of those powers, and a setling of those Governments in the Peoples Successive Assemblies. It is clear then, that Kings

[MP 93, 11–18 Mar. 1652]

257. *E omits:* In our last was proved; That the way of a free-State, or government by the People, setled in a due succession of their supreme Assemblies, is so farr from introducing of Community, and Levelling of Estates, that it is, and ever hath bin the only preservative of Property in all particulars.

258. Assemblies; which equality of Right in all to chuse and to bee chosen, is by Aristotle called Levelling.

259. Commonweal

260. are

261. and be chosen

262. *MP reads:* is not here to be determined; nor shall we presume to define what it ought to be in our own Nation hereafter, when it shall please God to extinguish the present Animosities, and unite us all in heart, under the form of a Free-State, as one People: In this Case a due Latitude (as aforesaid) cannot be accounted Levelling.

But as to a Common-wealth under the second Consideration, when it is founded or newly founded, in the close of a Civil War, upon the ruine of a former Government &c. In this case (I say) to make no distinction betwixt men, but to allow the Conquer'd part of the People an equal Right to chuse and be chosen, &c. with those that subdued them, and preserved the Common-wealth, were flat Levelling indeed: And truely this is the Levelling I ever condemned; because under a pretence of Universal Freedom, to admit all persons whatsoever, and by Consequence the Old Enemy, into an equal share and interest with the Common-wealth's Friends, to chuse and be chosen, &c. were not onely

263. reckoned

264. Common-wealths of Greece were

265. dead, devou[r]ing them to the deeps with Imprecations, and branding

266. Commonweal

267. Treason. This also hath been the practice of Florence, Luca, Siena, Millain

[MP 94: 18–25 Mar. 1652]

268. *E omits:* Our Position is, That a Free-State, or Government by the People, setled in a due and orderly succession of their supreme Assemblies, is the most excellent Form.

269. pretended

270. Commonweal

271. wrings

272. for ease and remedy

273. Councel

274. as we have heretofore sufficiently made manifest more at large, both by reason and example: Therefore all we shall do at present, is to add a little to the former part of our Discourse

275. Councell

276. continue as their standing Councell

277. *E omits:* And in Venice, though the People have no interest above that standing Senate, all Power and Authority being comprised in a great Councel, made up onely of that which they call the Patrician Order, in which great Council or Assembly they pass all Laws, and prescribe rules for Government, yet ever in the intervals of that meeting, they observ the same Method as hath bin us'd in States really free, committing the Arts & secrets of Government to a Councel, cald the councel of Ten, chosen by the great Councel, but with this difference, in regard they chuse them out of the Senatorian order, excluding the People.

278. Councel

279. Councellors

[MP 95, 25 Mar.–1 Apr. 1652]

280. size or Standard

281. above

282. *E omits:* But yet it will be said, that there were as many great and grievous Tumults after those Assemblies were in being. 'Tis true; but the

fault was not in the People, nor in the Freedom that they had gotten, but in this, that they never were so free as they ought, or might have been, had not the body of their Commonweal been infected with that rank mixture of an Hereditary standing Power, which was reserved still in the Senate. For, though all ultimate Appeals (the great Ensignes of Supremacy) were directed to the People, for that the Senate could not controll their Assemblie; yet the Senators being men of greater wealth, Power, and wit then ordinary, and having an Interest still in Affairs, as an hereditary distinct Order of men from the People (which is the Bane of all in a Commonweal) they by this means had such an influence, that they could perplex, puzzle, and over-reach the people (ever and anon) to serve their own ends, in the great Assemblies: which the people after-wards observing with regret, to see themselves baffled and cosen'd, was the true cause of most of those discontents, and Tumults that happened after the erection of their successive Assemblies; and this, with the like, might be made evident from time to time, not only by the Roman, but Athenian Stories, were not the multitude of Particulars more fit for a Treatise then a Pamphlet.

283. such as become their, Leaders. Thus
284. Liberty
285. Leader
286. the occasions were
287. an height
288. before, and after, but
289. Story
290. and the
291. Virginius
292. consequents


[MP 96, 1–8 Apr. 1652]

293. the form of Free-State
294. attends
295. Domination
296. called to account
297. their particular
298. First, Because it is
299. instate

300. remain

301. Common-weal

302. accusare; which being Englished saith, It most

303. reach them, nor have any ordinary course allowed for the keeping of them (as it becomes all earthly powers)

304. of the horrid tumults

305. ever

306. Common-weal

307. Process

308. them

309. *E omits:* We might be much larger, and shew you what miseries our own Nation hath endured for want of this liberty against our Kings and their grand creatures, such as Strafford, &c. [W]e might hint also, what adoe there was in and about London, in the year 1647 when the corrupt party then shelter'd themselves in both Houses under a pretended priviledge of Parliament, so that they could not be brought into question, till it pleased God that the Army, with extream hazard, brought in a Charge against them; which hazard of a new War (by God alone happily prevented) had never been, if there had been any ordinary way left for the management of their accusation.

310. the

311. Commonweal

## [MP 97, 8–15 Apr. 1652]

312. own hand

313. confederates; and now again at this instant, between the Court and the Princes, wherein

314. farther

315. same also in

316. grand game

317. betwixt

318. all Tyranny, and

319. seems

320. This was remarkable in the late Tyrant Charles

321. and fixt

322. *E omits:* How closely his son also hath troden the Father's steps, appears by the last Game with the Presbyters in Scotland, where he

plaid fast and loose with the Covenant and the stool of Repentance. It is memorable too, how Hollis, Stapleton, and the rest of those impeached grand stagers, diserted the Peoples interest, and all the pure pretences of their first engaging, so that had not the People been more constant, firm, and resolute, we might then have bid farwell to the Liberties of England.

323. Scipios, (of whom you had a hint in our last:) the cause

324. themselves within the rules of a Free-State, in an equability or moderate condition, by permitting

325. all these

326. own

327. what

328. Reputation that

329. Liberty

330. and access of power and greatnessions

331. ever

332. suiting with the Interest of Liberty

333. Antonius

334. unworthy dealing is the naturall effect

335. *E substitutes this paragraph for:* But the more large disquisition of all these things is referr'd to a better leisure and Oportunity, than this of a Paper-kite or Phamphlet; only thus far I have presumed (week after week) in sincerity of heart, and in honor to the Founders of our Commonwealth, to make it appear how highly they deserve of our Nation and the whole world, who have laid the Foundations of Freedom, upon that noble and declared interest of a Free-State, which consists onely in a due and orderly succession of the Peoples Assemblies, and without which I dare say I have fully proved, there can be no superstructure of true Liberty in a Nation. Therefore here we make an end of our Reasons, and Answers to the most material Objections; which are not to be taken apart, but compared one with one another, and consider'd alltogether, if you mean to judge aright of particulars.

## [MP 98, 15–22 Apr. 1652]

336. *E omits:* Before we proceed to any new Discours, Let us have Leave to bring in that last, which should have bin handled first, and is indeed the very Foundation of all the rest; to wit, That the originall of all just Power and Government is in the People.

337. upon

338. describes (as Salmasius and all the Royal Interpreters would have use beleeve) but

339. we

340. Right

341. their form

[MP 99, 22–29 Apr. 1652]

342. Having already proved

343. Israel's

344. by the Church-Nationall Pretenders

345. bringing

346. sanctified, &c. Not

347. My Kingdom is not from hence; My Kingdom is not of this world, &c.

348. certain

349. whose kingdom being not of this world, depends

350. *MP reads:* Orthodox (they said) as themselves. This tyranny of Bishops being reformed, then our late Clergy-Reformers cam in play, who did wel in banishing Prelacy, but yet retain the old Principle of a distinct powerful body, and of being Quartermasters & Sharers with the Civil power, which having obtained for a little time, they began to persecute those they called Independent, because they embraced Principles of a purer nature than theirs, which they branded too with Errour and heresie.

I fear I have bin too large, but could not avoid it, in regard you have not half my minde, therefore to conclude, he that will conscientiously and seriously consider how from this specious pretence of suppressing Error and Heresie, all these monstrous enormities did spring; and how that very pretence of Clergymens having worldly power to defend truth, hath from time to time bin the great impediment of its progress and discovery (their worldly interest ever lying in the present establishment;) And if it be considered likewise

351. Civil, or any thing like it, must

352. Errors received in

[MP 100, 29 Apr.–6 May 1652]

353. that

354. that

355. Monarchick

356. *E omits:* I should now shew you also, how that Venice it self is no more but (as a man may call it) a multiplyed Monarchy, a particular Senate of men (who call themselves Nobility) being seated there in an hereditary, arbitrary, uncontrolable, unaccountable state of domination over that poor people.

357. is evident also

358. crept into the United Provinces, the relicks whereof are not yet extinct, as appears by some humors of the people that you may observe there, even in this weeks Intelligence.

Now what use is to be made of this discourse? Onely this,

359. the Interest of Monarchy may reside in the hands

360. barring

### [MP 101, 6–13 May 1652]

361. to be taken notice of

362. shared all Authority

363. Interests

364. maxim; that ignorance

365. among a people setled in a State of freedom

366. Commonweal

367. reigne again

368. and levelled

369. State, all their

370. *E omits:* So much also of a Free-State we finde practised in Venice, though the benefit extend only to the Nobility themselves, and not to the people; for (as we told you once before out of one of our Countrimens [*James Howell's*] Collections) she puts limitations to the wealth of the Senators, that none of them grow over-rich, but to such a proportion; because accesse of wealth inclines men to high thoughts, and ambitious attempts, and drawes peoples affections after them: therefore one of her prime principles of State is, to keep any man, though never so meritori-[o]us, from being too pow[e]rfull and popular.

371. cost the Low countreymen their Liberty

372. been strangely prevented by a miracle of Providence, might

373. of command, power, and authority

374. large in heretofore, but it must not be omitted in this brief abstract now intended, so far as concerns a few more Instances for its confirmation. The

375. Emylian

376. est, &c. This

377. Emylian (*E has:* Emiliam)

378. that Ides

379. Epistle

380. were

381. *E omits:* For the other Rules, you are referr'd to the next, having been to large here already.

## [MP 102, 13–20 May 1652]

382. *MP begins:* Wee have noted the third error or default in Policy, to be a keeping the people ignorant of those ways and means that are essentially necessary for the preservation of their Liberty; and the remedy thereof we judged to be a publication of those Rules, which have been practised in time past by divers Nations, for the keeping of their Freedom when they once had gotten it. Three of those rules you had in our last.

A Fourth is,

383. one (*E has:* own)

384. is very evident

385. Commonweal

386. State in the Republick of the

387. sometimes winking

388. whereas (*E has:* whertas)

389. to the publick

390. Cosmus

391. doubting to

392. Columna

393. certainly that people could never have had so far an opportunity as they now enjoy, (the Cockatrice being but in the Egg) to reduce

394. to

395. *E omits:* Thus they were served too by his Nephew Octavius (better known by the name of Augustus) who was a ripe youth, and began betimes; for being scarce 20. years of age, he drew his Army also to Rome,

and sent messengers to the Senate to demand the Consulship; but when the messengers saw a kinde of slackness and unwillingness to make him consul, then Cornelius a Centurion (one of the messengers) told them plainly to their faces, setting his hand upon the hilt of his sword; *Hic faciet, si vos non feceritis,* If you wil not do it, this shall. When they saw that then (the messengers being withdrawn) they soon agreed to give them a satisfactory answer.

This was a just punishment upon the Fathers, that the same Freedom should be taken from the Senatick power, by such kinde of Practises as themselves had first contrived, to overthrow the free suffrage and authority of the people in their Assemblies.

396. preserve

397. *E omits:* More of these Rules are yet behind.

## [MP 103, 20–27 May 1652]

398. *E omits:* In order to the discovery of those waies and means, that are essentially necessary to the preservation of a Commonweal in a state of Freedom, we proceed in the setting down of such Rules as have been observed in past Ages, and Nations, upon the like Occasion. Five have been published already.

399. their own Consent

400. speciall care περὶ ὅπλησιν καὶ γυμνασίαν,

401. because (saith he) the Commonweal is theirs who hold

402. attempted severall

403. Common-weal

404. the Senate and people

405. River Rubicon

406. trajicito (*E also has:* trajicito)

407. all, and march

408. Commonweal *[In E, the corresponding word may or may not be hyphenated.]*

409. Praetorian, in stead of a publick popular Militia

410. Tyrant

411. *E omits:* Were Venice a State, so free as it is called, we might then have seen them in another posture of Militia then now they are: For, the Nobility, as the grand secret of State to uphold their own power, do not intrust thee Arms in the hands of the people but hold an Army

ever in pay, mixt partly with Natives, partly Foreiners, who depend onely upon themselves, being enabled thereby to do what they please with the people.

It were a wonder to consider, how the United Provinces have so long kept their Liberty, though they have held a constant Army in pay under the conduct of one and the same Family, did we not withall consider, that both the Army and its Commander were ever exercised with continual action and necessity. For no sooner was a peace made with the Spaniard, but that Nation immediatly felt, and we have observed the sad consequences that befell them.

## [MP 104, 27 May–3 June 1652]

412. *MP begins:* A Seventh Rule, essentially necessary for the preservation of a Commonweal in a State of Freedom, is this; that Children

413. muzled

414. *E omits:* I remember a discourse of a very subtile Politician *[Machiavelli. In* The Case of the Commonwealth, *where this passage of MP also appears, Nedham gives his source as "the Florentine's subtile Discourses upon Livy" and refers to bk. I, chaps. 16–18, of that work: Knachel, pp. 111–12],* very pertinent to our purpose, who shewing of what force education is in respect of Government, compares such as have been educated under a Monarchy, to these beasts which have been caged, or coop't up all their lives in a Den, where they seem to live in as much pleasure as other beasts that are abroad: And if they happen to be let loose, yet they will return again, because they know not how to use their Liberty: So strong an impression is made likewise by education and custome from the Cradle, even upon men that are indued with reasonable souls, that they chuse to live in places and forms of Government under which they have been bred, rather then to submit to better which might make more for their happinesse and advantage. Hence it is (as we have once observed before, but cannot now omit it) that those poor slaves under the Turk, Persian, Tartar, Muscovit, Russian, French and Spaniard with other Eastern, Northern, and Western Lords, are so inamor'd of their chains, that they admire their own condition, being bred up in it, above all others, and like the Indians, adore the Devil that torments them, because their education hath made them ignorant of a better Deity to protect them.

Seeing therefore, Education hath such a force in molding mens minds after every form in Government or profession, without doubt that Rule is of excellent use, which in all times hath been observed by the Rulers of States and Kingdoms, *Aliter educanda est juventus in regno; aliter in optimatum imperio; aliter in populi;* The education of youth is to be ordered one way in a Kingdom, another way in the government of a few great ones; and after a different manner from all in the government of the people; it being varied and regulated according to the nature of every form.

415. this ground

416. called the Druides

417. of Commonweal

418. *E omits:* How comes it to passe, that the Jesuits have so readily furnished themselves with Instruments and Agents for the carrying on of their designs to the embroylment of Christendom, but that they have been permitted to erect Colledges and Seminaries in every Corner, where their Novices are suckled onely with such doctrine as may inable and dispose them for the ruining of States and Kingdoms? so that whether it be to a good purpose or a bad, you see all the efficacie lies in the education.

419. and under such

420. Commonweal

421. a free Commonweal

422. in every Institution


## [MP 105, 3–10 June 1652]

423. *E omits:* Of those Rules that are essentially necessary for the preservation of a Commonweal in a state of Freedom, you have had seven already.

424. into a Monarchall

425. confute it is; that they doe

426. be a just

427. Commonweal

428. out of our past discourses, which are not to be repeated here: But the sense

429. that notable one

430. and that is

431. Actings among his souldiery

432. upon the senate and People

433. noble

434. *MP reads:* point of behaviour. For, if we reflect upon these 30. years past, we shall find how cautious the Parliaments and People of England have been before they proceeded to Arms, the utmost and most desperate Remedy.

435. late Tyrant's

436. *E substitutes that sentence for:* Though all these Tyrannies of his were sufficiently felt and known, yet such was the wisdom and caution of our nation, from time to time & Particularly of this Parliament, that they used all the waies under heaven by Petitioning, Declaring, Remonstrating to God and man, in hope to reduce him: and though all would not doe, yet notwithstanding, that desperate Remedy of the Sword was forborn till after he had first taken it up, and that invincible necessity did put it into their hands, for the preservation of Themselves, with the Rights and Liberties of the People.

437. Commonweals

438. Liberty.

## [MP 106, 10–17 June 1652]

439. *E omits:* As concerning those Rules that have been put in practice heretofore by divers Nations, and which have by them been reputed essentially necessary for a preservation of their Freedom, we have published eight already. The Eighth Rule mentioned in our last, was; That a People being once possessed of Liberty, ought to use it with moderation, least it turn to licentiousness; which as it is a Tyranny in it self, so in the end it usually occasions the corruption and conversion of a Free-State into a Monarchy. For prevention whereof we gave one Caution in our last. More Cautions there are, which (that I may drive on the main discourse to a period) shall be summ'd up this week in brief; whereby a People in a Free-State may understand how to demean themselves for the avoiding those pernitious enormities of Tumult, Dissention, Sedition, &c. charged upon them by Kings, Grandees, and their Creatures:

440. or

441. surely

442. farther

443. or

444. Commonweal

445. Commonweal

446. fift

447. Commonweal

448. instances

449. in the whole Series of affairs in the Roman State

450. heat

451. accusations, and calumniations

452. and so

453. Commonweal

454. called S C. Turpilianum

455. Commonweal

456. course (*E has:* course course)

457. fail

458. concerns a people established in a state of Freedom so to regulate

459. Thus

460. *E omits:* so that in this case, that maxime of our English Law is very pertinent, *Abundans Cautela non nocet.* There can be no hurt in extraordinary caution.

### [MP 107, 17–24 June 1652]

461. *MP begins:* Touching those Rules that have been reputed essentially necessary, and accordingly put in practice by divers Nations, for a preservation of the Publick Freedom, you have had Eight already.

The Ninth and last Rule is this

462. *E omits:* This was Treason of the grossest kind.

463. Commonweal

464. Commonweal

465. this

466. Cases, as they are collected and set forth by a Countriman *[James Howell]* of our own in English

467. 2. The second point of Treason is

468. this Crime, *aut vivi exurebantur,* &c, were either

469. *E omits:* And for the avoiding of those Inconveniences that follow a discovery, they have a speciall care in Venice to keep all those especially from the Priests, as they did in Rome from Women. The former are Persons alwaies, and in all Places, of a distinct Interest from the Civill; The latter, by the nature of their Sex, not fit for such kinde of Communications[.]

470. 3. It is Treason, and death without

471. heathen

472. Compliances. Hence it is, that the Pope's Conclave have ever been more hot and tedious in their debates and determinations, than any other Assembly of men in the world; For, most Princes have ever held them in Pension, some one way, and some another. But in

473. *E omits:* And that it may appear how extreme strict they are in this Particular, it cannot be amiss to let down here a very sad story concerning Antonio Foscarini one of the senators, as it was written by Sir Henry Wotton *[whose words, in* Reliquiae Woottonianae *(1651; repr. 1672, p. 309), MP loosely reproduces]*; who being Ambassador at Venice, chanced to be there at that very time when the Tragedy was acted. There in (saith he) in the Partitions of this Government a very awfull Magistracy entituled *Inquisitory distato,* who recieve all secret accusations in matter of practise against the Republick, and then referr the same, as they see caus, to the Councel of Ten, who are the suprem Tribunall in Criminal Cases. To these Inquisitors came two men, and capitulated for a reward to discover some Gentlemen, who at unseasonable times, and in disguised Forms did haunt the Houses of forein Ministers; in particular they named the spanish Agent, being likeliest to gain a favourable hearing upon that subject. In the head of their secret list they named one of the senators called Antonio Foscarini, who being of the senate was thereby restrained upon pain of death from all conference with publick ministers, unless by special permission. And to give some Colour to their discovery, they did, besides their own Testimonies, alledg one Giovan Battista, who served the aforesaid Spanish Agent, and had, as they said, acquainted them with the accesses of such and such Gentlemen unto him. But first they advised, or so the Inquisitors thought fit to proceed against Foscarini, without examining the aforesaid Giovan Battista, lest it might caus a noise, and then perhaps those other that they meant to accuse might escape.

Hereupon Foscarini coming from the next sitting of the Senate at night down the Palace, was by order of the Inquisitors suddenly muffled, and so made close Prisoner: And after usual examinations, his own single denial being over-ruled by two agreeing witnesses, he was by sentence at the Councel of Ten, about fifteen daies after his apprehension strangled in prison, and then hanged by one leg on a Gallows in the publick Piazza, from break of day till Sun set, with all imaginable Circumstances of Infamy. But not long after it fell out, that the Accusation of these men was found and by themselves confessed to be a devilish plot of their own to get money; so that the business was husht up with the hanging of the fals accusers, and a Declaration of the innocence of poor Foscarini. This is the story and by it you may see the severity of the Venetians in the afore named particular.

474. their
475. have before you
476. a Free Republick

### [MP 108, 24 June–1 July 1652]

477. *MP begins:* For Order's sake, let us run back a little, and see how our Discourse hangs together. The first thing we dispatched was to prove the Excellency of a Free-state above all other Forms; for which you had divers Reasons. After this, Answers were given to divers Objections comonly made against the Government of a free-State[.] Next, wee noted divers Errors that have been received in the course of Christian Policy; whereof wee have as yet set down onely Three; and the third Error is noted to have been a keeping the People ignorant of those wayes and means that are essentially necessary for the preservation of their Liberty; the remedy wee judged to be a publication of those Rules which have been practised in times past by divers Nations, for the keeping of their Freedom. The Eighth Rule was that which more especially related to the People themselves in point of Behaviour; for the due Regulation whereof, wee did in the next place set down a few Cautions; and after them the Ninth and last Rule which you had last week; so that having run through all these Particulars in order, wee naturally revert now to the former

478. our
479. not the strict

480. honesty

481. fear I be

482. called Reason of state, you had about this time Twelvemonth, Numb. 60 *[MP 24–31 July 1651, p. 959; LP, p. 210]*, which wee transplant hither, as into it's more proper Place:

483. That which wages

484. *E substitutes the opening of this paragraph for:* This passage being taken notice of, and quoted by an ingenious Gentleman in a Book of his in Print, he was pleased in opposition to this sandy Foundation of policy, called Reason of State, to point out a more sure and Noble way:

485. he

486. By-Actings or Engagements

487. *E adds this paragraph.*

488. in the behalf

489. Horses back

490. Harry the seventh

491. prosecute

492. *MP reads:* sad destruction. Yet reason of State is still the grand Idol of the present Youngster. It made him first resolve to joyn with the Irish; but things not falling out to his minde there, it made him wheel about into Scotland, and turn Covenanter. Afterwards, it made him cast off the Covenant and Covenanters both together; and therefore, no doubt but the next wheeling wil be towards Rome, or any way, if reason of State require it, that he may finish the transgressions of the Family.

I had thought to have touched upon the late powerfull Presbyterian party in England, and our Neighbours beyond Sea, the former having had the Cup of vengeance fill'd out in part to them already, and to the other it is filling out, because they have made Reason of State their God, and the Rule of all their Actions. But I want Room; and these

### [MP 109, 1–8 July 1652]

493. occasion, there lies a grand Secret of Liberty and good Government

494. wills were law

495. to

496. *MP reads:* the Senate. This was the main Caus, for, the Rape of Lucrece did but quicken them to lay hold of an opportunity. Kings

497. Standing senate

498. Commonweals

499. those

500. Councells

501. failer

502. *E omits:*

By the constitutions of the Kingdoms of Poland and Bohemia, their grand Diets or Parliaments have long enjoyed the Legislative power, but the execution of Law hath been left in their Kings, who were (no more than what all Kings should be) meere elective officers in Trust for that end, by which means Poland keeps its Liberty to this time in a good measure, though they begin to lose it every day by letting in French Interests and humors among them. As for Bohemia it is quite lost there already, the Emperor having by force of Arms turned both the Powers into the Channel of his own will and Prerogative. But this is more than ever he hath been able to doe at home; for, though he be the first in dignity among Christian Princes, yet so limited and restrained, that he cannot by law so much as wage warr, nor make Levies of men or money, but by consent of the German diet or Parliament; so that the power of Lawmaking being lodged here, and the Execution left in the Emperor, whilst these Powers run in two distinct Channels, those Countries may make a shift to retain their Freedom. But if ever he turn the Cours of one of them into his Cabinet at Vienna (as he often hath attempted) and so both of them into one, then there will be an end indeed of the Libertyes of Germany.

503. late Tyrant in England

504. and his

505. *MP reads:* himself and his family.

Now, I suppose whosoever takes a serious view of these instances, and examples, will easily conclude, That a permitting the two Powers of making and executing Laws, to rest in one and the same hands, hath been a notorious Error in Policie; since it appears, that the keeping them distinct hath

[MP 110, 8–15 July 1652]

506. Interests

507. loyall

508. shares

509. cleanly

510. Commonweal

511. domination

512. deserted

513. in

514. *E omits:* It is remarkable also in the State of France, how peace-ably, happily, and orderly their nation was governed, so long as their affairs were managed in a publick way by the three Estates, in their successive suprem Assemblies, as their stories will inform you. And no sooner were those Assemblies laid aside by the craft and power of Lewis 11 and the succeeding Kings, and the publick affairs and interests of the Nation in-grossed by them, and the Princes of the Bloud, and some few of their Creatures and Dependants, but their peace, liberty, and welfare became lost for ever. For, that Countrey hath ever since been the stage of bloud, and a perpetuall Civill war, the poor people being tost and banded to and fro to serve their ends and designes; who, as all Junto men and Grandees in the world, however they may seem to comply, collogue, and cog with one another for a time, in the carrying on their common design of usurpation, yet no sooner is the prey before them, but they ever fall to cutting one an-others throats (as we see in France at this day) for their shares in the tyranny.

515. *MP ends:* pernicious Error in the practices of other times and Nations.


[MP III, 15–22 July 1652]

516. A Seaventh Error in Policy, observable from the practises of other times and Nations, hath been the Driving

517. Commonweals

518. (or rather) malice

519. Commonweal

520. *E omits:*

We read also, what hazard that state ran many times by division and Faction, exposing themselves thereby as a Prey to their publick enemies. They received that notable defeat given them by the Veians, which had like to have cost them the loss of their Country, through the divisions at that time betwixt four of their chief Commanders. That other Desper-ate defeat which they received also at Cannae, was occasioned by the Spleen of two Factions; the one being headed by Paulus Aemilius, and

the other by Terentius Varro, so that Hanibal hereby gained a fair Oportunity; which had it been fairly prosecuted, he might with ease have set
an end to the Roman Power, and reduced their City under the Yoak of
Carthage.

521. befell Carthage in After-time

522. with such unanimity

523. dissensions

524. *E omits:* It hath often invited the Spaniard into France; but he
had never so sure a Footing as in the Guisian League. At this day we see,
he is gotten in again, upon occasion of the two Factions, banded betwixt
the Court and the Princes; which hath inabled him to give a fair Check
already to the growing greatnes of the French Monarchy.

Nor must it be forgotten what hazard our own nation hath run of late,
through the malice, falshood, and Faction of the late Presbiterian Drivers. He that will remember what they did in the year 1647, 48, 49. 50. and
51. must needs confesse, that great hath been the deliverance of this Commonweal, and the manner of it almost incredible, considering the waies
and meanes whereby we have been rescued out of the Claws of the old
Tyranny; which (through their faction and fury) was at the very point of
returning in again upon us.

525. Commonweal

## [MP 112, 22–29 July 1652]

526. An Eighth Error observable in the practise

527. Christian

528. I find it fully express'd in Machiavel; who as he hath left many
noble Principles and observations upon record, in defence of the liberty of
the people, so we find in some of his Books many pernitious sprinklings,
unworthy of the light, and of him who in other things was master of a
very solid judgement, and most active phant'sie. But the vile reason, which
he gives why Statesmen may be excused for this prodigious crime, is this;

529. have

530. those

531. Carthage & suffer.

532. *E omits:* For the rest, touching this particular, I refer you to another time; this being but an introduction to what I intend you in my
next, when I shall descend to the practices of later times and Nations.

[MP 113, 29 July–5 Aug. 1652]

533. *E omits:* The Eight Error in Policy observable from the practice of other times and Nations, we noted in our last to be, A violation of Faith, Principles, Promises and Ingagements, upon every Turn of Time and Advantage. An Impiety (we told you) that ought to be exploded out of all Societies which bear the name of Christian: and yet we find it often pass among the less discerning sort of men for admirable Policy, and those Imposters that use it, have had the luck to be esteem'd the only Politicians.

534. and avoid them, give me leave a little to

535. verbatim out of the English Translation

536. *MP reads:*

CHAP. XVIII.

In what manner Princes ought to keep their words.

How commendable

537. *MP ends.*


[MP 74, 30 Oct.–6 Nov. 1651]

538. Now, since

539. Upon any occasion: This indifferent Divell usually bears the character of the honest peaceable man, among the ordinary sort of people: But this

540. *E omits:* Many Pretences may be against it, many suppositions of danger; the sonnes of Anak may be said to be in the way, and therefore no entring into the promised Land: But had such Bugbears been regarded; had Phlegmatick reasonings taken place in time past, there is a Nation under the Sun (which shall be nameless) that had been undone before now in being kept from new moduling of an Army, which proved afterwards the most victorious Army that ever was in Christendom.

541. way then


## THREE OTHER EDITORIALS

*The following editorials, written during the period of the sequence from which* The Excellencie *was mostly taken, were omitted from it.*

## [MP 89, 12–19 Feb. 1652]

To prove the second part of that Reason, which was produced in our last, we shall (according to promise) proceed, to shew that the permitting of any Sort, Ranke, or Order of Men, to assume unto themselves the State and Title of Nobility, is altogether inconvenient in a Commonwealth, and must needs occasion many dangerous opp[o]rtunities of introducing Tyranny into a Free-State. The principal caus (as was then declared) is this, in regard such petty Titular Tyrants alwayes bear a naturall and implacable hatred against the People: so that if at any time it happen, that any great Man or Men whatsoever arrive to so much power and confidence as to think of usurping, or to be in a condition to bee tempted thereunto, these are the first will set them on, mingle Interests with them, and become the prime Instruments in heaving them up into the seat of Tyranny. And the main reason lies in this, That it is their Interest so to doe, because being seated in a higher degree and station then ordinary above the People, they will bee then in the fairer way of satisfying their hereditary Appetites of Covetousness, Pride, Ambition, and Luxury; and with the greater Impunity exercise and ease those passions of the Spleen, which usually break out into all extreames upon the People, for the maintenance of their Lordly interest and dignity.

Now for the evidencing of this Truth by example, the whole world affords variety in every corner. In Greece wee finde, that in the island of Cous, in Rhodes, and Megara (which were al free-States) they might have bin a free People indeed, had they but taken care to knock off those golden Fetters, wherein they were held bound by a titular Nobility: For, the People being prest under them, were forced once to drive them out, but afterwards most foolishly letting them in again into their former State and Order, they soon improved their Return to an undermining, and an utter extinction of the Peoples Freedom. We read too that in the free-State of the Argives, the standing titular Nobility would never be at rest, but always broaching one design or other, and at length the State having occasion of war against the Lacedemonians, did very foolishly intrust many of those Nobles with Commands in the Army: But what followed, the war being over, and they by this means gotten into Arms, immediately made use of the present opportunity to attempt the ruin of the Peoples Liberty, and the Republick. The innate Treachery in the same order of men was the ruin of the Syracusan Freedome too; For, they never left pecking at the poor people, til they were reduced to such extremity, that they were forced to put more power into the hands of Dionysius than ever they could get back again, which proved an occasion for his introducing an absolute Tyranny; wherein all the Nobility that formerly had been his Enemies, did side with him, after hee was once seated, because they saw their own interest provided for by his establishment in a Tyranny. In the Isle also of Corcyra they never left, till they brought that State to the utmost hazard, at which time that free and generous People made a shift to surprize them in their design, and give them the bloody reward of their Treason. In Athens, they destroyd that generous Free-State, first under their Τριάκοντα Τύραννοι, by ingrossing all power into the hands of their own Order, which was afterwards usurpt by thirty of their fellows; and when that Tyranny could hold no longer, then in process of time they erected a new one, called Ἄρχοντες, the Decennall Governors, which swayed all, for Ten years; and with no less Tyranny than the former, because they had an Interest distinct, being of a rank Superior to the People. In Heraclea likewise it is very memorable, that the Great ones were the men that drove out the Tyrant Clearchus, but with an Intent (it seems) to set up themselves in his Tyranny; wherein the People preventing them by making the State free, they were so impatient of the Peoples freedom, that rather than suffer it they called home the Tyrant againe, which nevertheless turn'd afterwards to the destruction of their owne persons, though not of their Interest and Families.

From Greece let us travell to Rome, where after the expulsion of Kingly Tyranny, a new one was substituted in its place by permitting those that called themselves the Nobility, to arrogate all authority unto themselves. This wrought so disastrous an effect, that the people allowing of a standing Titular Order of Nobility, soon lost all other enjoyments, as well as their Liberty; for, those grand Tituladoes made it their business every way to vex and keep them under, insomuch that they were forced into continuall mutinies for remedy; one while against the usury and exaction of their Nobles; another while for Land, & sometimes for Bread; sometimes also for liberty of Marriage, and lastly for the liberty of the whole State, when they procured the Tribunes and free Suffrages, with power of electing and calling their supreme Assemblies; but yet for all this, they could never enjoy any thing in quiet, but that they were still plagued with the subtilties and encroachments of their Nobles, all along, from before Appius Claudius; but especially then, and afterwards downe to Caesar; yea, and after him too, til the memory of the Roman liberty was buried in an odious Tyranny, which was erected first by force, but afterwards established by the Treachery and compliance of the Nobility in the Senate.

For Modern Instances, the truth of this hath been alwayes evident in the Republick of Genoa, where the People could never be quiet nor secure, till they puld down the pride of those hereditary petty Tyrants that were among them, and opened the Senate dores to the free Suffrages of the People in the election of their Duke, even out of themselves (if they pleased) and in all other affairs of concernment. But the Case is far otherwise in Venice, where the People are not in any capacity to elect, or be elected to the Dukedom, nor any other Office of Dignity. But all Officers and affairs of State and Authority are imbezled in the Senate, by an hereditary Titular Nobility; for which caus, though the State be called Free, yet if you please to proportion your Judgement by the Schemes of true Policy, you will finde it hath not so much as a face of Freedom, nor so much as the Forme of a reall Republick, as the people have ever found in all their Territories by sad experience.

And that you may Perceive what an Inconsistency there is between Liberty and those Titular toyes, it is very observable, that in many Parts of the world they have been the only obstacles to Freedom; witness the Countries of Latium, Aemilia, Flaminia, Insubria, Milain, Sicily, and Naples, in all which Places the multitude of Titular Powers and dignities, hath been the only cause wherefore the People have ever had so much difficulty to attain, or preserve themselves in the state of a Republick; and in Naples now, we see it is the Spaniards policy to uphold an innumerable frie of Hereditary Nobility, for the more sure bridling of the People; which cours was taken also by the Medicean family, first to weaken the Peop[l]es Interest, then to banish it, and ever since to extinguish the very hope of Liberty, in those *quondam*-free states of Florence, Siena, and Luca; as the People, and other Princes have don in the rest of Italy.

In France also, they were main Instruments in the loss of that Nation's Liberty: For, it so hapned, that when the most part of France was possest by the English, there was a necessity to discontinue the Assembly of the 3. Estates, which was the Bulwark of the French Liberty, and to put an absolute power into the hands of Charls the 7th during the war; which

Lewis the eleventh, having a minde to continue in his own hands after the war was don, took care to oblige the nobility unto himselfe by large Immunities, so that they were easily drawn to betray the Peoples Liberties, and leave them to the mercy of the King, since when an absolute Tyranny hath been continued there to this very day, wherein the nobility having a share allowed joyn issue ever with the King, to a miserable inslaving of the poor People.

We know the Case hath been the same here with us too in England, all along since the Conquest, and in Holland, it may be observed as one principall Cause of their long subsistence against the Spaniard, that the main authority hath been reserved in the peoples hands, and not much allotted to the Nobility, so that they have been the less considerabl[e] for effecting any designe against the publick Liberty, their power being small, and they but few in number. But the Switzers took a surer course for the preservation of their Liberty, and banish'd them; which had they not done, it had been almost impossible for them (as things then stood) to stand against that shock of Fury wherewith they were assailed on every side, by the French, Burgundian, and Austrian Tyrants.

Now, what we have here said of a Titular Nobility, extends likewise to all Hereditary or Standing Powers whatsoever, because they are in effect equivalent, and have the same influences and interests to the prejudice of Freedom, being concerned to preserve themselves in a Station above the ordinary standard of the People, and therefore are naturally inclined to side any way (as they see occasion) with any powerful persons whatsoever that are able to gratifie them in the increase of their Lordly Interest and domination. And therefore, from all these Instances and Examples, as we may easily conclude our Position; that a Titular Nobility, or Hereditary Powers, are not only inconvenient, but altogether inconsistent with a Common-wealth, because of their implacable animosity, and natural compliance with any Power against the Peoples Interest; so it cannot but make mightily for the honour of all Founders of Free States, that have or shall provide for the Peoples Interest, and block up the way against Tyranny, in keeping a due proportion, equability, or harmony of condition among all the Members, by placing the Authority in the Peoples hands; that is, in a due and orderly succession of their Supream Assemblies.

## [MP 90, 19–26 Feb. 1652]

That a Free State, or Government by the People, setled in a due and orderly succession of their suprem Assemblies, is more excellent than any other form, we shall more clearly Evidence by Reason.

A 14th Reason is, because all new Acquisitions in this form, made by Conquest tend not only to the ease & benefit of the People Themselves, but also to the content of the conquer'd Party; whereas under Monarchs and Grandees it hath been ever seen that in such cases they arrogate all unto themselves, and take Advantage by every new Conquest, for the in-slaving of all the rest that are under their Power. For in Story we seldom find them upon Terms of Indulgence to their Subjects, nor do they use to naturalise, incorporate or imbody them into an Enjoyment of the same Privileges with their Natives, but rather use the one as Instruments to oppress the other, and in the end to deprive them all of their Immunities.

But in States governed by the People, the case is much otherwise; for they ever deale more nobly with their Neighbors upon the like occasion, admiting them into a participation of the same Liberties and Privileges with themselves, by which means they hold them the more Fast in the bonds of affection and obedience. As for Example, in all the free States of Greece they ever did so, except only in Sparta, who being governed by a standing senate erred in this Point of State so far as to denie an Incorpo-ration, not only to their conquer'd Neighbors, but even to all the Pelope-nesians that were their Confederates and Associats: But what followed? nothing but loss and Vexation; for within a few years, upon the first occa-sion given, which was no more than a Suprisall of the Castle of Thebes by certain desperate Conspirators, there ensued immediatly a generall Re-volt & defection of all their neighbors and Associats, which was the ruin of their state, never after to be recovered by any Art or Industry: Now the Athenians took another cours during the time that they were under the government of the People; for, by naturalising and incorporating those that were conquer'd by them, or confederated with them, & letting them partake of the same Liberty with Themselves, they were bound so fast, being involved in the same Interest, that they stuck close in the midst of all storms, & never flinch't, when the poor Athenians were assailed by the united Powers, of the Lacedemonian and Persian Forces.

If we observe the actions of King Philip the Macedonian, we find that after he had got footing in Greece, first by confederacy, and after by Conquest, he, instead of indulging the People after the fore-mentioned manner took away their old Liberties and allowed them no new ones, but after he crush't one Commonweal, made use of it to suppress another till in the end having master'd them all, he improved his Conquests abroad to an increase of Tyranny both there & at home, & left both his old & new Subjects ful of discontent, and dissatisfaction. But what was the Consequence? Story will tell you the People never forgot it, but waited for an opportunity; and after the death of his son Alexander, having a fair one to be revenged, they were the first that cast off the Family of Philip; and submitted to Cassander, when he and his 3 Fellow Captains shared their Masters Conquests between them.

In old Rome, as long as Liberty was in fashion, it was their constant custom to admit such as they conquer'd into the Priviledges of their City, making them free Denisens. The first Instance I shall give is of that memorable union which was made between them and the Latins, which continued a long time, till some question arising between the Romans, and them, and some other of the Incorporated Nations, about this very point of Incorporation, it occasioned that War which was called *Bellum Sociale,* being the most bloudy and pernicious War that ever the Roman State endured, wherein after infinit Battels, Sieges, and surprises of Towns, the Romans with much ado made a shift to prevail, and master the Latins: But then looking back, and considering into what perdition and confusion they had like to have been brought, they naturalised them all, and confirmed their Incorporation, as the only means to extinguish the seeds of future enmity for ever.

Thus also saith Cicero, *Offic.* 1. did our Ancestors, and for the same cause, receive the Tuscu'ans, the Aequans, the Volsci, the Hernicini, and the Sabins, into a participation of the priviledges of their City, as succeeding Times did others afterwords that were willing to imbrace them, *at Carthaginem, & Numantiam funditus sustulerunt,* but as for such as refused, or scorned the Favor, and by an implacability of spirit rendred themselves incapable of it, those they utterly opprest or destroyed, as they did in Carthage and Numantia. This course of indulgence was ever practised (we observe) in the Roman State, even under Kings, and also under their standing Senate, so long as those For[ce]s were in their Infancy, and kept honest through necessity; but in a short time increasing their

Dominion abroad, they soon forgot to propagate the Interest of Liberty, but made use of their growing Conquests only to heighten their Power at home, up to a Tyranny over their own people, and to an inslaving of the world; as is evident in the continued practises of the Senators, and their Lieutenants in the Provinces. S[ti]ll, as that State lost its Liberty, first under the standing Form of Senators, and afterwards under Emperours, so all new Conquests and Acquisitions served only to bring in People, to serve as fewel for the Covetousness and Luxury of particular persons, and to fill the world with Combustion and misery.

There was, in these latter days, a time in Italy, when all Conquerors made no other use of their Counquests, than to maintain the common Interest of Liberty, as Castuccio of Luca, and Soderino of Florence, with others, till Caesar Borgia in Romania, and the Medicean Family in Florence, set the Italian Commanders to learn a new L[e]sson, which way to improve their new Conquests, by grandising and garbing many petty States into a formal Tyranny, without any allowance of Priviledge, more than what depended upon their own particular favor, to those whom they subdued and conquered: The effect of which hath been only this, that all the new Acquests of Borgia soon came to nothing, and while he possest them they were very uncertain; And as for the Mediceans, it was long ere they could sit easie in the saddle, by reason of the frequent Revolts of the Florentines. It is observed too, that the City of Pisa having been united to the State of Florence, the Grandees there not conceiving it would be for their Interest, to naturalise or allow them the benefit of Incorporation, the People thereupon being little satisfied with their condition, did upon the sight of Forein Assistance, by the Expedition of Charls the 8 of France into Italy, immediately revolt.

In Venice, where the Power is lodged in a standing Senat, there is little of Liberty left wherewith to indulge their own, or other people, so that if they chance at any time to make a Conquest of any Place, the People not being obliged upon the Score of Common Liberty, take so little content, that they either revolt, or yield up themselves, upon the first oportuinity.

In Spain, there is indeed a mutuall incorporation of Leon, Castil, Valentia, Andaluzia, and Granada, but this is not done upon the Account of propagating Liberty, but rather out of designe to hold them together, that the King may be the better inabled to domineer, and maintain an absolute power over the divided parcels of his new Conquests up and down in Milain, Sicily, Naples, and his new Inheritance in the low Countries; so that if ever those States finde an oportunity, they will soon bid him far-well, and follow the Example of Portugall and Catalonia. Arragon may after them too in time, for the same cause, because the Arragonians are not only despoiled of their old famous Liberties, but totally disobliged, not being gratified with the benefit of an Incorporation.

In France it was not the Act of their Kings, but of the Assembly of the three Estates of the People, that there was an Incorporation of those Conquests made in Britany, Normandy, Guien, Aquitain, and Burgundy. The Supream power in those days, was deposited in the hands of the People in that Assembly; the King was then but a Cipher, or otherwise it would hardly have been effected, it being the reputed Interest of Kings, wheresoever they have the power, to straiten, and not inlarge the Immu-nities of such as are reduced under their Obedience.

In England it was a long time ere our Kings would yeild to an Incor-porating of Wales. Edward the first, having extinguisht the Line of the Princess, and utterly subdued the Nation, did indeed give them leave to send Deputies to our Parliaments, who had liberty of Voting there, yet only in order to the Interests of their own Countrey; but this did no good, for, as long as they were abridged in a distinct way of Voting there, it put them still in minde, that once they were a distinct Nation, and therefore they were never quiet, but ever and anon breaking out, till after long experienc[e] of the many inconveniences hapning thereby, it was at last thought fit by Henry the 8. to take away all marks of distinction by Incorporating them with England; since which time they have ever been quiet, being brought under the same Laws, and made partakers of the same Liberties and immunities with the English Nation.

And as the incorporating of that People was neglected by Edward the first, so he neglected it also in Scotland, after his Conquests there, where (according to the Custom of all Monarchs and standing Powers) seeking to rule rather with a Rod of Iron, than a Golden Scepter, and taking no course to oblige or alter the disposition of the People, by an Incorpora-tion with us, or any other way, the consequence was, that all the time he held them (which was but short) they put him to a perpetual expence and trouble by continual Insurrections, and afterwards taking an occasion of Vertue by his son Edwards Infirmity, they soon cast off all Respects and obedience to the English—I might inlarge (were I not too large already) to shew, that all standing Powers (whether Monarchs or others) are so far from propagating, that they ever make it their studie to obstruct the common Interest of Liberty, upon new Acquisitions of Power, as well as all other occasions; which Inconvenience being provided for, and the common cause of Liberty ever promoted by the People in their Government, by Indulgence to other Nations, upon the same opportunity, must needs conclude it, as in all other Particulars, so likewise in this, much more excellent th[an] an[y] other Form whatsoever.

## [MP 114, 5–12 Aug. 1652]

I Am now come to set a Period to this Discourse; the Ninth and last Error in Policie, observable from the Practise of most Times and Nations, hath been the persecuting and punishing of men for their opinions in Religion.

This Error is grounded upon another, asserted in al times by the Furious drivers of the Clergy, under every transition and Revolution of outward Forms, viz[.], that there ought to be an establishment of some certain chief heads, Articles, and Principles of Faith, as Fundamentall and Orthodox, which all men must be bound to hold and beleeve, or els incurr the Censure of Hereticks, Sectarians, and Schismaticks, &c. This Position (I say) under what disguise so ever it come, with whatever Pretences it be clothed, or by what Persons so ever it be owned, is *ipsa Ratio formalis*, the very Spirit and Principle of the Pope and Antichrist; It hath been the dam of that white-Devill called Eccelesiasticall Politie, or Nationall Uniformity, a device subservient to that inveterated Project of Nationall Churches; which is in a word the Interest, not of Christ, but the Clergy; for these Errors depend upon one another, as Links of the same Chain of darkness, which hitherto hath shackled Truth in its progress, bound up all the Christian world in ignorance, and hinder'd the propagation of the Gospel, in it's more glorious degrees and discoveries of Light, life, and Power.

This unreasonable Position was it which set on the Edg of Papall Fury and persecution against that light which brake out among the Albingenses and Waldenses in France; against that also which was professed by the Hussites, the Wicklevists, the Lutherans and Protestants in Germany and England, who all successively received the Brands of Hereticks and schismaticks, being deliver'd up to fire and destruction, because they held forth greater measures of Trueth, than would fit the size of that state Religion which was established in their respective

Countries. And when all other Forms had fulfill'd their Periods of Domination, and laid down, then at last the Presbytery came in Play, and took up the Cudgels, laying about them with as much Fury as any of their Predecessors; so that you see this Papall Spirit and Principall hath run down through all these Times and Forms, since the very first dawnings of Reformation, to the great Impediment of the Gospel. And truly, it were to be wished, this Spirit might be at a stand in this last form of Presbytery, and not wind it self into any other more refined. For, as a Godly Preacher saith in an Epistle to a printed sermon of his, which he preached to the Parliament, on Novemb. 5 1651 [*Peter Sterry,* England's Deliverance from the Northern Presbytery *(London, 1652). Until the final paragraph, the rest of this editorial reproduces material from the epistle dedicatory, with minor abbreviations and adjustments, and pp. 8–18 of Sterry's text.*] I have desired in my Prayers to work with God, even for the opening of the eies of men to see; that the same spirit which lay in the polluted Bed of Papacy, may meet them in the perfumed bed of Presbytery; that the Fornications and sorceries of this whore are then greatest when they are most Mysterious; that she is able by her Sorceries to bewitch those that have atteined to a great degree of Spirituality, as the Galatians. To this purpose have I represented the same spirit, which dwells in the Papacy when it enters into the purer Form of Presbytery, as fuller of mystery, so fuller of Despight, of danger, not to make the Form or Persons, but that Principle, that Spirit unfit to be cherish't by any Person in any Form. The highest Godlinesses, and the highest wickednesses, are those which are most Spirituall.

In his sermon he proceeds thus, most excellently. I profess not at all to speak against the Form of Presbytery, if consider'd in its simplicity, as a way, and order, in which saints have Communion with God, and each with other, according to their present light; as it kisses the golden sceptre of the spirit, submitting, and subordinating it self to the Rule of that spirit, being desirous of no more, no other power, authority, or esteem, than what the spirit shall put forth upon it, by putting forth it self in it. Much lesse would I grieve or cast contempt upon any little one, that walks in that Form with humility and Integrity: believing that so it ought to worship God. But that Presbytery which I compare with the Papacy, is such as appropriateth to the Outward forme, those things which pertain onely to the Power of the Spirit: such as by vertue of an Outward Church forme, assumes a Spirituall and Civill power to it self; such as out of the

Golden cup of a glorious profession, makes it selfe drunk with the wine of Fornications with Earthly powers and Interests: such as takes to it self the Iron Mace of fleshly force and fury, to break in pieces at pleasure, Common-welths, Crownes, Consciences, Estates, and Hearts of men. This is that Presbytery, on which those Enemies, whom the Lord hath last of all subdued before you, had founded, and built up that Interest and Strength, by which they opposed the Glorious out-goings of God before you, and endeavoured your Ruin. This is that, which I call the Scotch-Presbytery, and now compare with the Romish Papacy.

1. The Comparison is first to be made in those things which I call Agreements between them, and these are Six.

1. Agreem. Both join setting up the Scriptures the Word of God out-wardly exprest, as the Letter of that Law, by which all things of Christianity and Religion are to be judged. So Scotus himself teacheth in his Preface to his Disputes upon the sentences, that Religion must be grounded upon a Revelation. In this, not only the Romish-Papist, and Scotch-Presbyter, but all who pretend with any face to any thing of God or Christ, do concurre. But there are two things in a Revelation. There is Lex Revelata: and Lumen Revelationis, that is the Law Revealed, and the Light of Revelation. One is the Subject, or Matter: but the other is the Form, the Life, the Essence of a Revelation. Now these two parties meet in this, to magnifie the first of these, the Law Revealed. This they make the foundation of their Throne, the Scepter of their Government, which as taken singly by it selfe is but a breathlesse Carkasse, or a Dead Letter. Herein a Living Member of Jesus Christ is in this point distinguished from all others; He receiveth, ownes, bowes down to the Law revealed upon this account, because it comes down from Heaven into his heart in a Light of Divine Revelation.

2. Agreement. These two of whom we speak, do Both assert a visible Judge on Earth, upon whom all Particular Persons are to depend for the Determining of those two Grand Questions; First, what is scripture; Secondly, what the sense of that Scripture is. The Romanists say, That this Judge is the Pope, or an Oecumenical Councell. The Scotch Presbyter is for a Nationall Assembly, or rather an Oecumenicall Assembly, if the Civil Government would bear it. This Presbyter condemnes the Papist justly because he suffereth not the People to read the Scriptures, in their own Tongu[e]. But who art thou, O man, who condemnest another, and

dost thy self the same thing, while thou forbiddest private persons to read the Scriptures with their own eys? Thou confinest them to Spectacles of the Assemblies making, while thou permittest the reading, but prohibit-est the interpreting of the Scriptures according to that sense, which the holy Spirit brings forth to every man in his own spirit, if it be not stampt for currant by the spirit of the Generall Assembly. Why dost thou judge the Papist for exalting unwritten Traditions to an equall Authority with the Scriptures, when thy way maketh the Scripture it selfe in the letter and meaning of it, a Tradition of the Elders.

3. Agreement. Both these Sects have a very great jealousie over the Spirit of God. As the Pharisees said Concerning Jesus Christ, John 11. 48. If we let this man alone, all men will believe on him, and the Romans shall come and take away both our place and Nation: So say these two, the Romish and Scotch principles in the hearts of men: If we yeeld to this, to let the Spirit alone, & to suffer all men to believe on the holy Ghost, as the only witness and evidence of divine truth: If we give way to this, as sound doctrine, that it is the proper office of the third Person, the Spirit, and of him alone, to apply truth authoritatively, as it is of the second Person to act, of the first Person to decree that it belongs to this Spirit alone au-thoritatively to testifie in the spirits of Men, what those words are which himself hath taught, what the meaning of the spirit is in those words: if this be once granted, that nothing is to be received, as Divine Truth, but that which brings an Epistle of commendations along with it, written by this finger of the living God upon the heart, then farewell all Religion: All manner of Sects, Heresies, Heathenisme, will break in upon us, and take way the very face of a Church from amongst us. It is said of Jesus Christ, that He was numbred amongst transgressors in his death. Such usage as our Saviour himselfe found on earth from Pilate, and the Priests, such doth his Spirit find to this day from the Papacy, & that Presbytery of which we speak. The holy Ghost, as he appears, and gives forth his Ora-cles in his Temples, which are his Saints, is numbred amongst whimsies, fansies, fanatick furies, enthusiasmes; and so is condemned, is suppressed.

4. Agreement. A watchfull Opposition to all Growths of truth above the pitch and stature of opinions commonly received. Nothing is ac-counted so dangerous in things pertaining to the Gospel, as Innovation; although St. Paul command us still, to be transformed in the renew-ing of our Minds, that we may prove what the good and acceptable will of God is; and this to Saints already converted, as a continuall duty, in

which they are ever to be exercising themselves, that they may have new minds to day, in comparison with those which they had yesterday, and new minds again to morrow, in comparison with their minds to day; yet the same Jesus, yesterday, to day, and for ever. As in some places of the River Thames you have Wyers set up quite crosse the River, and basket-nets laid in those Wyers, to catch those Lampries that come swimming up against the streame: so both in Papacy, and in rigid Presbytery; all Constitutions, Methods, Frames of Doctrin and Discipline seem to be as wyers with nets in them, set cross the whole stream of civil and religious conversation, to catch every discovery of Christ, every manifestation of the Gospel, which comes up against the present Tyde, the general current of Principles and Positions. They labour as to hedg in the winde, to binde up the sweet influences of the Spirit, they will not suffer it to blow where it lists, because they know not whence it comes, or whither it goes.

5. Agreement in annexing the Spirit to outward formalities. Like Simon Magus, both seem to believe, that the Gifts, and Ministry of the Spirit may be purchased by the coyn of Education, Parts, Morall honesty, formall qualifications, Ceremonious Observations of outward Rites. So is their way laid, so are all their practises managed, as if by a kind of Simoniacall Magick, that power which alone can awe, or secure us from, the devil, were shut up within the circle of their customary, and solemn Forms. When the Lord saith, Neither on this Mountain nor in Jerusalem, but in spirit and truth shall all men worship the Father: Yea, say they, but Spirit and truth dispense themselves within the Jerusalem of this Church-order, on the Mountain of these rituall observations, these consecrated forms.

6. Agreement in making Religion a rise to civil pomp, and power. Jesus Christ saith, My Kingdom is not of this world. But say these two Factions, Our Kingdom is over this world. We rule in earthly things, by an earthly strength, though not from an earthly title. The Heavenly power of the Spirit is the Scepter in our Hand: but the fleshly power of the Magistrate is the Sword in the hand of our Minister, and Guard, which is to be subordinate to our Scepter. By this means they bring all manner of civil affairs within the compass of their Cognisance, by vertue of their spiritual Judicatories: They dispose of Governments, Nations, Crowns by vertue of their Ecclesiastick censures.

Now what hath been said of this form of Presbytery, by that pious man, is apliable to any other form, or forms, though never so refined, that shall admit the same Papall and Antichristian Principle.—So here is an end of the whole discourse, having with sincerity run over all the principall points of Policy, in fortifying you with Reasons, refuting Objections, prescribing Rules, and Cautions, and noting the prime Errors; whereby suppose that all being put together have made a sufficient proof of my Position, which was this; that a Free-State, or Government by the People; setled in a due and orderly Succession of their Supream Assemblies, is much more excellent then any other Form whatsoever.—And yet, being confined to a few pages weekly, I have been able to give you but the bare hints of things done in haste, which may (perhaps) appear abroad in a more accomplished manner hereafter.

# INDEX

This book is set in Adobe Caslon Pro, a modern adaptation by Carol Twombly of faces cut by William Caslon, London, in the 1730s. Caslon's types were based on seventeenth-century Dutch old-style designs and became very popular throughout Europe and the American colonies.

This book is printed on paper that is acid-free and meets the requirements of the American National Standard for Permanence of Paper for Printed Library Materials, z39.48-1992. ∞

Book design by Louise OFarrell
Gainesville, Florida
Typography by Apex CoVantage
Madison, Wisconsin
Printed and bound by Worzalla Publishing Company
Stevens Point, Wisconsin